I0837161

REV. W. M. LEFTWICH, D.D.

MARTYRDOM IN MISSOURI

A HISTORY OF

RELIGIOUS PROSCRIPTION, THE SEIZURE OF CHURCHES, AND THE PERSECUTION OF MINISTERS OF THE GOSPEL, IN THE STATE OF MISSOURI

DURING THE LATE CIVIL WAR

AND UNDER THE

"TEST OATH" OF THE NEW CONSTITUTION.

BY

REV. W. M. LEFTWICH. D. D.

FIRST SERIES—FOURTH EDITION.

SAINT LOUIS:
SOUTHWESTERN BOOK AND PUBLISHING COMPANY,
510 AND 512 WASHINGTON AVENUE.
PUBLISHED FOR THE AUTHOR.
1870.

Dedication.

TO THE

MARTYRS OF MISSOURI,

AND THE

CAUSE FOR WHICH THEY SUFFERED,

THIS BOOK

IS RESPECTFULLY INSCRIBED,

BY THE AUTHOR.

PREFACE.

"We are making history," was the convenient and popular boast of certain politico-religious fanatics during the late civil war, and for a few years subsequent to its close. It will not be considered impertinent, now that the "piping times of peace" have come, and men are permitted to look back upon the cooled passions and crystallized events of that dreadful period with somewhat of calm philosophy, if the fact should be announced that "we are writing history." It is one thing to make the history, it is quite another thing to write it. If others could afford to "make history," and, then, in popular cant and with prurient vanity, boast of it, we can well afford to write it up for them. And if our part of the task be fairly, candidly and correctly done, they will have little reason to complain if they appear before the world and go down to posterity in the light of the history they have made, and with their true character brought out by the shadows they have thrown forward upon the future. History is valuable, not merely as a catalogue of events and an inventory of things, but for the principles involved and the lessons taught. The events herein narrated are notorious, the principles involved are vital, and the lessons important.

Missouri will ever be conspicuous in the annals of history as the only State in the American Union to inaugurate and authorize a formal opposition to Christianity, as an institution, and legalize the persecution of ministers of the gospel, as a class. The fact will not be denied, and the history furnishes the saddest, wisest lessons. Ministers of the gospel have been robbed, arrested, imprisoned, and even murdered, for no other cause than that they were ministers of the gospel. They have been indicted by grand juries, arrested and imprisoned with common felons, mobbed and put to death for no other cause than that of preaching the gospel without taking the "Test Oath" of the New Constitution. A pure, unsecular Christianity owes much to the moral heroism of the Missouri ministry. The faith once delivered unto the saints, the integrity of the Church of Jesus Christ, as a kingdom not of this world, the purity of the gospel, the divine authority of the ministry, the liberty of conscience, and the rightful sovereignty of Christ in his Church, with every principle and phase of religious liberty, have been illustrated in the lives and sublimely vindicated in the sufferings of the ministers of the gospel in Missouri.

The author fully appreciates the delicacy and difficulty of dealing with such recent events and so many living names—events, too, which belong to the catalogue of crime, and names that will pass into history associated with the persecution and stained with the blood of the Lord's annointed. But if the task is difficult and the questions delicate, the duty is no less imperative. It is due alike to the martyrs, living and dead, and to the holy cause for which they suffered, that their names and deeds be preserved, and that their unswerving fidelity and sublime devotion to a principle and a cause, equal to the purest heroism of the ancient martyrs, should not be lost to the Church. It is one of the gravest responsibilities of the hour, and one of the most gracious opportunities of the Church, to preserve the history, vindicate the faith, maintain the principles and impress the lessons of the turbulent past upon the peaceful future, that grace may abound through suffering and God may be glorified in his servants.

A diluted charity says, "Let the dead past bury its dead, and let the living present draw the mantle of charity over the unfortunate by-gones." This might be well enough if the "dead past" did not contain the imperishable germ of a resurrection life that speaks to us with authority in the vital principles of yesterday, to-day and forever, and tells us, amongst other things, that the chief of the Christian virtues—a pure, discriminating charity—has no mantle for crime, however Christ-like may be its compassion for the penitent criminal.

Both Federal and State legislation shield those who committed the crimes of the war from legal prosecution; but such enactments possess no control over the pen and the press.

In presenting this work to the public the author is fully conscious of its many literary defects. But for all that, he dare not sacrifice the facts of history, even to literary excellence. Many subjects possess an importance and a grandeur wholly independent of those who handle them.

If, in treating of so many men and such recent events, injustice has been done the living or the dead, the author pleads the absence of intention and claims the benefit of a discriminating charity.

Both the work and the author will receive the severest criticism—perhaps censure—possibly abuse. The first—he would not escape if he could; the second—he could not escape if he would; the third—well—it is no new thing under the sun for those who are set for the defense of truth and righteousness to be abused.

The following prefatory notes, furnished by Dr. M'Anally and Bishop Marvin, together with the Introduction by Dr. Summers, will not only assure the timid and establish the doubtful, but will be as grateful to the Methodist and general public as to the author:

PREFATORY NOTE.

"In the following pages the reader may find an account of some of those horrible outrages perpetrated on Christian ministers in Missouri, chiefly because they were Christian men and Christian ministers; but scarce a tenth of all such outrages have been, or likely ever will be, placed before the public. They have cast a foul and ineraseable blot upon the fame of the State of Missouri, and must consign the immediate perpetrators to an infamy as lasting and as hateful as that of the most cruel persecutors of Christians in gone-by ages. And what deepens, blackens and renders more odious the guilt of these things is, they were for the greater part done by, or under the sanction of, men professing to love and follow the Lord Jesus Christ; with a claim to, and under the pretext of, a purer patriotism and holier Christianity, they committed atrocities that would disgrace barbarians and savages.

"It is well the record of these horrible deeds be preserved, that the better portion of the people in this and other States may have some knowledge of what was done and suffered here during the dark and bloody days, from 1861 to '65.

"Many of those, directly or indirectly, implicated in these deeds of cruelty and shame are now loud and earnest in their entreaties for 'by-gones to be by-gones,' and profess great grief that anything should be said or done 'to keep alive the feelings of the past.' It is not strange they should feel thus; but can they reasonably expect an honest and outraged people should continue to cover up such abominations, receive those who committed them into respectable society, and treat them as though they were innocent, honest, high-minded, Christian gentlemen? That would be strange—passing strange! No! Truth and righteousness, justice and mercy, alike demand that a faithful record of all such inhuman outrages be made, extensively circulated and carefully preserved; that all the perpetrators, instigators and abettors be consigned to that infamy they so deservedly earned. Of such a record this is the first volume, and it is hoped another, and another, and, if need be, yet another, will be forthcoming, until the whole matter shall be placed in its true and proper light.

"Of the manner in which the author has performed his work in the pages following I need not speak. Each reader will judge for himself, and each will find something to interest and instruct. The facts developed are exceedingly suggestive, and suggestive, too, in regard to all the interests of society.

"The thoughtful reader will naturally inquire as to the cause of, and reason for, such things, as well as to their natural and legitimate effects, and this may induce an honest, healthful inquiry as to what influences should be brought to bear to make men better, and thus prevent the recurrence of such things as are here detailed. Let the book be extensively circulated, carefully read, and its contents well considered.

"D. R. M'ANALLY.

"CARONDELET, Mo., December 29, 1869."

"ST. LOUIS, December 24, 1869.

"REV. W. M. LEFTWICH:

"*Dear Sir*—I have seen the proof sheets of a large portion of the first volume of 'Martyrdom in Missouri,' now soon to come from the press.

"The publication of this book meets my hearty approval. I have met with some who say, 'Let the past sleep; let all its crimes, and the bad blood engendered by them, be buried forever.' I have not so learned Christ. He, the Incarnate Love, charged the blood of the prophets upon the sons of their murderers. The true work of Christian charity is to *eradicate* crime, not to ignore it. The maudlin sentiment that would daub over the great public crimes committed by the highest dignitaries of the Nothern Methodist Church and their representatives in the South and along the border, is *not* charity. It is at best a clumsy counterfeit of that chief of the virtues. True charity will seek to bring them to confession and recantation of their deeds.

"To all their former misdeeds they now add, to avoid the shame of the past, denials, equivocation and, as in the case of the Holston property seized by them, false recriminations. The sober truth is that they never hesitated during the time of our public trouble to use the influence an active partisanship gave them with the party in power, to take possesion of our property, either by military order, or terrorism, or mob violence. The public conscience of that Church seems to have been debauched by their efforts to defraud us of our property at the time of the division of the Church.

"But the stench of these recent atrocities is so strong in the nostrils of the people that the perpetrators resort to the ever open refuge of the evil-doer—denial. This book is opportune. The great body of the preachers and members of the Church North are honest men. The denials made by their leading men and Church papers they suppose to be true. Here are facts in detail, with places, names, dates, and copies of legal proceedings taken from official sources.

"Before the war, when Northern preachers were objects of suspicion, and public demonstrations were sometimes made against them, the editor of the St. Louis *Christian Advocate*, Rev. D. R. M'Anally, raised his voice against all mobs and mob violence with a will and an emphasis that left no covert suggestions of encouragement to those who might have been disposed to resort to violent measures. Led by the *Advocate*, the whole Southern Church in the State gave its influence, publicly and privately, against all violent proceedings. If that paper and our Church had, at that time, pursued the course that the Northern preachers and papers did towards us during the war, they would have been driven from the State. As it was, in order to get credit for persecution, they had to resort to the most remarkable tricks. Take, for instance, the case, given with proper names in this book, of one of their camp meetings being broken up by the preacher in charge of it being caught in the act of adultery—broken up by their own members. This they published to the world as a case of persecution by Southern people.

"While I do not agree fully with all the views set forth in the preliminary chapters of this volume, I am prepared to say that the *facts* bearing on the main topic have been collected and verified with great care, and that there can be no doubt of the accuracy of the statements. You have been pleased to hold yourself responsible, giving proper names, dates, etc. I do not hesitate to invite upon myself a full share of the responsibility.

"Hoping that you will soon have the second volume, containing the names of our other murdered brethren, ready for the press,

"I am, very respectfully,

"E. M. MARVIN."

INTRODUCTION.

BY

REV. T. O. SUMMERS, D. D.

The author of the following work has desired an expression of our opinion in regard to its publication. We have read the manuscript with painful interest, and are free to say that we have had some misgivings as to the expediency of sending it forth to the world. The facts here brought to light are so revolting, and their record is so damaging to the reputation of those by whom they were perpetrated and their aiders and abettors, that we might well hesitate as to the propriety of their publication. As Methodists, in particular, we are strongly tempted to throw the veil of oblivion over those scenes of oppression and outrage, in which many of our co-religionists of the North bore so conspicuous a part.

But the cause of truth and righteousness demands the publication. There is a measure of retribution which must not be relegated to the "judgment to come," but which must be dealt out in the present world.

We owe it to "the noble army of martyrs," whose lives were sacrificed to appease the demands of fanaticism, bigotry, cruelty, and hate, that their murderers shall not go unwhipped of justice—at least, such castigation as the truth of history can inflict.

We owe it to those who were made widows and orphans by the monsters who enacted these bloody scenes, to let the world know that the husbands and fathers of these innocent sufferers were not rebels and traitors, but good men and true, "of whom the world was not worthy."

We owe it to the institutions of our country to let it be known that the appalling scenes that were enacted during the late reign of terror were not the result of the principles which underlie our Federal and State governments, but of the palpable contravention of them.

We owe it to the ecclesiastical bodies of the South that posterity shall be told who invaded their rights; who robbed them of their churches, parsonages, cemeteries, and seminaries; who murdered, scourged, and plundered, and banished many of their ministers and lay members, including even women and children, because they would not compromise principles which they held dearer than life itself.

It is well for the world to be told that moral heroism has not, like Astræa, left the earth and ascended to the skies. Thank God! there have been heroes in our times; and we are encouraged to believe that the race will not soon become extinct. The night of persecution would bring such stars to view again. Daniel and the "three children," the Maccabees, the Apostles, Polycarp,

Ignatius, and other victims of Pagan persecution in primitive times—the Albigenses, Waldenses, Huguenots, the Marian martyrs, and other victims of papal persecution—Noncomformist and Remonstrant confessors, who "took joyfully," or at least patiently, "the spoiling of their goods," imprisonment, exile, and sometimes death—these have had their successors in the fearful times through which we have passed, and the record of them gives us a guaranty that under similar circumstances such heroes will appear again.

In perusing this work one is constantly reminded of the saying of the wise man, "Is there any thing whereof it may be said, See, this is new? it hath been already of old time which was before us." He had seen similar evils to those which we have seen and suffered. "There is an evil which I have seen under the sun as an error which proceedeth from the ruler: folly is set in great dignity, and the rich sit in low place. I have seen servants upon horses, and princes walking as servants upon the earth." "So I returned and considered all the oppressions that are done under the sun; and behold the tears of such as were oppressed, and they had no comforter." Then, as in our late calamitous times, good men mourned as they were forced to

—— bear the whips and scorns of time,
Th' oppressor's wrong, the proud man's contumely,
The insolence of office, and the spurns
That patient merit of th' unworthy takes.

The history of these terrible transactions is valuable, too, as an admonitory lesson, teaching us that no sect is absolutely proof against the seductive influence of political power and ascendency. Down to the present decade the Methodists could plume themselves with an honest satisfaction upon the fact that while nearly all other sects had risen to power and abused it to persecuting purposes, they never had. It was, indeed, sometimes insinuated that they never had persecuted because they never had the power to do so. But they contended, and, it was thought, with good reason, that the principles of Methodism, being so pure, spiritual, and catholic, would be a sure safeguard from political alliances, worldly ambitions, and persecuting practices; but, alas! that ground of boasting is taken away. The devil came with his "third temptation" to Northern Methodists, including even bishops of the Church, and they did not say, "Get thee hence, Satan!" They ascended by the devil's ladder to "thrones of power," and played such tricks during the continuance of their brief authority as made the angels weep! The wrongs of 1844 and 1848 developed into horrible atrocities in the sun of political prosperity which shone upon them during the war which subjugated the South. The lesson, we repeat, is admonitory. We trust in God no such temptation will ever be set before the Southern Church; it seems to be "a test for human frailty too severe."

It is not intended by these remarks to inculpate all the ministers and members of the Northern Methodist Church. God forbid! There are thousands among them who have not bowed the knee to Baal. They are attached to the Northern connection because of their location—they denounce the evil deeds of their brethren; indeed, in many instances they are not apprised of them, or honestly believe that they are gross exaggerations.

These enormities, however, are, to a great extent, charged upon the Northern Methodist Connection because they were perpetrated by its bishops and other agents; endorsed, or at least not disowned, by General and Annual Conferences, and have not been repented of until this day. Need any one seek further for a reason why the Southern Church wants no fellowship with those who murder, rob, oppress, and slander its ministers and members, or sanction those who do?

It must not be supposed that we lay all the blame upon Northern Methodists—other Churches furnished their quota of persecution and oppression, though, for obvious reasons, Southern Methodists suffered more from their Northern co-religionists than from any other parties. Thus was it with pagan and popish persecutions—a man's foes were frequently those of his own household. Apostates have ever been the most bitter and unscrupulous persecutors. This is a painful reflection. The eagle is pierced by an arrow feathered from an eagle's wing! Thus history repeats itself.

The perusal of this work will teach us not to put our trust in man, not even in princes; no, nor in institutions of our own framing, written constitutions, compacts, and the like, which upon occasion may prove to be worth no more than the parchment on which they are engrossed.

Nothing is perfectly true, and just, and good, and stable, but the kingdom of God. Nevertheless, the recital of the horrors portrayed in this book, which contains a mere modicum of what might be narrated, ought to lead us to thank God most devoutly that these calamities are nearly overpast, and we have the prospect of civil and religious liberty, which we know better than ever how to appreciate. The changes which have taken place in the government of the United States lead many to entertain gloomy anxieties for the future, and to despair of the permanency of republican institutions; yet we venture to hope that a wise, gracious, and powerful Providence will so interpose in behalf of our country that these forebodings will not be realized.

We may just state that we are assured of the truth of many of the details in this work by other testimonies; and for the rest we depend confidently on the accuracy of the author, who has taken great pains in collecting his materials from the most trustworthy sources. He is a reputable minister of the Missouri Conference of the Methodist Episcopal Church, South, and holds himself responsible for all that he narrates.

T. O S.

Nashville, Tenn., Nov. 22, 1869.

CONTENTS.

CHAPTER I.

MISSOURI DISTINGUISHED FOR RELIGIOUS PERSECUTION.

CHAPTER II.

POLITICAL EXCITEMENT OF 1859 AND '60.

CHAPTER III.

CHARACTERISTICS OF THE POPULATION.

CHAPTER VI.

FROM 1845 TO 1861, CONTINUED.

CHAPTER VII

CHARACTER OF THE STRIFE IN MISSOURI.

CHAPTER VIII.

ANOMALOUS CONDITION OF THE STATE—GREAT EXCITEMENT.

CHAPTER IX.

THE PULPIT AND PRESS ON THE SITUATION IN MISSOURI.

CHAPTER X.

PILLAGE, PLUNDER, BLACK-MAIL—MURDER OF THE REV. J. FEWEL—3,050 NEW ENGLAND CLERGYMEN.

CHAPTER XI.

SEIZURE OF CHURCHES—CHURCHES IN KANSAS CITY AND INDEPENDENCE.

CHAPTER XII.

CHURCH SEIZURES—CONTINUED.

CHAPTER XIII.

CHURCH SEIZURES—CONTINUED.

CHAPTER XIV.

CHURCH SEIZURES CONTINUED AND MADE GENERAL.

CHAPTER XV.

MARTYRDOM—REVS. J. M. PROCTOR, M. ARRINGTON, J. M'GLOTHLIN AND JAMES PENN.

CHAPTER XVI.

REVS. W. CLEAVELAND AND JESSE BIRD.

CHAPTER XVII.

ELDERS J. DUVAL, ISAAC ODELL AND ALLEN SISK.

CHAPTER XVIII.

WOOLDRIDGE, MARQUIS, PUGH AND BREEDING.

CHAPTER XIX.

REVS. R. N. T. HOLLIDAY AND GREEN WOODS.

CHAPTER XX.

REVS. A. MONROE, W. M. RUSH, NATHANIEL WOLLARD.

CHAPTER XXI.

REV. B. H. SPENCER.

CHAPTER XXII.

REVS. D. B. COOPER, H. N. WATTS AND THOS. GLANVILLE.

MARTYRDOM IN MISSOURI.

CHAPTER I.

MISSOURI—A DISTINGUISHED STATE.

Missouri Distinguished for Religious Persecution—Religious Liberty Secured to every Citizen by the Constitution of the United States, by every State Constitution, and every Department of the Federal and State Governments—Religious Liberty Protected and Enjoyed for two Centuries—The Stephen Girard Will Case—Mr. Webster's Great Speech—Religious Rights Defined—General Assembly of Missouri Refuses to elect a Chaplain—Legalizes Sunday Beer Gardens—A Card—A Renegade Minister—Reflections.

The State of Missouri is justly entitled to the distinction of being the first and only State in the American Union to inaugurate and authorize a formal opposition to Christianity, as an institution, and to legalize a systematic proscription and persecution of ministers of the gospel, as a class. Her constitution, statute books and judicial proceedings alone reproduce the ordinances, enactments and proscriptive decrees of the "dark ages," with the gross darkness that covered the people left out. Her prison walls and military bastiles have re-enacted the scenes of persecution, and her officers, courts and mobs have repeated the history of religious intolerance and proscription which we had associated *only* with the ignorance, superstition and tyranny of the long, silent past.

But the fertile soil of Missouri has been stained with the blood of real martyrs, and the "seed of the church" has been scattered all over her broad prairies and along her winding streams. Unmarked graves and marble monuments here and there fix the eye of God as he watches the dust of his martyred servants awaiting the resurrection, and a double portion of his Spirit is given to the living watchman in answer to the brother's blood that cries from the ground.

The Spirit of the Divine Master, in whose service they fell, inspires charity for the living, and will not rebuke the tears that fall for the dead. We have both, and it is profitable to indulge them, while we accord to Missouri the distinction she has justly won in reviving the laws and repeating the religious persecutions which an enlightened Christianity vainly hoped had passed away with the barbarous times which produced them.

The right to worship God without molestation, according to the dictates of conscience, was not only secured by the Federal and State Constitutions, but was always sacredly preserved and defended by the three co-ordinate branches of the Federal Government, and by the executive, judicial and legislative departments of the several State governments, until it had become so thoroughly interwoven with every form and feature, every principle and fiber of our institutions, and had penetrated so deeply and permeated so generally the popular heart, that its defenses were considered impregnable and its sacredness inviolable.

Every attempt to abridge the religious liberties involved in the rights of conscience, from whatever quarter and under whatever disguise, has been met and resisted by a public sentiment that pronounced it the most dangerous and unwarranted invasion of the dearest rights of American citizens. The enactment of laws to restrain the liberties of the citizen in any other direction might be tolerated, but whenever and wherever the enactment of laws, the decision of courts or the exercise of power have impinged upon the rights of conscience, or placed religious institutions under disability, the American people have moved to a resistance that subordinated all minor differences and distinctions and put their hearts and lives, their all, upon the defense.

The strenuous efforts made to break the will of Stephen Girard, in the courts of Pennsylvania, in 1839 and '41, and in the Supreme Court of the United States in 1844, are too fresh in the minds of American jurists and many of the American people to require more than a reference to one single item in this connection as an illustration.

The founding of the institution in the city of Philadelphia that bears the name of Girard, and his princely bequest for that purpose, would have passed his name down to the generations to come as one of the great benefactors of his race, but for one restrictive clause in his will; and it was in the light of that clause that the case assumed a national importance, and enlisted some of the ablest advocates of the American bar, prominent amongst whom was Mr. Webster.

After providing for all the college buildings that would be necessary, and the enclosure of the grounds by high stone walls, with iron gates for ingress and egress, he adds the following restrictions:

"Secondly—I enjoin and require that no ecclesiastic, missionary or minister of any sect whatever shall ever hold or exercise any station or duty whatever in the said college, nor shall any such person ever be admitted for any purpose, or as a visitor, within the premises appropriated to the purposes of said college."

Mr. Girard had a right to dispose of his estate in any way that his wisdom might direct, provided, however, the rights of others were duly respected; and Mr. Webster's unanswerable argument clearly sets forth the relations of Christianity to the State, and shows that such disabilities are in direct conflict with the institutions of the country, against the public policy of Pennsylvania, and every other State in which Christianity is recognized as the law of the land, and must be subversive of the dearest rights and liberties of the people.

What is the value of Mr. Girard's bequest, however great or munificent, when it touches the very foundations of human society—when it touches the foundations of religious liberty, of public law, and endangers the well-being of the State?

The restrictive provisions of Mr. Girard's will, in the opinion of Mr. Webster, distinctly repelled Christianity in the person of its accredited ministers; for whatever proscribes the minister of Christianity proscribes Christianity itself. The ministry is a part of Christianity, divinely instituted and authorized, and whoever makes war upon ministers of the gospel, as a class, makes war upon the Christianity they teach and represent.

In the light of these facts the State of Missouri, by her military and civil officers, her conventions, her General Assembly and her courts, has fairly won the unenviable distinction here announced, the painful history of which is recorded in these pages.

The ground work of this persecution was laid in the public mind years before its manifestation. The first out-croppings of the anti-Christian spirit was in the session of the General Assembly of 1858–9, in declining to elect a Chaplain, and in the refusal to repeal what was called the "Sunday Law." The encouragement given to this infidel spirit by a large portion of the press of the State, and by many so-called benevolent associations of foreigners, and from other influential sources hereafter noticed, prepared the public mind for the legislation, the military and civil despotism, and the mob-violence which authorized and executed a system of persecution, the history of which presents a catalogue of crime and scenes of blood and murder disgraceful to the State and revolting to the whole civilized world.

The refusal of the General Assembly to elect a chaplain, December, 1858, derives its importance, not from the fact, but the *animus* of the debates, and the sentiment reflected by the action.

The journal of the House of Representatives, of Dec. 29th, 1858, contains the following:

"EVENING SESSION.—Mr. King, of St. Charles, offered the following resolution: *Resolved,* That the House do now proceed to the election of chaplain. Mr. Edwards, of Dallas, offered the following amendment to the resolution: 'And that the individual members of this House pay said chaplain for his services out of their private means;' which, on motion of Mr. Sitton, was tabled by a vote of 79 to 43.

"Dec. 30th, 1858.—The House resumed the consideration of the regular order of business, viz., the election of chaplain, when Mr. King, of St. Charles, nominated Mr. Leftwich; Mr. Brisco, of Cass, nominated Mr. Williams; Mr. Boulware, of Callaway, nominated Mr. McGuire; Mr. Lenox, of Miller, nominated Mr. Litsinger; Mr. Davis, of Buchanan, nominated Mr. Welch. Mr. Ament moved to reconsider the vote on the adoption of the resolution to proceed to the election of chaplain, pending which motion Mr. Morris, of Barton, nominated Mr. Crow. Mr. Welch moved to lay the motion to reconsider on the table, which was negatived by a vote of 49 to 69.

"Afternoon Session.—Mr. Ament offered the following resolution as a substitute for the resolution of Mr. King, of St. Charles, in regard to the election of chaplain for the House: '*Resolved,* That the speaker be authorized to invite, each alternate week, the services of the respective resident ministers of this city, in opening, daily, this House with prayer.'"

This resolution awakened a lively discussion, which consumed much of the time of the three succeeding days—at a cost to the tax-payers of the State of not less than $20,000—and was finally passed under the operation of the previous question. Several efforts were made afterward to reconsider, but to no effect. The Senate, after some discussion, adopted a similar resolution.

The debate upon this resolution was very spirited, and drew out the sentiments of the people's representatives quite fully. Party lines were drawn clearly between the chaplain men and the anti-chaplain men, and this resolution was considered by both parties a compromise upon the vexed question. But why compromise such a question? Why make it a vexed question at all? Former Legislatures had elected chaplains and paid them, and thus recognized Christianity, not only as an element of national character, but as an accepted institution of the State, the doctrines of which were confessed in the oath of office and in all judicial tribunals, and the institutions of which conserve the highest interests of public weal, as they appeal to the most sacred guardianship of the State.

If the position taken by Mr. Webster, in his great speech before the Supreme Court of the United States, in the Girard will case, is accepted as true—and it is so accepted by all the right-thinking men of the country—there is nothing in the New Testament more clearly established by the Author of Christianity than the appointment of a Christian ministry; that the ministry is a necessary part of Christianity, divinely ordained for its propagation, and whoever rejects the regularly authorized minister of the gospel rejects the Christianity he teaches and represents; whatever repels the ministry repels Christianity, for it is idle, and a mockery and an insult to common sense, to pretend that any man has respect for the Christian religion who yet derides, reproaches and stigmatizes all its ministers and teachers.

The action of the House of Representatives was spread upon the journal, but the *animus* of the members could only be gathered from the speeches, and then only by one who was present to hear and see. The kiss of betrayal precedes crucifixion.

It was in view of the spirit developed by this action,

more than the action itself, that three of the resident ministers of the city held a council, and after due deliberation published the following card in the city papers:

"A CARD.

"We, the undersigned, resident ministers of this city, believing that the discussion just closed in both branches of the General Assembly, on the office of chaplain, is a virtual repudiation of the claims of Christianity by that body; and that the action had is only a compromise measure, designed to reconcile the hostility of members somewhat to that office; and believing that for us to comply with any request to officiate in that capacity, under existing circumstances, will compromise the dignity of our office and the gospel which we preach; therefore,

"*Resolved,* That we will not sacrifice our self-respect and ministerial dignity to the enemies of Christianity by officiating in the office of chaplain for either branch of the General Assembly.

(Signed) "W. M. LEFTWICH,
Pastor M. E. Church, South.
"S. D. LOUGHEED,
Pastor Presbyterian Church.
"R. H. WELLER,
Rector Episcopal Church.

"JEFFERSON CITY, Mo., Dec. 31, 1858."

It is due alike to Christian integrity, ministerial fidelity and the truth of history to state that Rev. Mr. Lougheed did subsequently officiate as chaplain to the Senate, upon the solicitation of one or two members of that body, and under the operation of the unrescinded action of December 31st, 1858, after he had solemnly affirmed and formally announced to the world, through the public prints, that to do so would "compromise his self-respect and ministerial dignity."

This same session of the Legislature was made famous by the failure to repeal what was known as the "Sunday Law," which was passed merely upon its title, and in disguise, by the previous session, and which legalized the opening of beer gardens, play-houses, and many other places of drunken licentiousness on the Christian Sabbath in St. Louis. Pending the effort to repeal this unchristian law the discussions in both Houses and in the public press assumed an importance and a gravity which greatly alarmed the Christian people of the State for the freedom and safety of all religious institutions, and awakened the faithful watchmen upon the walls to the real issues that the enemies of Christianity would make, and to the real danger that threatened the peace and well-being of society in the not distant future.

CHAPTER II.

Political Excitement of 1859 and '60—Foreigners—Know-Nothingism —Foreign Element in Politics—Class Legislation to Encourage Immigration, Develop the Resources, and Subvert the Religious Institutions of the State—German Rationalists and Christianity—The True Interests of a State—Modern Spiritualism—Its Pretensions—Phenomena—Influence upon the Credulous—Circles—Mediums—Agents—Lecturers—Free-Loveism—Thousands of Disciples—Midnight Lamp in Thousands of Homes—Many Turned from the Faith to Serve Tables—Most Dangerous and Powerful Form of Infidelity—Free-Thinkers—A Novel Encounter with an "Improved Monkey"—Napoleon's "Moral Combinations" at Work upon the Public Mind.

Many will remember with unfeigned regret the political excitement that began to agitate the whole country in 1859, and which increased in violence and intensity the nearer the Presidential election of 1860 was approached.

In times of great popular excitement, when partisans are using their utmost efforts to carry elections, it is less surprising than hurtful that politicians should appeal for support to every class of citizens. The German population of St. Louis, St. Charles, Franklin, Cole, and some other counties and cities had increased rapidly in the past few years, and now for the first time began to make their presence and power felt in Missouri politics. They had fairly recovered from the effects of Know-Nothingism, if, indeed, the existence and labors of that singular political freak did not precipitate the foreign born citizens into a distinct political element and foist them into political prominence.

Being courted, and flattered, and fawned upon by political place-seekers, they were easily induced to believe that they held the balance of power at the ballot-box in many of the largest cities of the State, and they began to claim the right, not only to vote, but to be represented as a distinct class in the city and State governments—to hold office and control municipal patronage.

To secure the support of this class of citizens politicians stood ready to enact special laws for their relief, to grant privileges and immunities to them as a class, and to accommodate their social peculiarities and religious castes and creeds. The statutes of the State and the ordinances of cities show that they were the *privileged class*, and that class legislation, which always endangers the well-being of society, was accommodated in this instance to those peculiarities of the foreign element which looked to the subversion of the Christian institutions of the State, and the protection of an infidel sentiment that dared to invade the sanctity of the Christian Sabbath, disturb the peace of Christian worshipers, and strike down the supreme authority of the Word of God as a code of morals and a system of law.

To encourage foreign immigration for the development of the resources of the State, to build railroads, open coal beds, work lead mines and melt iron mountains, special legislation may have been necessary, but a State consists of something other than broad, fertile acres for agricultural purposes, or coal beds, lead mines, iron mountains and railroads.

These may be fruitful sources of material wealth, and

may be necessary to support and sustain a vast population, but they can not create intelligence, promote virtue, regulate the social system, or in any way define and adjust the higher duties and prerogatives of citizenship.

The wisest legislation protects equally the rights of all and confers exclusive privileges upon none, and the best government guarantees equal rights to all its citizens.

It is natural to expect that foreigners coming to these shores and settling in these States would accept the institutions with the protection of the government, and not seek to supplant the institutions of the State that offers them home and shelter; and yet it will not be denied that the foreigners in Missouri, taking advantage of the readiness of politicians to truckle to their passions and prejudices, have made strong demands upon the peculiar institutions of the State, and their demands have not been unheeded. It could not be expected that German rationalists, who could scarcely speak English well enough to carry on the most ordinary traffic, would understand, or care to understand, those institutions of the State which characterized the State as a Christian commonwealth.

Nor did legislators, politicians, editors or preachers consider the moral forces they were starting and fostering for evil, and the subtle agencies that would work with all deceivableness of unrighteousness in them that perish, and whose coming was after the manner of Satan, with all power, and signs, and lying wonders, deceiving the very elect, and spending its force and fury upon the desecrated altars and martyred ministers of Christianity.

Other and different agencies were at work, and had been for years, which could not be reached or affected by State legislation, and which contributed no little to that state of the public mind which put the institutions and ministers of Christianity under disability—what was commonly denominated "Spiritualism." It existed in a multitude of forms, had many names, and manifested itself in many strange phenomena. Professing to hold communication with the spirit world and receive intelligence from departed spirits, it appealed strongly to the curious, the credulous and the superstitious.

Those who believed in the supernatural, or whose hearts of grief kept them near the "region and shadow of death," or whose caste of temperament made them supersentimental, or who, by some constitutional or cultivated peculiarity, easily take up with every wild fancy and foolish vagary that produces a new and novel sensation ; and many others, too, who had credit for intelligence, refinement and piety—and as for that, some of the most gifted minds of the State—were led away by it, and became its deceived disciples, in one form or another, without suspecting its deceitful moral tendencies.

Lecturers came into the cities and traversed the State, circles were formed, mediums constituted, spirits rapped and wrote, tables moved and turned, and men, women and children forgot their meals, and stood in superstitious awe within the enchanted circles. Thousands of people lost their relish for the Word of God and forsook his altars of worship. Men neglected their fields, women their homes and children their schools, and for whole days and nights hung with bated breath upon the supposed communications from departed spirits, made often through the most ignorant mediums. Not only in the cities full, but throughout the vast populations of the rural districts, all classes seemed more or less affected by and interested in it. In thousands of homes in Missouri the midnight lamp shone upon tables surrounded by groups and circles of people so intent upon the unintelligible incantations and messages of spiritualism, so-called, that sleep was banished from swollen eyes and pillows brought no rest to aching heads. By it many were disqualified alike for secular, domestic and religious duties.

A peculiarity of spiritualism was that night and darkness were necessary to evoke the spirits. They would rarely communicate to mortals in the day time, or perform any very remarkable feats, such as playing on musical instruments, untying mediums, singing in the air, etc., except in total darkness. Evil spirits, like evil men, "love darkness rather than light, because their deeds are evil."

This modern spiritualism—neither the history nor philosophy of which it is necessary here to discuss—organized itself into bands, circles and societies of men and women in the larger cities, had their places of secret nocturnal meetings, rented halls for public Sabbath exercises, had their rituals and creeds, their priests and prophets, their altars, incantations and genuflexions, which answered to some sort of public worship. The first female lecturers and public speakers were spiritualists, and in the spiritualists' church, so-called, women are the high-priests ; and the scriptural teachings in regard to the relation of men and women and their duties in the church are reversed.

Indeed, to call them a church at all is a misnomer, and a shameful reflection upon every idea, principle and function of a true church of Jesus Christ, for by believing in a revelation direct from departed spirits in the spirit world they reject God's revelation.

They commissioned mediums to write, women and men indiscriminately to preach, to heal the sick, to see through the material and reveal the spiritual, to break up the marriage relation, to destroy parental affection, to form new standards of private and social virtue, to disturb and destroy all the old foundations and safeguards of society, and reconstruct the social system upon the modern ideas of socialism and the most offensive forms of free-loveism.

Religious liberty with them meant social licentiousness, and the social virtues were sacrificed to the lustful passions.

These things can not all be affirmed of all spiritualists, and yet the inevitable tendency is the same, and the extremest consequences are legitimate. To say that thousands of people in Missouri, through the subtle agencies of spiritualism, renounced their religion, forsook the church, neglected to read God's Word, turned themselves away from paths of piety and works of righteousness to serve tables, and became downright infidels, is not half of the whole truth. To a large extent the minds of men became detached from the foundations of Divine truth, and wandered, like the "unclean spirit, seeking rest and finding none."

Systems of infidelity, and infidelity without system, sprang up in every direction and found supporters amongst those that were least suspected, and the church began to tremble for the "faith which was once delivered unto the saints." Free-thinking, so-called, took the place of solid, religious faith, and every form of doctrine received encouragement in the public mind. The tendency in the public mind to skepticism was never more alarming, and the mystic vagaries of Andrew Jackson Davis stood in defiant competition with the New Testament. Lecturers appeared in every city and centre of population, haranguing the people upon the vain philosophies of men and questions of science, falsely so-called, seeking to turn away their ears from the truth unto fables, and "doting about questions and strifes of words" that would and did disturb the foundations of godliness. Nor could both the religious press and pulpit countervail their influence upon the public mind. Infidel clubs and associations were formed under different disguises, and many mischief-makers began to believe and teach "unwholesome doctrines" and deceive the ignorant and unwary. It was a common thing to hear of men lecturing in the principal towns on spiritualism, a higher civilization, phrenology, pathology, physiology, hygiene, and other kindred topics, and selling maps, charts and cheap books. In some places they drove a brisk trade, and set all the old women—and young ones, too—men and boys to talking and querying over the new ideas and theories advanced by these flippant, and often immodest lecturers.

The character of such teachings can not better be illustrated than by relating a somewhat novel adventure which the author had in the spring of 1859 with one of these lecturers.

While stationed in Jefferson City I was invited by the Moniteau County Bible Society to deliver a lecture in California on the Bible cause, and aid them in raising funds to supply the destitute of the county with the Word of God. Arriving in California by the afternoon train I was informed that a gentleman, a stranger, had been there lecturing for several evenings, and would lecture again that evening, in a public hall. My informants had not heard him, and could not tell exactly his subject or his object. When informed that his lectures were free, and that he was selling some kind of books, I was not long at a loss to reckon his moral latitude and longitude, and, indeed, to "guess" whence he came, and what he came for, and hoped that some lucky chance would throw us together.

The meeting of the Bible Society that night was quite a success, but my anxiety to see the lecturer seemed fated to disappointment. The next morning, in company with a friend, I went to the hotel, near the depot, to await the arrival of the down train. A goodly number of gentlemen sat and stood about in the public room awaiting the train also. My friend soon opened the way (as he knew many of them) for an appeal to them for contributions to the Bible cause, to which they pretty generally declined to respond. About this time a rather queer looking genius entered the hotel from the street, hastily and boisterously relieving himself at once of what seemed to be a meal sack half filled with books, and several rather pert exclamations and general salutations, taking a seat near me. I did not at first suspect his identity, but his inveterate loquacity brought him into notice, and my eye soon measured a small, thin-visaged, sharp-nosed, squint-eyed, thin-lipped, cadaverous, nervous specimen of humanity, a stranger to every sense of modesty, propriety and decency, and who believed that with himself all wisdom would die. He soon learned that I lived in Jefferson City, and the following conversation occurred. Turning to me, whom he had evidently been regarding for some time with uncivil curiosity, he said:

"You live in Jefferson City?"

"Yes, sir."

"On your way home now?"

"Yes, sir."

"Will you be good enough to make an announcement for me to lecture in your city next week?"

"Well, I don't know. Our people are not good lecture-goers."

"Why, don't you think I can have a good house?"

"That depends upon circumstances."

"What circumstances? My object is to do good."

"What subject do you propose to lecture on?" I asked.

"Various subjects; but especially treating of the construction and functions of the human body, the laws of physiology and hygiene."

"You may possibly do some good by lecturing on such subjects," said I, "and as we both are trying to do good, but in different ways, possibly if you will help me I may be able to help you."

By this time, of course, we had the eager attention of all present.

"How can I help you?" he inquired.

"I am trying," I replied, "to raise money to supply the destitute of this county with the Bible, and as I have applied to all of these gentlemen for help, perhaps you would give me something."

"No, indeed," said he, with emphasis, "I would rather give my money to have all the Bibles in the county burned up."

"You don't believe much in the Bible, then?"

"Not a bit of it," he replied. "It has deceived the people long enough already. If the people would only read my books on physiology and hygiene, and learn something of the nature and laws of their own physical organization, and what will promote the health, growth and action of all its parts, and let that 'old fable' alone, they would be healthier, happier and better off every way."

He said this with an air of assurance and authority which he evidently thought and desired would settle the matter with me, at least for the present, as he rose and walked the room nervously.

But I had seen too many men in the West to be bluffed off after that style, and my interest in him was too intense.

"Well, my friend," I said, after he subsided a little, "If you do not believe the Bible, what do you believe?"

"I am a free-thinker, sir."

"And what is a free-thinker?"

"One who thinks freely, and as he pleases, upon all subjects, without the shackles and 'leading strings' of the Bible, or any other old book—who has the independence and manliness to think for himself."

"I have long desired to see a free-thinker," said I, rather coolly.

"Look at me, then, and you will see one," he replied, rather curtly.

"Will you be kind enough," I asked, "to tell me what you think, 'freely,' upon some subjects of grave importance of which the Bible treats?"

"What subjects?"

"The origin of man, for instance. If you reject revelation, how do you account for the origin of our race?"

"Easy enough," he replied. "In the same way that I account for the origin of plants and animals—by growth and development."

"You believe, then, in what is called the 'development theory?'"

"I do, most fully and freely."

"From what is man a development?" I asked.

"From the lower animals, and immediately from the animals whose organism is nearest like ours."

"What animal," I asked, "do you think furnishes the resemblance so striking that leads you to believe that man is a development from it, and an improvement on it?"

With evident embarrassment, he answered, "I suppose the ape or the monkey."

"Then," said I, "I think I can have you a fine audience in Jefferson City next week, if I can make the announcement according to your theory."

"How is that?" he inquired.

"I will tell the people that an improved monkey will lecture to them."

The excitement of the man was scarcely less than the evident pleasure of the listeners.

"And, moreover," I continued, "I will readily excuse you for not giving me anything for the Bible cause, and can no longer be surprised that you desire to see all the Bibles destroyed."

"Why?" he asked, turning upon me sharply.

"Because," said I, "I can not expect a monkey, however developed and improved, to appreciate a revelation from God."

He became furious, sprang to his feet, and with gesticulations as rapid and violent as the volubility of his tongue, and as threatening as the intensity of the mingled chagrin and anger that burned in his countenance, delivered himself somewhat as follows:

"You are a Methodist preacher, going about trying to make the people believe that they can get religion—that God can convert them. It is all a deception—a delusion. God can do no such thing. I was deceived once, too, and was fool enough to join the Methodist church and believe that God could convert me. I went to the mourners' bench, where you try to get people to go; they sang, and prayed and shouted over me, and beat me on the back, and tried to make me believe that I was converted. But it was no such thing. God could not convert *me*. How could he get into me? Where would he come in at? At the mouth? or nose? or ears? All the men in the world could not make me believe that I could be converted. God 'lmighty could not convert *me*."

He closed, pretty well exhausted, and yet with his feelings somewhat in the ascendant, and with marked interest awaited my reply.

"I am not at all astonished at the fact," said I, "that God could not convert you."

"Why? Do you not teach the people that God can convert and save men?"

"Certainly I do. But, then, I read in the Scriptures no provision whatever for the conversion and salvation of monkeys, however improved."

Without another word he wheeled and "went away in a rage," snatching up his sack of books in his flight, and muttering something that could not be heard above the roar of laughter that followed him. I never saw him afterward. From that moment he went his way, and I mine. Our paths never crossed each other, or at least we never met. Our encounter lasted about half an hour, and when he disappeared so unceremoniously nearly every gentleman present walked up and gave me a dollar for the Bible cause, as the best way of testifying their appreciation of the victory.

This aptly illustrates the pernicious character of the teachings then rife through the State, and this "improved monkey" was a fair specimen of the class of itinerant lecturers that were then talking to thousands upon thousands of the people every week.

The rejection of the office of chaplain by the State Legislature, and the passage of the "Sunday law," and other class legislation affecting the religious institutions of the State, meant more than the temporary freak of a few irreligious politicians. It was the expression of a wide-spread and growing sentiment amongst the people, and the first bold demand of a fast-maturing infidelity.

The great Napoleon said that "there are certain moral combinations always necessary to produce revolution; and if they do not exist it is impossible to revolutionize a government or interrupt its peaceful administration. Without them a few ambitious leaders, inspired by selfish motives, may struggle in vain for political power."

If civil revolutions attest the wisdom of this remark of the great military chieftain, much more the moral and religious phases which revolutions assume under given conditions.

The foreign element, with its rationalism, anti-Sabbatarianism and abused Romanism; the irreligious element, with its Spiritualism, Universalism, Free-lovism and open and disguised infidelity—these furnish to the reflecting "moral combinations" sufficient to produce, or at least to control and direct, the great moral agencies that were so efficient during the civil revolution in burning churches, breaking up religious associations, hunting down and dragging ministers of the gospel "to prison and to death," and adding to the horrors of civil war, this, that the comforting ministrations of Christianity are proscribed, or altogether prohibited, under the penalty of imprisonment or death, or both imprisonment and death, to the man of God whose enlightened conscience teaches him to fear God rather than man.

CHAPTER III.

Characteristics of the Population—All Nationalities and all Social Peculiarities Fused into a Common Mass—Missourian—First Settlers of the State—Where From, and their Type of Domestic and Social Life—The "Kansas-Nebraska Bill"—Its Effect upon the Population of Missouri—"Emigration Aid Societies"—Extremes Brought Together in Missouri—Reflex Tides of Population—Rapid Increase—Unique Social Formation—Social Peculiarities Fuse—Religious Characteristics Become more Distinct—Religious Thought and Feeling, Doctrines and Dogmas, Sharply Defined and Fearfully Distinct in Missouri—Sects and their Peculiarities—Sectarian Strife Uncompromising—Why—Religious Controversy—Published Debates—Their Effect—Sectarian Bigotry and Intolerance—Differences, Essential and Non-essential—History Repeating Itself—Persecution the Same in Every Age—Early Martyrs and the Missouri Martyrs—"The Altar, the Wood and the Lamb for a Burnt Offering."

The population of Missouri differs in some respects from that of any other State. There is a greater variety of nationalities blended, of blood mingled, and of national, political, social, domestic and religious characteristics crossed and intermixed than can be found in any other State.

Other States may have more nationalities represented in their population, and the political, social and ecclesiastical characteristics may be more sharply defined; but that fact only confirms the position taken—that in Missouri these characteristics lose their identity, to a greater or less extent, and become fused in the common mass Nearly all the nationalities of Europe, and many of Asia, are represented in Missouri, but only a few years' residence is sufficient to either destroy or modify their national characteristics.

The social and domestic peculiarities of every State in the Union, with many foreign states, are exotics here; while many of them die out altogether and are abandoned, others compromise and intermingle, until the type of social and domestic life is somewhat of a hybrid, and is peculiarly Missourian.

The bulk of the old population of the State was from Kentucky, Virginia, Maryland, North Carolina, Tennessee and Ohio, with a respectable number from Indiana, Illinois and New York. Up to 1855 and '56 the types of social life existing in these several States were scarcely disturbed in Missouri. After the passage by Congress of the somewhat notorious "Kansas-Nebraska bill," in 1854, and the organization of these Territories, the population of Missouri increased rapidly and became of a more general character.

"Emigration aid societies" in New England and the Eastern States threw into these newly-formed Territories thousands of families who represented in their social and religious lives the extreme of New England ideas and New England faith.

Emigration from the Southern Atlantic and Gulf States, whether by aid societies or otherwise, rushed to these Territories, bringing the extremest types of Southern life. The middle and Mississippi Valley States furnished their share, until the swelling population of Kansas presented a scene of contrasts and conflicts turbulent and exciting beyond anything before known in the history of territorial settlement.

It is true that it was the struggle of political parties for dominion, each seeking to incorporate its peculiar class of ideas and cast of policy into the corporate structure of the future State by controlling the Territorial election; yet the effect upon the social and domestic peculiarities of Missouri, as well as the peculiar institutions of the State, was marked and decided.

Missouri caught the reflex tide of population, and her fertile soil, mineral wealth and commercial advantages not only retained this reflex population, but supplied an effective appeal to thousands more from all parts of the country—North, East and South—until for a few years her population increased at the rate of nearly one hundred thousand per annum. And yet, in her extended area of territory, this immense influx was scarcely perceptible. Along her rivers and railroad lines her population thickened, and her great commercial centres felt the life and power of multiplied agencies and resources.

Either the rapid growth of cities, the stir and excitement of trade, the strife for fortune and fame, the magical charm of Western life, or something else peculiar to the climate, the country or the people, all of these distinct and opposing types of social life began soon to lose their "type force" and blend into a conglomerate social mass, with fewer Northern, Eastern and Southern peculiarities than Western—a rather unique social formation, which the modern socialogists have not yet classified.

Few Southern men and Southern families long retained their purely Southern style of life, and few Eastern or Northern men and families long retained the social and domestic habits that were peculiar to the latitude from which they hailed. It is easy to see how the social life that derives its characteristics from such different and distant systems would be peculiar in itself and to itself.

People lose their social characteristics much sooner and more easily than they do their religious peculiarities. The former are based on education, taste, association and habit, the latter on principles vital and divine. As every national and social characteristic known to American society has become mixed and blended in Missouri, so every shade of religious thought and feeling, every form of religious doctrine and dogma, together with every type of ecclesiasticism known to modern American civilization, exists in the hearts and homes of Missouri—at least to some extent. Nearly every shade of religious belief has a representative in Missouri, and stands out more or less distinct upon the moral phases of society.

These do not blend. No moral alchemist can fuse the distinct religious peculiarities of a people. Men may relinquish their social and domestic characteristics because they are matters of taste or convenience; but to give up their distinctive religious characteristics is considered a sacrifice of principle and conscience.

Men do not struggle long to maintain and propagate that which was peculiar to their former social life, but will contend forever for that which is peculiarly distinctive in their religious belief. That which men hold lightly and esteem of little value to them elsewhere assumes an importance and a value in the West, and will not be surrendered tamely. Religious ideas which in Massachusetts and South Carolina existed in the mind crudely or loosely, exerting no influence upon the life, would in Missouri take a permanent shape, seek affinities, and ultimately grow into churches struggling for a place in the great moral agencies of the State. Men whose religious habits were scarcely formed, and whose lives had not assumed any positive ecclesiastical type in the older States, on coming to Missouri became positive, decided, unequivocal, sectarian partisans, and often uncharitable bigots. Men who would contend fairly for their distinctive tenets elsewhere contend fiercely here, and very few live long in this State without espousing, to some extent, the cause of some religious sect.

There are causes for this state of things. Society is, to a great extent, in a formative state. In very few places, if any, has society settled down into grooves, and channels, and circles, and social and church castes, as in the older States; and then society exists in a great variety of unassimilated elements, Northern, Southern, Eastern, Western; English, French, German, Scotch, Irish, with a hundred different shades of social and domestic life, which are too distinct to become homogeneous, and which seek in church creeds and church associations their social as well as religious affinities.

The result is that, perhaps, no other State can furnish as great a variety of distinct sects, or denominations of Christians, with the religious population so liberally distributed amongst them. There may be more sects in States that have a much larger population, but in proportion to the population, no State has a greater variety of churches which accommodate such a diversity of belief, each of which has so large a hold upon the public mind.

It would, indeed, be anomalous if all of these sects

could exist together in peace. Missouri can not claim such exceptional distinction. In, perhaps, no State or country has denominational contention and strife been more general and uncompromising.

Not willing to accept the standards of doctrine published and recognized by each church, nor to abide by the verdict of learned debates upon all questions of difference, ministers and members, with astonishing freedom and with defiant presumption, enter the arena of controversy, public and private, with a zeal and a spirit equally hurtful to Christian charity and the general cause of true piety. Nothing can awaken a community more generally and excite the people more intensely than a public debate, formally arranged and pitched by two noted champions. The notoriety gained by the *antagonistæ* outlasts, if it does not outreach, the settlement of disputed questions. And, then, each man or woman, however old or young, must become an adept in religious controversy, and convert every road side, street corner, shop, office, counting room, kitchen and parlor into a place for petty, spiteful theological disputation. Instead of edifying one another in love, and deepening the work of grace in the heart by appropriate religious conversations, they embitter the sectarian spirit, destroy Christian charity, alienate personal friendship, "and dote about questions and strifes of words, whereof cometh envy, strife, railings, evil surmisings, perverse disputing of men of corrupt minds, and destitute of the truth."

With many, sectarian jealousy is equaled only by sectarian bigotry, and the great work of soul-saving is made only tributary to denominational success. Indeed, many go so far as to deny the virtue of saving grace to all but themselves, and vainly imagine that the saving virtues of the atonement are transmitted to the hearts of men only through their church ministrations and distinctive ordinances.

Nothing excites sectarian jealousy more thoroughly than great religious awakenings and revivals in any given church. It is natural that the minister of the gospel who, as a human instrument, is very successful in winning souls to Christ should be "highly esteemed in love for his work's sake," and yet nothing exposes him more to the unjust criticisms and unchristian detractions of his less successful brethren in the ministry. Let a revivalist be successful in stirring the religious life of a whole community and in producing a general religious awakening, and the ministers and members of other churches, instead of joining heartily with him in the great work and laboring together for the general good, will watch with jealous interest the progress of the work, discuss with uncharitable criticism its character, and seize the first opportunity to begin a meeting of their own, that they may make the religious awakening of the community inure to their denominational advantage. Should the revival occur in a small town where the whole population Christianized could not more than adequately support one healthy church organization, with one pastor, instead of assimilating all the religious elements, it would act like a moral solvent, disparting and isolating each shade of religious belief and thought. "Where two or three are gathered together" of the same belief they will organize, send for a pastor and set up for themselves.

Thus the little community becomes divided into little sectarian factions, each to drag out a half-conscious, miserable, contentious existence, instead of uniting in one large, healthy, self-sustaining congregation, with all the benefits and advantages of a first-class minister well supported, a good church and Sabbath school, with all the regular ministrations of the gospel.

These things can not be affirmed of all ministers of the gospel, nor of all churches and communities in Missouri; but the facts are too common, too prominent and deplorable to be overlooked in any legitimate search for the *animus* of sectarianism in Missouri.

Where the differences between denominations are essential they are agreed upon their differences and live in peace, each pursuing a distinct line of operations in its own way unmolested, and their lines rarely, if ever, cross each other. On the other hand, where the difference is non-essential, they will not agree to disagree, and wrangling and contention, disputings and debates, mark the conflict. Where the difference lies in fundamental doctrines, debates are rare and formal. If the difference lies in ecclesiastical polity, or in forms of worship, or in sacraments or modes of ordinances, the discussions are interminable and the petty disputations endless. The nearer denominations approach each other in all that is essential in doctrine, worship and works of righteousness, the deeper seated and more bitter the jealousy and strife between them. Non-fraternization and non-intercourse are maintained with much punctiliousness between those Churches which are one in origin, one in doctrine, and one in all of their essential characteristics, but which have separated from each other upon questions of ecclesiastical polity, or for some other like cause.

Judging from the character of the strife between them, their methods of ecclesiastical warfare, and the downright animosity that enters into and characterizes these strifes, one would readily suppose that, according to their own interpretation, their peculiar commission is to overcome, root out, exterminate and supplant the church that bears the same "image and superscription." Particularly is this true when the essential grounds of difference are political.

For confirmation of this position it is only necessary to refer to the two Methodist, the two Presbyterian, and recently the two Baptist Churches of this State, which are divided, not upon doctrines or ordinances, but upon questions of ecclesiastical polity—whether ecclesiastical bodies, *as such*, have the right to legislate upon or intermeddle with questions that belong to the State, and must be controlled by the State.

This allusion is sufficient for the present purpose. It only remains to be noted here how readily ecclesiastical partisans take advantage of everything in political and civil strife that will confer upon them power and position. How readily they identify themselves with dominant parties, if by so doing they can damage their ecclesiastical opponents and gain position and power for themselves! How heartily they endorse the policy of the party in power, if by it their own disability is exchanged for temporary enfranchisement, and their own minority is invested with temporary power to oppress and persecute the hated majority!

History repeats itself; and the genius of religious

persecution and proscription has discovered very few new expedients and adopted very few new instruments since the days of the Master. The manger of Bethlehem cradled the Incarnate Innocence, and Pilate's judgment hall gave birth to the diabolical genius of persecution, which was equal to the task, in that it did there and then invent and employ the only expedient that could at once be successful in the crucifixion of Incarnate Innocence, and in transmitting itself to every country and age with undiminished efficiency to pursue to prison and to death the followers of its first and greatest Victim as long as time should last. The cry of disloyalty and treason made by ecclesiastics is now, as it always has been, the strongest appeal to the guardians and defenders of the State; and as that was successful before Pilate, and forced him to sign the death warrant of the Master, so it has been successful in every tribunal of earthly power, and procured the death warrant of all the martyrs in every country and age, and under every form of government and every phase of ecclesiasticism from that day to this. "We found this fellow perverting the nation, forbidding to give tribute to Cæsar, saying that he himself is Christ—a king." "If thou let this man go thou art not Cæsar's friend; whosoever maketh himself a king speaketh against Cæsar." Such declarations made by the High Priests of the Church could, and did, influence the Roman Procurator against the convictions of his better judgment, against reason, against all the facts, against right and against innocence. What were all these to the life-blood of their victim?

In some form or other these charges have been repeated in every systematic persecution of ministers of the gospel and martyrs for the truth, from Stephen,

Antipas, Polycarp and Barnabas to the Bartholomew Massacre in Paris, and from the revocation of the Edict of Nantes and the Papal Inquisition to the last great tragedy in the drama, occurring during and since the late civil war in America, in free Missouri and under the ægis of institutions that boast of religious liberty, and the sanction of men who profess to represent the advanced Christian civilization of the age.

But, then, "the disciple is not above his Master, nor the servant above his Lord." "Remember the word that I said unto you, The disciple is not above his Lord. If they have persecuted me they will persecute you."

They beheaded John, crucified Christ, stoned Stephen, murdered Paul, "and others had trial of cruel mockings and scourgings, yea, moreover, of bonds and imprisonment; they were stoned, they were sawn asunder, were slain with the sword; they wandered about in sheepskins and goat-skins, being destitute, afflicted, tormented; of whom the world was not worthy."

Every age and country have reproduced in some form the altar and the victim, the persecutor and the persecuted, the Caiaphas and the Christ, without material alteration in the charge or the trial. Missouri has provided the altar, the wood, the fire and the sacrifice for the offering demanded by this age and country in the interest of the Church. Woods, Sexton, Glanville, Wollard, Robinson, Wood, Headlee and others supplied the sacrifice.

While this chapter prepares the way, in an important sense, for the better understanding of the subject in hand, it will also embody a standing declaration and testimony against the peculiar spirit and character of sectarian strife in Missouri.

CHAPTER IV.

Division of the Church in 1844—Slavery only the Occasion—Action of the General Conference in 1836—Slavery in the Church in 1796 and in 1836—No Change of its Moral Aspects in 1844—Facts Perverted—Constitutional Powers of the Church—Bishop Andrew, a Scapegoat—Protest of the Southern Conferences—Resolution and Plan of Separation—Dr. Elliott and Schism—The Vote—The Question in the South—Louisville Convention in 1845—Division—The Bishops of the M. E. Church Accept the Division the following July—Failure to Change the Sixth Restrictive Rule—General Conference of 1848 Pronounce the Whole Proceedings Null and Void—Dr. Lovick Pierce Rejected—Fraternization Denied—Responsibility of Non-Fraternization—Northern Church Refuse to Make any Division of Property—Appeal to the Civil Courts—Decision of the United States Circuit Court for the Southern District of New York—Justice McLean—United States Circuit Court for the Southern District of Ohio—Judge Leavitt's Decision—Supreme Court of the United States—Points Decided—The Decision of the Supreme Court in Full.

It is due to the uninformed that a true statement be made here of the causes, conditions, plan and immediate results of the great division, in 1844, of the Methodist Episcopal Church in the United States. This is made the more necessary by the misrepresentation of the facts made by the press and pulpit of the Northern wing of the Church, and the political and other uses a perversion of the facts was made to subserve in Missouri.

1. Slavery was not, in any proper sense, the *cause* of division, but was made, incidentally, the *occasion* only. American slavery had existed in the Church for sixty years in the same form, and under the same civil and religious sanctions that authorized and covered it in

1844. If it was the "sum of all evils" in 1844, it was the same in 1796; and the moral character of the institution was not changed in 1836, when the General Conference in Cincinnati, by a vote of 120 to 14, adopted the following *preamble* and resolutions:

"WHEREAS, Great excitement has prevailed in this country on the subject of modern abolitionism, which is reported to have been increased in this city recently by the unjustifiable conduct of two members of the General Conference, in lecturing upon and in favor of that agitating subject; and, whereas, such a course on the part of any of its members is calculated to bring upon this body the suspicions and distrust of the community, and to misrepresent its sentiments in regard to the points at issue; and, whereas, in this aspect of the case, a due regard for its own character, as well as a just concern for the interests of the Church confided to its care, demand a full, decided and unequivocal expression of the ideas of the General Conference in the premises; therefore,

"*Resolved,* By the delegates of the Annual Conferences in General Conference assembled, that they disapprove, in the most unqualified sense, the conduct of two members of the General Conference, who are reported to have lectured in this city recently upon and in favor of modern abolitionism.

"*Resolved,* That they are decidedly opposed to modern abolitionism, and wholly disclain any right, wish or intention to interfere in the civil and political relation between master and slave as it exists in the slaveholding States of this Union."—*Bangs' History of the Methodist Episcopal Church, vol. 4, pp. 245, 246.*

This is rather strong language, but not more so than the pastoral address issued by the same General Conference. In that address the following language is used: "It can not be unknown to you that the question of slavery in these United States, by the constitutional compact which binds us together as a nation, is left to be regulated by the several State legislatures themselves, and thereby is put beyond the control of the general government *as well as that of all ecclesiastical bodies*, it being manifest that in the slaveholding States themselves the entire responsibility of its existence or non-existence rests with those State legislatures; and such is the aspect of affairs in reference to this question that whatever else might tend to meliorate the condition of the slave, it is evident to us, from what we have witnessed of abolition movements, that these are the least likely to do him good." Reasons are given amply sufficient to prove that abolition speeches and publications all "tend injuriously to affect his temporal and spiritual condition, by hedging up the way of the missionary who is sent to preach to him Jesus and the resurrection, and thereby abridging his civil and religious privileges."

"These facts," the address continues, "which are only mentioned here as reasons for the friendly admonition which we wish to give you, constrain us, as your pastors, who are called to watch over your souls, as they who must give an account, to exhort you to abstain from all abolition movements and associations, and to refrain from patronizing any of their publications, and especially from those of that inflammatory character which denounce in unmeasured terms those of the brethren who take the liberty to dissent from them." * * * * "From every view of the subject which we have been able to take, and from the most calm and dispassionate survey of the whole ground, we have come to the solemn conviction that the only *safe, scriptural* and *prudent* way for us, both as ministers and people, to take, is wholly to refrain from this agitating subject which is now convulsing the country, and consequently the Church, from end to end, by calling forth inflammatory speeches, papers and pamphlets. While we cheerfully accord to such all the sincerity they ask for their belief and motives, we can not but disapprove of their measures as alike destructive to the peace of the Church and the happiness of the slave."—*Bangs' History of the M. E. Church, vol. 4, pp. 258, 260.*

It is patent to every candid observer that the Church in 1836 did not consider the subject of slavery as the "sum of all evils," and therefore to be extirpated at whatever cost to Church and State, but rather that the danger to the peace of the Church and country was not in slavery itself, but in the "abolition movements," "speeches and papers" that were "convulsing the country and Church from end to end," and "that the only *safe, scriptural* and *prudent* way for both ministers and people was wholly to refrain from this agitating subject." Slavery was, according to this address, "*beyond the control of all ecclesiastical bodies,*" and it would have been fortunate for the peace and welfare of both the Church and the country had it remained beyond their control, and had the teachings and deliverances of all ecclesiastical bodies upon this subject remained just as this General Conference expressed it in 1836.

Slavery remained unchanged; and if it was "safe, scriptural and prudent" for the Church in '36 to let it alone, and leave it under the "control of the State legislatures," where "the constitutional compact which binds us together as a nation placed it," why was it not "safe, scriptural and prudent" to do the same in '44? Did slavery, as a domestic, moral or civil institution present any new aspects in 1844? What civil or moral questions were applicable to slavery in 1844 that did not equally apply in 1836 or 1796? Had slavery just been admitted into the Church for the first time, then those who contend that it was the cause of division would have some show of reason. If slavery was the "sum of all villainy" in 1844 it was in 1793, unless time can change the character of "villainy," for it *did not* change the character of slavery. If a slaveholder was "a thief, a robber, a murderer and a sinner above all others" in 1844, he was the same in 1836. Nathan Bangs, George Peck, Charles Elliott, Orange Scott, and many others were members of the General Conference of 1836, but they did not discover such mighty man-defrauding, God-defying wrongs in slavery and slaveholders then. Their optics were different when, in 1844, the effort to make the institution of slavery a proper subject for ecclesiastical legislation, by deposing Bishop James O. Andrew from the Episcopal office because his wife had inherited slaves, revealed the dangerous advances the Church had made toward the control of civil questions.

In this case "certain constructions of the constitutional powers and prerogatives of the General Conference were assumed and acted on, which were oppressive and destructive of the rights of the numerical minority represented in that highest judicatory of the Church." It was upon the "construction of the constitutional powers of the church" that they differed, and in the discussions and decisions that followed "certain principles were developed in relation to the political aspects of slavery, involving the right of ecclesiastical bodies to handle and determine matters lying wholly outside of their proper jurisdiction."

No candid man who will study the philosophy of that memorable Conference in the light of the plain facts can believe that slavery was more than the occasion for the separation.

When men willfully pervert the facts of history, or misrepresent the connection and bearing of these facts, they must have a motive, and candid men are justified in suspecting an end that can not be reached by straightforward, honorable means.

Northern Methodist preachers had become fanatical on the subject of the abolition of slavery—had recently discovered great moral wrong in the "peculiar institution," and commenced a war upon everything that favored the existing relations of master and slave. All at once it was discovered that all the resolutions and pastoral address of 1836 were in sympathy with the "sum of all villainies," and for that reason should be disregarded. It was discovered that ministers of the gospel were slaveholders—which had been the case from the beginning—and the most noted instance then existing was James O. Andrew, a man of unblemished character, unswerving integrity and singular purity of heart and life. Why not take him for a scapegoat? They needed one, for many of them had been connected with the same institution in one way or another. But how could they reach his case? Did the law of the Church cover the case? Did the constitution of the Church confer upon the General Conference the power to depose a Bishop because his wife had inherited a slave, and the laws of the State would not admit of emancipation? Could not a majority of the General Conference so interpret and construe the law that the case could be reached, and the "abolition movement" that had been unequivocally condemned eight years before be just as unequivocally indorsed now and greatly advanced by the great Methodist Church in the United States? And what if this assumption of constitutional power should be rejected? Aye, there was the rub. *This was the cause.* Admit the authority of the General Conference to depose a man from office for incidental or even positive complicity with slavery, and with it the right is established to depose a man from the ministry for complicity with democracy, republicanism, or any thing else purely political. The same authority extends to the ballot-box and all the distinctive privileges of citizenship.

There were other questions incidentally brought out at the Conference of 1844 which tested the *animus* of the delegates from the North, and disclosed the construction placed by their leaders upon the constitutional prerogatives of the college of Bishops.

Any one at all acquainted with ecclesiastical government can readily see how these questions could divide the Church whether slavery had an existence or not.

The same questions have produced division in ecclesiastical bodies since slavery was abolished.

It was not the three cents a pound upon tea that caused the American revolution of 1776, but the right to tax tea to that amount involved the right to make every man in the British colonies a slave; and the right to depose Bishop Andrew implied the right to depose every man from the ministry who differed from the numerical majority upon any political question whatever.

To all sober, unbiased, right-thinking, candid men this position will be undeniable—unanswerable. To others it will be like "casting pearls before swine."

2. The *plan* of division provided a remedy for the *cause* of division. The one stands in the light of the other. When the action in the case of Bishop Andrew was taken in the General Conference of 1844 the delegates from thirteen Annual Conferences, making fifty-one in all, drew up a declaration in which they set forth the fact that in the slaveholding States the objects and purposes of the ministry would be defeated by it. Upon this protest the General Conference raised a committee of nine, six from the Northern Conferences and three from the Southern Conferences, to whom the declaration was referred. After deliberation they submitted what is known in history and in law as the "Plan of Separation."

It begins thus:

"WHEREAS, A declaration has been presented to this Conference, with the signatures of fifty-one delegates of the body from thirteen Annual Conferences in the slaveholding States, representing that, for various reasons enumerated, the objects and purposes of the Christian ministry and church organizations can not be successfully accomplished by them under the jurisdiction of the General Conference as now constituted; and,

"WHEREAS, In the event of a separation, a contingency to which the declaration asks attention as not improbable, we esteem it the duty of this General Conference to meet the contingency with Christian kindness and the strictest equity; therefore,

"*Resolved 1,* Provided that should the Annual Conferences in the slaveholding States find it necessary to unite in a distinct ecclesiastical connection, all the societies, stations and Conferences bordering on the line of division, adhering by vote of a majority of the members of the society, station or Conference to either the Church in the South or the M. E. Church, shall remain under the unmolested pastoral care of the church to which they do adhere."

The rule was not to apply to interior charges, which shall, in all cases, be left to the care of that church within whose territory they are situated.

It should be observed that the Plan of Separation was thus agreed upon by the General Conference: "Should the Annual Conferences in the slaveholding States find it necessary to unite in a distinct ecclesiastical connection." They were to be the sole judges of the *necessity* of such "distinct ecclesiastical connection." The "plan" also provided for "ministers of every grade and office" adhering either North or South, "without blame," and for a change of the sixth restrictive rule by a constitutional vote of all the Annual Conferences, so that in the event of separation an equitable *pro rata* division of the Book Concerns at New York and Cincinnati, and the Chartered Fund at Philadelphia, could be made. It provided, also, for the division of the property by a joint commission, in which N. Bangs, S. Peck and J. B. Finly were to represent the Church North; and the ninth resolution was as follows:

"*Resolved 9,* That all the property of the Methodist Episcopal Church in meeting-houses, parsonages, colleges, schools, conference funds, cemeteries, and of every kind within the limits of the Southern organization, shall be forever free from any claim set up on the part of the Methodist Episcopal Church, so far as this resolution can be of force in the premises."

It is pertinent to the case to state here that on the day the "committee of nine" was raised, and before it was formed or announced, the following resolution was passed, without debate:

"*Resolved,* That the committee appointed to take into consideration the communication of the delegates from the Southern Conferences be instructed—provided they can not, in their judgment, devise a plan for the amicable adjustment of the difficulties now existing in the Church on the subject of slavery—to devise, if possible, a constitutional plan for a mutual and friendly division of the Church."

The adoption of this resolution, without debate, embodied and announced the decision of the General Conference upon the constitutional powers of the body to divide the Church.

An effort was made to strike the word "constitutional" from the resolution, but it failed, and the resolution as passed forms a part of the history of the division, bearing directly upon the constitutional prerogatives of the General Conference.

Dr. Charles Elliott, who subsequently made himself notorious by denouncing the Church, South, as a secession, and by making war upon the "Plan of Separation" and all that it accomplished, was the first man in the General Conference to move the adoption of the report of the committee of nine, and in a long speech he urged, with many arguments, the practicability, the propriety, the necessity and the expediency of a division of the Church, avowing distinctly that "were the present difficulty out of the way there would be good reason for passing the resolutions contained in the report. The body was too large to do business advantageously. The measure contemplated was *not schism*, but separation for their mutual convenience and prosperity.

After much debate and a full and free discussion of every possible point that could be raised by that able body of men, amongst whom were many of the best constitutional lawyers of the Church, the report was adopted; the vote on the several resolutions varying from 135 to 153 in the affirmative, and from 22 to 12 in the negative. These were certainly very large majorities, and show plainly the *animus* of the General Conference of 1844.

With implicit confidence in the sincerity and good faith of this action, the Southern Conferences proceeded to ascertain whether there existed a necessity in the Southern States for the separation thus provided for.

The Southern Conferences were to be the *sole judges* of the necessity for such action as would make this provisional separation a real one; and that in their judgment such necessity did exist, the history is in proof. However greatly the opinions and purposes of men may change, the facts of history that have gone to official record can not change. Upon such facts intelligent judgment alone can rest, and to such facts an honest public will always make a final appeal.

"The Annual Conferences in the slaveholding States" *did* "find it necessary to unite in a distinct ecclesiastical connection," and for that purpose met in convention, in Louisville, Ky., in 1845, and reduced the possible contingency to fact. In the organization of a "distinct ecclesiastical connection" the Louisville convention adhered strictly to the plan adopted by the General Conference of 1844. The division of the church into two distinct co-ordinate branches, which was considered a contingency, and, as such, provided for in 1844, was, by the action of the "Annual Conferences in the slaveholding States" represented in the convention at Louisville, made an accomplished fact in 1845. After this convention erected the "Annual Conferences in the slaveholding States" into a "distinct ecclesiastical connection" the Bishops of the M. E. Church (North) met in New York, July, 1845, and passed, among others, the following resolution:

"*Resolved,* That the plan adopted in regard to a distinct ecclesiastical connection, should such a course be found necessary by the Annual Conferences of the slaveholding States, is regarded by us as of binding obligation in the premises, so far as our administration is concerned."

They also gave instructions respecting the voting of

"those societies bordering on the line of division, to decide for themselves whether they would adhere to the Church North or South." And they further declared that they did not feel justified in presiding over the Conferences South, and struck them from their plan of Episcopal visitation. Thus the Bishops of the Church, North, quietly and gracefully resigned their jurisdiction over the Southern Conferences, because they considered the "Plan of Separation" adopted in 1844 of "binding obligation."

The division of the Church was recognized by the Bishops of the North as an accomplished fact, and the "Plan of Separation" as of "binding obligation." And it may fairly be assumed that, had there been no property interests to be divided according to that plan, *pro rata*, there would have been "a mutual and friendly division of the Church." But after the separation had been accomplished and recognized as legitimate and of "binding obligation," the Northern wing of the Church discovered that the required vote of the Annual Conferences to change the sixth restrictive rule was not obtained, and the pretext was furnished them to refuse a *pro rata* or any other division of the property that was held by the Northern Church, which consisted of a Book Concern in New York, what was known as a Chartered Fund in Philadelphia, and a Book Concern in Cincinnati.

To ignore and set aside the claims of the Church, South, to the common property it was necessary to pronounce the General Conference of 1844 incompetent to divide the Church, and to declare the "Plan of Separation null and void," so that "there should exist no obligations to observe its provisions." This was done by the Northern General Conference of 1848, after the separation had been acknowledged by their Bishops as an accomplished fact, and the "Plan of Separation" as of "binding obligation."

Dr. Lovick Pierce, father of Bishop Pierce, and the noblest Roman of all, was duly accredited to this General Conference of 1848 as the fraternal messenger of the Church, South, to express to that body the Christian regards and fraternal salutations of his Church. Upon the reception of his credentials the General Conference "*Resolved,* That as there are serious questions and difficulties existing between the two bodies it is not proper at present to enter into fraternal relations with the M. E. Church, South."

Fraternal intercourse was declined by official action. The door was shut, and the fraternal messenger of the Church, South, stood without, feeling most keenly the unchristian rejection. That he felt the dishonor, the humiliation, the insult thus offered to his Church most sensibly the closing words of his communication to that body, upon being notified of his rejection, is in evidence: "You will now regard this communication as *final* on the part of the Methodist Episcopal Church, South. She can never renew the offer of fraternal relations between the two great bodies of Wesleyan Methodism in the United States. But the proposition can be renewed at any time, either now or hereafter, by the Methodist Episcopal Church; and if ever made, upon the basis of the Plan of Separation as adopted by the General Conference of 1844, the Church, South, will cordially entertain the proposition."

His language to the General Conference of the Church, South, in submitting his report to that body, was worthy of the great cause he was delegated to serve, worthy of his Church, and worthy of himself. One single sentence of that report illustrates the whole, and reflects the highest honor on his head and heart: "Thus ended the well-intended commission from your body. Upon this noble effort I verily believe the smile of Divine approbation will rest when the heavenly bodies themselves have ceased to shine. We did affectionately endeavor to make and preserve peace, but our offer was rejected as of no deserving."

He returned home and, with his entire Church, had to accept the situation thus decreed by the M. E. Church, North. And with the responsibility of non-fraternization rests the shame and disgrace of the fact, in the estimation of the enlightened Christian world, as well as all the damaging results.

But the Church, North, knowing that the Church, South, could not be divested of her legal rights to the property otherwise, proceeded to set aside the Plan of Separation, to pronounce the Church, South, a schism, and to decline all fraternal intercourse. Thus cut off as illegitimate, as schismatics and as secessionists, by an action wholly *ex parte*, all claim upon the common Church property was denied, and all the authority of commissions to settle with the Church, South, was revoked.

An appeal to the civil courts was thus made necessary, and the strong arm of the civil law was evoked to force the unwilling conscience of the Northern Church, and to become "a judge and a divider over us."

It is unnecessary to give in detail the history of these civil suits. Suffice it to say, that the United States Circuit Court for the Southern District of New York and the Supreme Court of the United States both recognized and affirmed the authority of the General Conference to divide the Church, pronounced that body competent to provide a plan of separation, fix a boundary line, determine the *status* of ministers, adjust the rights of property, and erect two separate and distinct ecclesiastical bodies, of co-ordinate existence and authority, out of the M. E. Church of the United States. These highest judicial tribunals of the country did affirm the validity of the "Plan of Separation" adopted by the General Conference of 1844 to be of "binding obligation" in every part and particular; and, notwithstanding the failure of the sixth restrictive rule, the United States Circuit Court for the Southern District of New York caused a decree to be entered, November 26th, 1851, ordering a *pro rata* share of the property of the New York Book Concern, including both capital and produce, to be transferred to the agents of the M. E. Church, South, and it was referred to the Clerk of the Court to ascertain the amount and value of the property. When he reported, exceptions were filed, the Court could not agree upon some points, and the case was certified to the Supreme Court of the United States for decision.

Judge McLean, a leading member of the M. E. Church, and at the time one of the Justices of the United States Supreme Court, induced the Commissioners of the two parties to come together in New York. The result of this interview was an agreement between them about dividing the property of the New York Book Concern, which agreement was afterward made a part of the decree of the U. S. Circuit Court, December 8th, 1852. By this decree the property of the New York Book Concern was settled, of which the Church, South, obtained about $191,000.

It may not be out of place to insert here a part of the decision of the United States Circuit Court for the Southern District of New York, Justice Nelson and Judge Betts presiding. The former delivered the opinion of the Court.

After analyzing the Plan of Separation, the decision of the Court goes on to say: "Now, it will be seen from this analysis of the Plan of Separation that the only condition or contingency upon which an absolute division of the Church organization was made to depend was the action of the several Annual Conferences in the slaveholding States. If these should find it necessary to unite in favor of a distinct organization, by the very terms of the Plan the separation was to take place according to the boundary designated. It was left to them to judge of the necessity, and their judgment is made final in the matter. And when the division is made, and the Church divided into two separate bodies, it is declared that ministers of every grade and office in the Methodist Episcopal Church may, as they prefer, remain in that Church, or without blame attach themselves to the Church, South. The whole Plan of Separation confirms this view. As soon as the separation takes place, in accordance with the first resolution, all the property in meeting-houses, parsonages, colleges, schools, Conference funds and cemeteries, within the limits of the Southern organization is declared to be free from any claim on the part of the Northern Church. The general and common property, such as notes and other obligations, together with the property and effects belonging to the printing establishments at Charleston, Richmond and Nashville, and the capital and produce of the Book Concern at New York, was reserved for future adjustment. This was necessary on account of the restrictive article upon the power of the General Conference. * * * When the Annual Conferences in the slaveholding States acted, and organized a Southern Church, as they did, *the division* of the Methodist Episcopal Church into two organizations *became complete.* And so would the adjustment of the common property between them, if the assent of all the Annual Conferences had been given to the change of the restrictive article. The failure to give that has left this part of the plan open, the only consequence of which is to deprive the Southern division of its share of the property dependent upon this assent, and leave it to get along as it best may, unless a right to recover its possession legally results from the authorized division into two separate organizations."

The suit for a division in the Cincinnati Book Concern was brought in the United States Circuit Court for the District of Ohio, July 12th, 1849. The evidence agreed on by the counsel for both parties was the same used in the New York case. Justice McLean declined to sit in the case, because he had previously expressed his opinion that the Sixth Restrictive Rule could be constitutionally modified by the General and Annual Conferences so as "to authorize an equitable division of the fund with the M. E. Church, South."

Judge Leavitt presided, and reached the decision that "the General Conference possessed no authority, directly or indirectly, to divide the Church." And that, as the Annual Conferences did not change the Sixth Restrictive Rule, the Church, South, could not recover; and dismissed the suit. He said, however, that the power to divide the Church "rested with the body of the traveling ministry, assembled *en masse* in a conventional capacity." This was fatal to his whole decision; for since the first delegated General Conference in 1808, the whole body of the traveling ministry had been assembling by delegation every four years, and authorized to exercise all the powers of the entire body of traveling preachers, six clearly defined restrictions on its powers only excepted.

From the decision of Judge Leavitt the Commissioners of the M. E. Church, South, appealed to the Supreme Court of the United States. That august tribunal was then composed of Chief Justice Taney, and Associate Justices McLean, Wayne, Catron, Daniel, Nelson, Grier, Curtis and Campbell. (Justice McLean did not sit in the case.)

The cause was heard in Washington City, in April, 1854, and the decision in favor of the rights of the Church, South, was without dissent from any of the Justices. Judge Nelson delivered the opinion of the Court, April 25th, 1854. The main points settled by that decision are these: (1) That the Methodist Episcopal Church in the United States was divided. (2) It was not a secession of a part from the main body. (3)

By it neither division lost its interest in the common property. (4) The General Conference of 1844 had the power to divide the Church into two distinct ecclesiastical bodies. (5) The six restrictive articles did not deprive the General Conference of the authority and power to divide the Church. (6) The proposed change of the Sixth Restrictive Rule was not a condition of separation, but to enable the General Conference to carry out its purpose. (7) The separation of the Church into two distinct parts being legally accomplished, the "Plan of Separation" must be carried out in good faith, and a division of the joint property by a Court of Equity follows as a matter of course.

By this decision of the Supreme Court the M. E. Church, South, obtained from the Cincinnati Book Concern, in money, bonds, Southern notes and accounts, about $93,000.

These facts have all been gathered from official documents, and will not be denied. If they serve to place before the public, in a succinct form, the true history of the division of the Church, and by so doing countervail the many misrepresentations and mischievous falsehoods that have led to the unprovoked persecutions of the ministers of the M. E. Church, South, in Missouri and elsewhere, the end will be reached and the labor will not be in vain.

As the decision of the Supreme Court of the United States in the above case is not accessible to every reader, it may serve the purpose of history, while it serves the cause of truth and righteousness, to put in convenient form, and as a befitting close to this chapter, that decision in full—except so much of it as was necessary to carry out the decree of the Court in detail.

DECISION OF THE SUPREME COURT.

"WILLIAM A. SMITH, *et al.*, *vs.* LEROY SWORMSTEDT, *et al.*

"This was the appeal from the Circuit Court of the United States for the District of Ohio, which dismissed the bill.

"This cause came on to be heard on the transcript of the record from the Circuit Court of the United States for the District of Ohio, and was argued by counsel. On consideration whereof it is ordered, adjudged and decreed by this Court that the decree of said Circuit Court in this cause be and the same is hereby reversed and annulled; and this Court doth farther find, adjudge and decree:

"1. That under the resolution of the General Conference of the Methodist Episcopal Church, holden at the city of New York, according to the usage and discipline of said Church, passed on the eighth day of June, in the year of our Lord one thousand eight hundred and forty-four (in the pleadings mentioned), it was, among other things, and in virtue of the power of said General Conference, well agreed and determined by the Methodist Episcopal Church in the United States of America, as then existing, that in case the Annual Conferences in the slaveholding States should find it necessary to unite in a distinct ecclesiastical connection, the ministers, local and traveling, of every grade and office in the Methodist Episcopal Church, might attach themselves to such new ecclesiastical connection without blame.

"2. That the said Annual Conferences in the slaveholding States did find and determine that it was right, expedient and necessary to erect the Annual Conferences last aforesaid into a distinct ecclesiastical connection, based upon the discipline of the Methodist Episcopal Church aforesaid, comprehending the doctrines and entire moral and ecclesiastical rules and regulations of the said discipline (except only in so far as verbal alterations might be necessary to or for a distinct organization), which new ecclesiastical connection was to be known by the name and style of the Methodist Episcopal Church, South, and that the Methodist Episcopal Church, South, was duly organized under said resolutions of the said Annual Conferences last aforesaid, in a convention thereof held at Louisville, in the State of Kentucky, in the month of May, in the year of our Lord one thousand eight hundred and forty-five.

"3. That by force of the said resolutions of June the eighth, eighteen hundred and forty-four, and of the authority and power of the said General Conference of the Methodist Episcopal Church, as then existing, by which the same were adopted; and by virtue of the said finding and determination of the said Annual Conferences in the slaveholding States therein mentioned, and by virtue of the organization of such Conferences into a distinct ecclesiastical connection as last aforesaid, *the religious association known as the Methodist Episcopal Church in the United States of America, as then existing, was divided into two associations, or distinct Methodist Episcopal Churches, as in the bill of complaint is alleged.*

"4. That the property denominated the Methodist Book Concern at Cincinnati, in the pleadings mentioned, was, at the time of said division and immediately before, a fund subject to the following use, that is to say, that the profits arising therefrom, after retaining a sufficient capital to carry on the business thereof, were to be regularly applied toward the support of the deficient traveling, supernumerary, superannuated and worn-out preachers of the Methodist Episcopal Church, their wives, widows and children, according to the rules and Discipline of said church, and that the said fund and property are held under the act of incorporation in the said answer mentioned by the said defendants, Leroy Swormstedt and John H. Power, as agents of said Book Concern, and in trust for the purposes thereof.

"5. That, in virtue of the said division of said Methodist Episcopal Church in the United States, the deficient, traveling, supernumerary, superannuated and worn-out preachers, their wives, widows and children comprehended in, or in connection with the Methodist Episcopal Church, South, were, are, and continue to be, beneficiaries of the said Book Concern to the same extent and as fully as if the said division had not taken place, and in the same manner and degree as persons of the same description who are comprehended in, or in connection with, the other association, denominated, since the division, the Methodist Episcopal Church, and that as well the principal as the profits of said Book Concern, since said division, should of right be administered and managed by the respective General and Annual Conferences of the said two associations and Churches under the separate organizations thereof, and according to the shares or proportions of the same as hereinafter mentioned, and in conformity with the rules and Discipline of said respective associations, so as to carry out the purposes and trusts aforesaid.

"6. That so much of the capital and property of said Book Concern at Cincinnati, wherever situated, and so much of the produce and profits thereof as may not have been heretofore accounted for to said Church, South, in the New York case hereinafter mentioned, or otherwise, shall be paid to said Church, South, according to the rate and proportions following, that is to say: In respect to the capital, such share or part as corresponds with the proportion which the number of the traveling preachers in the Annual Conferences which formed themselves into the Methodist Episcopal Church, South, bore to the number of all the traveling preachers of the Methodist Episcopal Church before the division thereof, which numbers shall be fixed and ascertained as they are shown by the minutes of the several Annual Conferences next preceding the said division and new organization in the month of May, A. D. eighteen hundred and forty-five.

"And in respect to the produce and profits, such share or part as the number of Annual Conferences which formed themselves into the Methodist Episcopal Church, South, bore at the time of said division in May, A. D. 1845, to the whole number of Annual Conferences then being in the Methodist Episcopal Church, excluding the Liberia Conference, so that the division or apportionment of said produce and profits shall be had by Conferences, and not by numbers of the traveling preachers.

"7. That said payment of capital and profits, according to the ratios of appointment so declared, shall be made and paid to the said Smith, Parsons and Green, as Commissioners aforesaid, or their successors, on behalf of said Chuch, South, and the beneficiaries therein, or to such other person or persons as may be thereto authorized by the General Conference of said Church, South, the same to be subsequently managed and administered so as to carry out the trusts and uses aforesaid, according to the Discipline of said Church, South, and the regulations of the General Conference thereof."

CHAPTER V.

FROM THE DIVISION OF THE CHURCH, IN 1845, TO THE BEGINNING OF THE CIVIL WAR, IN 1861.

Provisions of the Plan of Separation — Time of Division — The Missouri a Border Conference — Vote on Adhering North or South nearly Unanimous—The Disaffected—Covenant Breakers —The M. E. Church in Missouri after the Division—Her Ministers and Members — How Regarded — Relative Strength of the Two Churches in Numbers and Property—Sympathy—Persecution—Tenacity in Spite of Opposition—Success the only Revenge —The Class of Northern Methodist Preachers—Their Connection with Clandestine Efforts to Free the Slaves—Their Condemnation and their Secret Service—Character of the Old Missourians—Their Vindication—Northern Methodists Condemned for being Secret Political Partisans, and not for Preaching the Gospel—The Anti-Slavery Element in Missouri Ten Years before the War—Lawful vs. Clandestine Means—"Underground Railroad" and other Nefarious Schemes to Run off the Slaves of Missouri—These Things Condemned by the Anti-Slavery Party—Public Meetings of Citizens in the Interest of Order and Peace.

The "Plan of Separation" adopted by the General Conference of 1844, to which attention is given in the preceding chapter, fixed the line of separation along the line of division between the free and the slaveholding States, for the most part, and provided as follows, to-wit:

"1. That, should the Annual Conferences in the slaveholding States find it necessary to unite in a distinct ecclesiastical connection, the following rule shall be observed with regard to the northern boundary of such connection: All the societies, stations and Conferences adhering to the Church in the South, by a vote of a majority of the members of said societies, stations and Conferences, shall remain under the unmolested pastoral care of the Southern Church, and the ministers of the Methodist Episcopal Church shall in no wise attempt to organize churches or societies within the limits of the Church, South, nor shall they attempt to exercise any pastoral oversight therein: it being understood that the ministry of the Church, South, reciprocally observe the same rule in relation to societies, stations and Conferences adhering by vote of a majority to the Methodist Episcopal Church; provided, also, that this rule shall apply only to societies, stations and Conferences bordering on the line of division, and not to interior charges, which shall in all cases be left to the care of that Church within whose territory they may be situated."—*General Conference Journal, vol. 2, p. 135.*

The Missouri Annual Conference was one of the Conferences "bordering on the line of division," and the question of adhering North or South was thoroughly canvassed and decided almost unanimously in favor of the South. Those ministers favoring the North were allowed to adhere North "without blame," by the "Plan of Separation." They were seven out of one hundred and thirty-six.

Prior to the session of the Conference in Columbia, in the fall of 1845, when the vote was taken, the "societies and stations," along the border particularly, were asked to decide by a vote of the members whether they would adhere North or South. The vote was so nearly unanimous in favor of adhering South that not a single "society or station" in the Conference gave a majority in favor of adhering

North, and in very few of them was there a division at all. In a few societies along the border, such as St. Louis, Hannibal, Lagrange and some others, and a few scattering societies in the interior, there was a small minority in favor of adhering North. These were generally men recently from the Northern States, or mal-contents who rejoiced in the occasion thus afforded to seek notoriety or revenge in a contentious faction. Such persons are found, more or less, in every community, and unfortunately for the peace of society some sections of Missouri unwittingly offered special inducements to that class of immigrants, and received quite a large surplus of them from the older States. Amongst the few disaffected of Missouri Methodists who would not go with the majority in this division may have been some honorable exceptions, but they were few and far between, and only prove the general rule.

The vote to adhere South was so general in the State that no one thought of accepting the "pastoral care" of the ministers of the M. E. Church, North, until after that Church had pronounced the "Plan of Separation null and void," and had proceeded to violate their plighted faith and disregard every "binding obligation in the premises."

The right and authority of one party to set aside and declare "null and void" a solemn contract or covenant entered into by two parties, without the consent of the other party, is not debatable. The failure of the sixth restrictive rule, according to the decision of the United States Supreme Court, did not vitiate the covenant, nor had the M. E. Church, South, up to 1854, by act or deed, according to the same high authority, forfeited the covenant to the other party by any failure to comply with its provisions.

The assumption of authority, therefore, by the M. E. Church to set aside the conditions of the covenant, to violate what their Bishops had pronounced its "binding obligations in the premises," to reject the fraternal messenger and ignore the claims of the Church, South, and proceed to "organize churches and societies within the limits of the Church, South," could only exhibit to the world their utter recklessness of moral obligation and place them before the public as covenant breakers, "truce breakers and false accusers."

In such light were they and their friends and abettors held in Missouri, after the Church in the whole State had decided so positively to adhere South. Indeed, so general was this decision, that for many years after the division the existence of the M. E. Church, North, in Missouri was scarcely suspected by the best informed.

There were but few places in the State where their presence was tolerated; not because of any religious or political proscription and persecution, but because their presence in Missouri was not only unauthorized, but in direct violation of the most solemn ecclesiastical compact, for which an instinctive sense of right in every community was disposed to hold the Northern Methodist preachers responsible.

All our best notions of religious toleration revolt at the idea of proscribing the largest liberties of any church in any country or community for any reasons. But, then, when a church deliberately proscribes herself and fixes her own limits of territory, transferring all her claims to property and privileges beyond her self-appointed boundaries to another and a "distinct ecclesiastical organization," a decent respect for moral obligation and the covenanted rights of others demand that every enlightened community should hold every such church to the strictest accountability for every violation of her self-imposed obligations. Covenant breakers forfeit their claims to all the benefits of the covenant broken, if they do not forfeit their claims upon the confidence and protection of the community whose rights and privileges the broken covenant respected.

Communities whose sense of justice and moral right are outraged by religious teachers, to whom neither civil nor criminal law will apply, have recourse only to a public sentiment which can place the guilty under the ban of public condemnation. The Northern Methodist preachers who were trying to "organize societies" and "exercise pastoral care" in Missouri, from the division of the Church in 1844 to the beginning of the civil war in 1861, need not be reminded how terrible and general was this ban of public condemnation. It was not a proscription which they themselves had not authorized; nor could they claim the benefits of a persecution for righteousness' sake without confessing to an indictment which truth and honesty found against them for obtaining said benefits under false pretenses. They raised the cry of persecution, but failed to enlist the popular sympathy due to such a cry, because the virtues and elements of a religious persecution were all wanting. They, nevertheless, managed to keep up a factious, feeble organization in some places in the State, sustained by missionary money from the North, which took advantage of every popular excitement against them to manufacture foreign sympathy, and, at the same time, furnished a convenient refuge for the disaffected, mal-contents, of the M. E. Church, South.

They sought, by maintaining a convenient proximity to the Southern Church, not only to catch the Methodist immigration from the North, but, also, to afford a convenient retreat for those who seek in prominence what they lack in piety, and to "beguile unstable souls" with the false plea of "Old Church" and "Old Methodism." Thus, while serving all the purposes of factious agitation, and furnishing in themselves an example of covenant breaking for covetousness' sake, which can never be reproduced and re-enacted, they have, also, served the purposes of peace and purity by receiving from other churches the contentious, the dissatisfied and the disaffected. It was an easy road to a miserable revenge, as it was often a happy riddance of a pestilent element, while the rule of loss and gain was reversed.

The relation of the two churches during that period to the people of the whole State will be seen in their statistics. At the time of the division the whole Church in Missouri numbered 26,310 members, served by 113 traveling preachers. In 1850 the M. E. Church, South, had 27,012 members and 126 traveling preachers in Missouri alone. In 1850 the M. E. Church, North, had 5,474 members and fifty-one traveling preachers in Missouri and Arkansas together.

The relative strength of the two churches in 1860 is seen in the following figures: The M. E. Church, South, had 48,797 members and 243 traveling preachers, and the M. E. Church, North, had 6,619 members and sixty-nine traveling preachers.

In church property there was a much greater difference. When the Church divided, all the property in churches, parsonages, cemeteries, colleges, Conference funds, and of every other description, passed into the hands of the M. E. Church, South, according to the "Plan of Separation." Those who voted to adhere North were not strong enough in any one place to set up any claim to the Church property. The Church, North, was thus left without houses of worship or any other property possessions in the State. By common consent, as well as by the decision of the courts, the division of the Church extinguished the right and title of the M. E. Church to all property in the State of Missouri. The struggle for existence, under the circumstances, was a forlorn hope, and the erection of churches in communities where they were not in sympathy with either the masses or the moneyed people was a slow and doubtful enterprise. They had to rely, for the most part, upon private houses in obscure neighborhoods for places of public worship, for it was not always that they could even get the use of school houses for that purpose. In St. Louis they had one Church, Ebenezer, which had to supply them with church facilities for the whole State for many years. They built a small church in Hannibal in 1850. In 1856 they added Simpson Chapel, in St. Louis, to the list, and then, in 1858, they erected a small brick church in Jefferson City, for which they had help from abroad. These were all small churches, but amply sufficient for all their wants. They may have had a few other small churches in different sections of the State, but their number and resources were quite small, and their influence for good in each community was unfortunately counteracted by the spirit of contention and strife they created. In 1860 the whole of their Church property in this State and in Arkansas was estimated in their statistics at $36,400.

Under these circumstances it is not surprising if they made up in bitter, spiteful jealousies what they lacked in the true elements of success, and repaid the public disapprobation in a dogged tenacity that seeks revenge in success despite all opposition.

They had no friendly feeling for the Church, South, and gladly and freely employed every means to disaffect and disintegrate the Southern organization, especially in obscure neighborhoods. Nor did they scruple at the grossest misrepresentations of the facts concerning the division of the Church.

Their preachers traversed the State and visited every family that was suspected of being in sympathy with them; and wherever two or three could be gathered together of kindred sympathy they were organized into a society, regularly visited, and made a nucleus around which to gather the disaffected and disappointed of the M. E. Church, South.

The preachers engaged in this work were not of the class and style of men whose ministrations would reach and affect the intelligent and cultivated portions of the people. They were, for the most part, rough, uncultivated and illiterate, and hence their social and intellectual affinities were found among the lower classes and the ignorant. They were the kind of men to be doggedly pertinacious, and to know nothing amongst men outside of one idea, one purpose, one cause. They looked upon everything that did not favor them and their cause as wrong *per se*, and considered their mission unfulfilled until it was righted or removed.

They had more patience than charity. They could bide their time, but could not tolerate opposition. They could proscribe, and even persecute, others for opinion's sake, but could not endure with fortitude the reflex influence of their own bigotry.

Public opinion and jesuitical policy required them to be discreet as ministers of the gospel in their public performances, but as partisans they were strangely indiscreet. They were sent into Missouri by the authorities of their Church distinctly and thoroughly indoctrinated in the belief that the success of the Church whose credentials they bore was in the success of the anti-slavery party; hence they were secret and earnest partisans *out of the pulpit*. They associated with abolitionists, and warmly espoused every measure for the abolition of slavery. Whether right or wrong, slavery existed then by the authority of the Constitution of the State and under the protection of her laws; and, like all other men, slaveholders could not surrender tamely their constitutional and legal rights to that species of property in which they had invested their money, much less could they look with indifference upon the presence and movements of men who were seeking by clandestine, "under-ground" methods to render insecure their property by means neither open nor honorable.

No class of men were more favorably circumstanced for the prosecution of such a work than these Northern

Methodist preachers, and they were considered by the abolition party as indispensable to final success.

It was in the character of partisans, and not ministers, that they were put under the ban of public sentiment. The fact that they were ministers of the gospel, and that they used the privileges of their profession to further the objects of a party that sought by unlawful and disingenuous means the extirpation of slavery, made their presence, character and work the more offensive to the people of the State. The common opinion among men who cared less for the institutions of Christianity than for the institutions of the State was that the Northern Methodist preachers in this State were wolves in sheep's clothing. Only by an unseemly torture of facts could they make it appear that they were opposed and persecuted because they were ministers of the gospel.

When ministers of the gospel become political partisans, and expect their high calling to protect them in a sinister attempt to abolish the institutions and laws under which the rights of property are protected, they should not complain if honorable men detect and denounce the hypocrisy.

The spirit of reckless insubordination that animated these fanatical preachers has often, of late, found emphatic utterance through their Church papers. This is its language: "We must teach people to make better laws, or trample upon such as are made, if we expect to meet God in peace."

But in those days the utterance was in the signs and symbols of secret societies, and the execution was in the by-ways, around the corners, in "Uncle Tom's cabin," in occasional doses of poison and midnight arson, with the aid of butcher-knives, axes and "under-ground railroads." For such work true ministers of the gospel are never held responsible; but when it is incited and aided by those calling themselves such, the verdict of double guilt can not be escaped.

It would be as unfair to say that all Northern Methodist preachers in the State engaged in this nefarious business as to say that none of them were respectable, Christian gentlemen. Suspicion rested upon all of them, because the grounds of suspicion were too strong and the evidence of guilt too general to make wholesale exceptions. Nor did the masses of the people know or care to discriminate.

It is true that very few men of worth, of ability, or of standing in the M. E. Church could be had for this work. They looked upon it as involving much toil, sacrifice, suffering, and perhaps martyrdom, for which they were not candidates. But men who had broken down in other fields, and were no longer wanted in other Conferences, and men who had despaired of distinction in the more honorable fields of competition with their brethren, embraced the opportunity thus afforded to win notoriety.

The men who could consent to do such work for a political party while they wore the cloth of a holy calling were the pliant tools of the John Browns and others who were prominent leaders in the great crusade against the institutions of the South.

It is due to the truth of history to state that the old settlers of Missouri and the slaveholders of that day were high-minded, honorable, intelligent men, who would scorn to proscribe and persecute men for opinion's sake, or protect and harbor men who would secretly and treacherously use the hospitality of the slaveholder to reach the slave and poison his mind against his master, and inspire him with the hope of freedom by the torch and the dagger.

Missourians were not hypocrites, nor would they abuse a generous hospitality, betray either public or social confidence, or seek by underhanded, sinister means the destruction of the rights of property and the guarantees of domestic and social order. However they may be characterized by ugly epithets and maligned by partisan hirelings, they will stand vindicated on the pages of history as humane, generous, peaceful, prosperous, intelligent, honorable and high-minded citizens, who could neither perpetrate a mean act nor tolerate, even in so-called ministers of the gospel, the abuse of confidence or domestic treachery.

In illustration of the abuse of hospitality to secret abolition purposes, one instance in a thousand must suffice.

In the spring of 1856 Mr. Thomas E. Thompson, of Palmyra, Mo., was returning home late on Saturday evening, when he found a stranger by the road side preparing to camp in a corner of the fence, with his wife and child. He had unharnessed his team and stretched his wagon cloth on the fence over them for a shelter from the inclement weather.

Mr. Thompson stopped and inquired why the stranger did not go into the city and obtain better accommodations; and when informed that he had no money, and thought of spending not only the night but the following Sabbath there, and that the stranger was a Northern Methodist preacher trying to get to Kansas, he told him it would not do, invited them to his house, and offered them a generous hospitality, which was accepted. The child had never seen negroes, was much alarmed at the sight, and would not remain in their presence.

During the night the preacher got to talking to one of the colored women, tried to persuade her that she was free, and that he would assist her to reach Illinois. She reported the facts to Mr. T.; and on Sabbath afternoon he overheard the preacher talking with the husband of this woman in the stable, telling him that he was not only a free man, but that he would do right in taking Mr. T.'s horse, or anything else by which he could gain his freedom. The negro told the preacher to go off and let him alone, that he had a good master, a good home and everything in plenty, and he did not want to be free. Mr. Thompson ordered the preacher to leave, telling him that he could not protect him from violence if the community were apprised of the facts. He let him depart in peace.

If Northern Methodist preachers were condemned, it was not for preaching the gospel and trying to save the souls of men, but for a palpable violation of plighted ecclesiastical faith, and more particularly for their partisan services in the cause of emancipation.

Let it be understood, also, that Missourians did not so much oppose the emancipation of their slaves as they did the means used to accomplish it. For thousands of slaveholders believed that the abolition of slavery would be a blessing both to the slave and the master, if it could be done in a lawful and peaceable way. Many of them were laboring to reach the result through a political organization, by open-handed, lawful means.

For ten years before the war it was a foregone conclusion with the more intelligent classes that slavery would be abolished in Missouri, and a system of free labor adopted that would be more successful in developing the resources of the State. But they looked for it to be done by a change of the Constitution and the necessary legislation; and, while they expected this result to be reached in a lawful way, they heartily detested the secret organizations and treacherous agents that were seeking to decoy the slave from his master, and furnish facilities for his escape from bondage, and his protection from the legal claims of his owner.

This was against law, in contravention of law, and in flagrant violation of constitutional guaranties, which all the courts and officers of the country were sworn to protect and enforce; and hence it was considered by the people and the courts—by the law and the gospel—a *crime* against the peace and dignity of the State. But it was one of those crimes which either could not be covered by statutory enactments, or in the commission of which the statute could be evaded or the guilty party concealed.

Legal processes could not be served; the law could be set at defiance while the mischief was being done; and the only recourse left to the people was in such protection as they could devise outside of the law. Some carried their slaves into the Southern States and disposed of them. And in some communities, where forbearance with these disturbers of domestic tranquillity had ceased to be a virtue, the citizens assembled together in a peaceable and lawful way, interchanged views, and devised the only lawful means left them to protect themselves and secure the public peace. They adopted resolutions, stating publicly and openly their grievances, and warning the abolition emissaries to desist from intermeddling with their property and their rights, and if they could not settle down and become peaceable, law-abiding citizens, then to leave the country for the country's good. In a few counties of the State these public meetings were held, and in no instance was there any indignities or outrages committed on the person or property of any man by such public assemblies or by their authority.

CHAPTER VI.

FROM 1845 TO 1861, CONTINUED.

Responsibility of Ministers, Editors and Publishers—Perversion of Facts, a Double Guilt—Public Meetings—Presses Mobbed—Fabius Township Meeting in 1854—Rev. Mr. Sellers—Review of the Preamble and Resolutions—Meeting at Rochester, Andrew County—Three Facts Affirmed of these Meetings—The Best Citizens Controlled Them—What the Author of the Fabius Township Resolutions Says—Jackson Seminary in Cape Girardeau County—The Jefferson City Land Company and the Great Northern Methodist University—The Transaction Transparent—Resolution of Missouri Conference of 1858—A. Bewley—The True Facts in his Case—That he was Hanged at Fort Worth, Texas, not for being a Minister of the Gospel, but for Complicity in the most Horrible Crimes—The Facts Analyzed—The Bailey Letter—Bishop Morris—Dr. Elliott—Truth is Mighty—Correct View of the Relation of the M. E. Church to the People of Missouri prior to the War.

When historical facts are perverted, or so detached from each other as to destroy their connection, and false impressions are made thereby, and bad feelings created in the interest of designing men, the moral wrong is twofold, and the perpetrators are doubly guilty—falsehood reaches its result on the credit of truth, and Christ, the truth, is fatally wounded in the house of his friends. Ministers of the gospel, editors and publishers are accountable to men and God for the most potent of all responsibility. They are a savor of life or a savor of death, and through them peoples and countries have peace or war.

The uses made by them of the public meetings of citizens held in various parts of this State prior to the war did much to aggravate the spirit of animosity between the Northern and Southern people in Missouri, and to embitter the scenes of war. Some papers were so severe upon certain classes of citizens as to provoke mob violence, when party feeling was at blood heat, and a few printing offices were visited by an insulted populace, and type, press, cases and fixtures thrown into the streets, or made to settle accounts at the bottom of the river, while the editors and publishers were driven off. Public meetings were called in many places by the best citizens, to prevent mob violence and promote the public tranquillity. This was their object.

Much has been said in the Northern press and pulpit about a meeting of the citizens of Fabius Township, Marion county, Mo., held February 18, 1854, just after fifteen slaves had walked off to Canada from that township. It was alleged by these preachers and papers, and the statement is reiterated by Dr. C. Elliott, in his book called "Southwestern Methodism," that the said "meeting was held by the citizens of Fabius Township for the purpose of carrying out a scheme to expel Rev. Mr. Sellers, a minister of the M. E. Church, from the country"—p. 39; and a great hue and cry was raised over the persecution of this Mr. Sellers by the aforesaid citizens. And all the cheap capital was made out of this heroic victim of pro-slavery malice of which the utmost torture of the facts was capable. But, after all, it is rather surprising to find that neither in the long preamble nor in any one of the five resolutions is the name of Mr. Sellers so much as once used; nor do they contain so much as a personal allusion to him or any other individual man. They refer to a class of men, and are directed against a dozen others as much as against Mr. Sellers.

The preamble sets forth, amongst other things, as follows: "And, *Whereas,* there is in our community considerable excitement, arising from the belief upon the part of many of our citizens that the ministers of the Northern division of said Church, who have for some time past been preaching in Fabius Township, are the representatives of a body whose sentiments upon the subject of slavery are decidedly hostile to our interests as slaveholders and dangerous to our peace; and that the leading object of their mission here is the destruction of slavery by the propagation—in any manner not inconsistent with the safety of their persons—of doctrines calculated to array against the institution the weak-minded and fanatical among us, and to create discontent, dissatisfaction and insubordination among our slaves; therefore," &c.

No one will doubt that these utterances were directed against the Northern Methodist preachers as political partisans, and not as ministers of the gospel, and that the cry of persecution for righteousness' sake failed of its sympathy where it failed of the truth.

The *first* resolution advises these men to "desist from visiting and preaching among us."

The *second* is a declaration of rights, and amongst them the following: "When the law fails to protect, we claim to have the natural right, as a community, to resort to the use of such means as will afford us protection."

The *third* affirms that "Northern fanatics have forced the question of slavery into all the churches," and claims protection under the Constitution and laws of the United States government for the institution of slavery thus endangered.

The *fourth* affirms the unity of Methodist doctrine and worship, the validity of the Plan of Separation, and "protests against the M. E. Church, North, sending ministers among us, and respectfully requests such ministers to make no more appointments in this vicinity."

The *fifth* is as follows: "That, as we are situated contiguous to Quincy, a city containing some of the vilest abolition thieves in the Mississippi Valley, and as we have already suffered so much at the hands of these incendiaries we regard it as absolutely necessary to the protection of our slave interests that we close our doors against abolition and free-soil influences of every character and shade, and that we shall, therefore, esteem it highly improper for any citizen hereafter to countenance or encourage the preaching or teaching in this community of any other minister or teacher, person or persons, the representatives of, or in any way connected with, any church or churches, any association or society, whether religious or political, or of any character whatsoever, who have heretofore or shall hereafter take ground, directly or indirectly, expressly or impliedly, against the institution of slavery."

That resolution is both special and general. It may apply to Mr. Sellers, and it may apply to Dr. Elliott, and a hundred others, as abolitionists and not ministers, or as abolitionists and ministers.

A similar meeting was held in Rochester, Andrew county, in June, 1856, at which resolutions of a similar character were passed. In a few other places, too, the people assembled peaceably and expressed their disapprobation of their course and asked them to desist. But whatever may be said to the contrary in partisan publications, the page of unerring history will affirm *three* facts of the people of Missouri in these meetings:

1. That the M. E. Church, South, as such, had nothing whatever to do with them; while her members, *as citizens,* were only equally interested and implicated in them with the members of other churches.

2. Whenever these meetings denounced the preachers of the M. E. Church, North, it was not because they were ministers of the gospel, *as such,* but because they abused the privileges of their profession, and were secret, active political partisans and abolition emissaries.

3. Mob violence was never instigated by these meetings, but prevented. No man suffered in person or property from them in Missouri.

In confirmation of this position it is only necessary to state the fact that the best class of citizens were the prime movers in these public meeting, and, indeed, they were only called when it became apparent that the peace and safety of the community demanded it; for in every community there are passionate, reckless men, who are ready to take the law into their own hands and vindicate their rights, at whatever danger to the public safety. But the best men of the country, and those who had the deepest interest in its peace and security, entered the most heartily into these meetings, as peace measures, and they now, and will ever, believe that such meetings were necessary to prevent mob violence and insure the general tranquillity.

The author of the Fabius Township resolutions, a distinguished citizen and lawyer of Marion county, and a colonel commanding a regiment of Missouri Militia in the Union army during the war, not only anthorizes the above statement, but affirms freely that, though he had been an anti-slavery man for many years, and rejoices in the emancipation of the slaves as he does in the restoration of the Union, yet he endorses that meeting and those resolutions to-day, and would conscientiously pursue the same course again should a similar state of things exist in the community to demand it. An old citizen of Missouri, a member of no church—friendly to all—a Union man from first to last, speaking, working and fighting to restore and preserve the supremacy of the Federal government, he would make affidavit to-day that, to the best of his knowledge, the three facts above stated are fully vindicated in the Fabius Township and all similar meetings held for similar purposes in Missouri. Thousands of the best citizens of the State are ready to affirm the same facts and vindicate the good people of Missouri against the aspersions of the Northern press.

Similar meetings to that of Fabius township were held in Andrew county, in Independence, Jackson county, in Cass county, and perhaps other places, and with similar results. In no single instance was the M. E. Church, South, implicated. In no single instance were the ministers of the M. E. Church, North, mobbed or murdered, and in no single instance was mob violence against the "vilest abolition thieves" coun seled or countenanced; and with all honest people who know the facts the hue and cry raised in certain quarters about religious intolerance, mob violence, persecution of ministers, and the martyrdom of innocent and holy men is as gratuitous as it is contemptible.

When the lower House of the Missouri Legislature, in February, 1855, refused, by a vote of sixty to thirty-six, to charter what was called the Jackson Seminary, in Cape Girardeau county, for the Northern Methodists, it was not because the representatives of the people opposed the establishment of literary institutions, or wished to proscribe any form of religion, but because, as then stated, the Northern Methodist preachers were the emissaries of abolitionism, and by encouraging them in establishing institutions in Missouri they encouraged their purposes and organization to subvert the lawful institutions of the State, which the law-makers did not hesitate to affirm would be encouraging a cowardly, clandestine treason against the laws and government of the State. Four years later the Legislature refused to charter a university at Jefferson City for the Northern Methodists, for the same reason.

The "Jefferson City Land Company," to encourage immigration, build up the city and enhance the private fortunes of its members, proposed a liberal grant of land to the Northern Methodists, or any others, who would build up and endow, with foreign capital, a university at the State Capitol. Though many of the members of this Land Company were slaveholders, and some of them large slaveholders, they believed that the introduction of free labor into the State would greatly facilitate the development of her material resources, by building railroads and opening her vast beds of coal, and lead, and iron to the markets of the world. They conceived the idea of inviting and encouraging free labor from the Northern States through the active agency of the Northern Methodist Church.

The class of immigrants they desired were opposed to negro slavery, and the Northern Methodist Church was opposed to negro slavery. Methodist ministers, more than any other ministers, were in sympathy with the anti-slavery surplus populations of the Northern and Eastern States, and could influence them more. Hence the alliance.

The proposition to donate so much land for a university, even at a fictitious value, was a splendid prize for that church in Missouri, backed, as it was, by the names and influence of some of the first men of the State, and located at the seat of political power—the State Capital.

On the other hand, the promise of the most extensive and efficient agency in the world actively working throughout the dense populations of the older States to put into operation a system of emigration that would fill up the State with industrious laborers, absorb the surplus lands and enrich the centers of settlement, was a tempting premium upon the cupidity of the "Jefferson City Land Company," for which they could afford to give up their slaves and their former principles.

The inevitable logic of facts does not compliment either the benevolence of the Land Company or the religion of the Church. The members of the Land Company may have been anti-slavery from principle, and their benevolent donation may have been unselfish if so, they were unfortunate in their schemes; if not so, they were unskilled in dissimulation.

They succeeded in this much, at least, in making the impression pretty general that their creed was a policy, and their policy was simply a question of loss and gain. Not that they loved slavery less, but that they loved money more; not that they loved the Northern Methodist Church more, but that they could use that Church better: while the success of the other party resolved itself into a question of deception; either deceiving themselves or deceiving others — possibly both.

Residing in Jefferson City at the time, and being personally acquainted with each member of the Land Company, as well as cognizant of all the facts, the author feels justified in thus making transparent the shrewd scheme about which so much was said at the time. The only motive for this *expose* is a vindication of the truth of history and an analysis of the spirit of the times before the war.

After the failure of the "Jefferson City Land Company" and the M. E. Church, North, to build up a Cambridge or a Harvard at the State Capital the Land Company subsided, and the Church directed attention to other expedients and sought a footing in Missouri through other agencies. Public sentiment was against them; political prejudices and social barriers denied them access to the people. All other religious denominations were unfriendly to them; their best preachers left them, and either went into the M. E. Church, South, or returned home. The better class of Northern immigrants, even from their own Church at home, found it to their interest to seek other church connections.

A suspicion followed them into the domestic, the social and the business relations of life, which manifested too clearly the instinctive sense of moral justice and religious fidelity in the public mind to be either mistaken or escaped by them as covenant breakers, false accusers and clandestine enemies to the property and peace of the State. It was natural for them under such circumstances to long for redress, and gladly embrace and use every means in their power to effect their purpose. They had a lively conception of the horrors of slavery, and more skill than conscience in magnifying them for the Northern press and the Northern public. By this means the Northern mind was misled, and many a victim of their misrepresentations was undeceived only on coming to Missouri and seeing for himself the system of slavery, not as it existed in a blinded imagination, but as it existed in the homes and on the farms of slaveholders; and abandoning their deceivers, they vindicated both the system and the people from the false impeachment of unscrupulous fanatics. This made against them and exasperated them, and when they found that they were not sufficiently successful in deceiving the public mind to secure even the letters with their bearers from their own Church in the Free States, the Missouri Conference, in 1858, uttered complaint in the following resolution:

"*Resolved,* That we hereby earnestly and affectionately request our brethren of other Conferences, in dismissing from their charges, by letter, members who intend immigrating to Missouri, that they be at pains to inform them that, under the blessing of the great Head of the Church, the Methodist Episcopal Church in this State is living and thriving, and urge upon them the propriety of attaching themselves to our Church here immediately on their arrival."

Several Quarterly Conferences took action on the subject, and set forth more fully the grounds of complaint, which even Dr. Elliott could not escape or overlook in his "Southwestern Methodism."

Perhaps no event in the history of those times furnished them more food for comment and capital than the hanging of the Rev. Anthony Bewley by the citizens of Fort Worth, Texas, in September, 1860. Out of this event the strangest system of falsehood was manufactured by designing men to fire the Northern Methodist heart against the Southern people, especially the Southern Methodists.

It was at a time when the country was convulsed with political excitement from one end to the other, and partisan politics, more or less, colored every report of the affair. It was almost impossible at the time to get a true history of the event, as the most extravagant statements were put in circulation to influence the Presidential election the following November. The reports in the papers made at the time, and under the pressure of the most exciting and embittered political campaign known to the history of this country, must be received with great allowance and heavy discount. After the heat of political excitement, when every ballot stood for a thousand bullets, and the fire and blood of the civil war that followed have all passed away, when passion and prejudice can no longer serve the purposes of party, the following facts appear upon the surface and bear the imperial image and superscription of truth:

1. That the Rev. Anthony Bewley, a minister of the M. E. Church, North, was hung at Fort Worth, Texas, September, 1860.

2. That the said Bewley had been living in Texas but a short time, operating when he could as a minister of his Church, but connected with an extensive secret organization for the purpose of freeing the slaves, at whatever risk to the peace, the property, and the lives of citizens.

3. That he was implicated in a nefarious plot to poison wells, fire towns and residences, and, in the midst of conflagrations and death, to run off the slaves. This fact rests upon much oral and documentary evidence.

4. That a Vigilance Committee had been formed to ferret out the plot, capture the guilty parties and bring them to justice.

5. That this Committee had cause to suspect Mr. Bewley, ascertaining which he fled the country and made his way to Missouri, whither he was pursued by them, captured, and taken back to Fort Worth.

6. That the evidence was so strong against him that neither the Vigilance Committee nor the officers of the law could protect him from the outraged and enraged populace, and about midnight he was taken by force and hung.

7. That if there was a member of the M. E. Church, South, on the Vigilance Committee, or in the mob that hung him, the evidence does not appear.

8. Neither the extremest torture of facts nor the most distorted construction of collateral circumstances can implicate Bishop Pierce, or any other Bishop, minister, or member of the M. E. Church, South, as such, in the murder of Bewley.

9. With all due respect to the character of the Northern Methodist publications of this affair, and to Dr. Elliott in his "Southwestern Methodism" in particular, it may be asked with some degree of consistency, "Was Bishop Ames Bewley's hangman?" Bishops Janes and Ames are responsible for Bewley's appointment to Texas; the latter for his re-appointment, after Bewley had made him acquainted with all the facts existing there that would prevent his usefulness and endanger his life. The Bishop sent him upon a missionary appropriation of $400, for which he pledged the Missionary Society of the Church. Bewley and Willet were sent to the Nueces country with specific instructions "not to organize societies next summer, but to correspond with the Missionary Board."

10. The evidence upon which he stood convicted in the public mind of complicity in the bloody plot to poison wells, burn towns, and, through fire and blood and insurrection, free the slaves, convicted others also, who were not ministers of the M. E. Church. It can not be made to appear, therefore, by any legitimate construction, that he suffered *because* he was a minister of that Church, but *because* he was a ringleader in the clandestine scheme of fire and murder, that was too diabolical to discriminate even in favor of women and children, but doomed all indiscriminately who might drink of the wells, or be the victims of midnight con-

flagrations, or in any way be exposed to the wide-spread negro insurrection thus instigated. *For this cause,* and not for preaching the gospel, he was hanged.

11. The following letter, written by one Rev. W. H. Bailey, addressed to Rev. A. Bewley, and acknowledged by him to have been received and subsequently lost, was the principal evidence upon which he was convicted. Bewley acknowledged to his brother-in-law, Mr. John Cook, that the letter was genuine, and had been received by him and lost. The letter was dated, "Denton Creek, Texas, July 3, 1860," and was found by the Vigilance Committee, authenticated, and extensively published by the secular and religious papers of the country, and is as follows:

"DENTON CREEK, July 3, 1860.

"*Dear Sir:* A painful abscess in my right thumb is my apology for not writing to you from Anderson. Our glorious cause is prospering finely as far South as Brenham. There I parted with Brother Wampler; he went still further South. He will do good wherever he goes. I traveled up through the frontier counties—a part of the time under a fictitious name. I found many friends who had been initiated, and understood the mystic Red. I met a number of our friends near Georgetown. We had a consultation, and were unanimously of the opinion that we should be cautious of our new associates; most of them are desperate characters, and may betray us, as there are some slaveholders among them, and they value the poor negro much higher than horses. The only good they will do us will be destroying towns, mills, &c., which is our only hope in Texas at present. If we can break Southern merchants and millers, and have their places filled by honest Republicans, Texas will be an easy prey, if we only do our duty. All that is wanted for the time being is control of trade. Trade, assisted by preaching and teaching, will soon control public opinion. Public opinion is mighty and will prevail. Lincoln will certainly be elected; we will then have the Indian nation, cost what it will; squatter sovereignty will prevail there as it has in Kansas. That accomplished, we have but one more step to take—one more struggle to make—that is, free Texas. We will then have a connected link from the Lakes to the Gulf. Slavery will then be surrounded, by land and water, and will soon sting itself to death.

"I repeat, Texas we must have, and our only chance is to break up the present inhabitants—in whatever way we can—and it must be done. Some of us will most assuredly suffer in accomplishing our object, but our Heavenly Father will reward us in assisting him in blotting out the greatest curse on earth. It would be impossible for us to do an act that is as blasphemous in the sight of God as slaveholding.

"We must have frequent consultations with our colored friends. (Let our meetings be in the night.) Impress upon their clouded intellects the blessings of freedom; induce all to leave you can. Our arrangements for their accommodations to go North are better than they have been, but not as good as I would like.

"We need more agents, both local and traveling. I will send out traveling agents when I get home. We must appoint a local agent in every neighborhood in your district. I will recommend a few I know it will do to rely upon—namely, Brothers Leak, Wood, Evans,

8

Mr. Daniel Vicry, Cole, Nugent, Shaw, White, Gilford, Ashley, Drake, Meeks, Shultz and Newman. Brother Leak, the bearer of this, will take a circuitous route and see as many of our colored friends as he can. He also recommends a different material to be used about town, etc. Our friends sent a very inferior article—they emit too much smoke, and do not contain enough camphene. They are calculated to get some of our friends hurt. I will send a supply when I get home.

"I will have to reprove you and your co-workers for your negligence in sending funds for our agents. But few have been compensated for their trouble. Our faithful correspondent, Brother Webber, has received but a trifle—not so much as apprentice's wages; neither have Brothers Willet, Mungum and others. You must call upon our colored friends for more money. They must not expect us to do all. They certainly will give every cent if they knew how soon their shackles will be broken. My hand is very painful, and I close.

"Yours truly, W. H. Bailey."

Should any one be tempted to doubt the genuineness of this letter, his attention is directed to what critics call internal evidence, to the testimony of witnesses on the spot, and the acknowledgment of Bewley himself to Mr. Cook, his brother-in-law, and others.

The disclosure of such a diabolical plot, to be executed simultaneously in all parts of the country, with these preachers and others in secret league and clandestine confederation, extending, perhaps, all over the South, and involving a negro insurrection with all the horrible crimes of St. Domingo intensified and aggravated a thousandfold, could not fail to enrage the populace and fire the passions of men to an uncontrollable point.

Upon such provocation Bewley and Bailey were both hung. And with all the efforts made to hold the Southern Methodist papers, Bishops and members responsible for the crime, no papers and no men more deeply regretted and more heartily condemned the act.

How the venerable Bishop Morris, of the M. E. Church, could write—"One of our godly and inoffensive ministers, A. Bewley, was hung by a Texan mob, for no other crime but connection with the Methodist Episcopal Church," it is difficult to conceive unless we assume that he was kept in ignorance of the facts. Surely the good Bishop would not suffer his prejudices to blind him to the true state of things as they will ever stand out in the history of that deplorable event.

Dr. Elliott says: "Mr. Bewley was suspended upon the same limb and tree upon which several negroes and a Northern man named Crawford had been hung." Were these negroes and this "Northern man named Crawford" hung "for no other crime but connection with the Methodist Episcopal Church?" and yet, so far as the facts appear, they were hanged for the same crime of which that "godly and inoffensive minister, A. Bewley," was convicted.

We could excuse the above declaration from the pen of Dr. Cartwright or Dr. Elliott; we could palliate it somewhat had it come from Bishop Ames; but from Bishop Morris! the astonishment can scarcely surpass the mortification.

"Truth is mighty and will prevail;" and from all the rubbish of falsehood and all the coloring of distorted facts the true history of this event will finally reach posterity, and vindicate Southern Methodism of every aspersion made by a subsidized press, and tear the martyr's crown from the victim who expiated his crimes upon "the Crawford limb."

This whole chapter will furnish the reader with a correct view of the relation of the M. E. Church, North, to the people, the property, the laws and the institutions of the State between the division of the Church, in 1844, and the breaking out of the civil war, in 1861. But this is subordinate to the prime object, which is to show, at least, one reason for the conspicuous and efficient agency of Northern Methodist preachers in the vindictive persecution of the ministers of the M. E. Church, South, the seizure and use of Church property, etc., under the constructive association of the latter with slavery, secession, rebellion, treason, &c., &c., during the civil war. A vindictive spirit put many of them in Missouri and in the army during the war. "Vengeance is mine; I will repay, saith the Lord."

CHAPTER VII.

CHARACTER OF THE STRIFE IN MISSOURI.

Conflict of Sentiment—Party Spirit—New England and Missouri Fanatics—Fraternal Blood—"Houses Divided—Three against Two and Two against Three"—Organized Armies and Predatory Brigands—Bull Run, Seven Pines, The Wilderness, Gettysburg and Vicksburg Reproduced on a small scale in every County and Cross Roads in Missouri—War upon Non-Combatants—The Bloodiest Records—Ministers of the Gospel—Their Troubles and Perplexities—Peculiar Trials and Persecutions—Military Fetters put upon the Conscience—Disloyal Prayers and Military Orders.

The mixed population of Missouri, presenting such diverse types of domestic and social life, and such different casts of political and religious belief, could not fail to be turbulent, contentious and almost self-destructive in any civil revolution. The people were not homogeneous, and could not unite upon any principles or policy, civil or ecclesiastical; but, on the contrary, each shade of political and religious faith stood out upon the face of society sharply defined, firmly set and fully armed for both offensive and defensive warfare. Party leaders were bolder, party spirit ran higher, party blood waxed hotter and party strife raged fiercer than in any other State.

When the Northern fanatics adopted a platform and announced a line of policy, the Missouri fanatics of the same school would not only fall into line, but glory in their excess of fanaticism, and push the extremest measures of their Northern masters to the most reckless results. Likewise the Southern fire-eaters, so-called, could always find in Missouri politicians the champions of their extremest measures. Hence it was a common "cant" saying among the politicians that "when the New England fanatics took snuff the Missouri fanatics would sneeze," and, indeed, some times the sneezing was done before the snuff was taken, and in all that was revolutionary and reckless in politics and religion they could "out-herod Herod."

The extremists, North and South, whether religious or political, found the heartiest supporters in Missouri; and that which brought the two sections together in organized warfare brought the citizens of the same neighborhood in Missouri, and even members of the same family, into the sharpest personal conflict. The great battles of Bull Run, Fredericksburg, Vicksburg, the Wilderness, Seven Pines and Gettysburg were reproduced on a limited scale in a thousand places in Missouri. The brush, the prairie, the glen, the road side all over the State sheltered concealed foes, and often witnessed the deadliest combats between neighbors and brothers. Here "houses were divided, two against three and three against two," "a man was set at variance with his father, and the daughter against her mother, and the daughter-in-law against her mother-in-law, and a man's foes were they of his own household." There was in many instances a literal fulfillment of the prediction that "the brother shall deliver up the brother to death, and the father the child, and the children shall rise up against their parents and cause them to be put to death;" and the spirit of contention was too rife to confine itself to the hostile armies, or even the lawless bands of armed men, who, in the name of one party or the other, satiated their diabolical hatred and inordinate cupidity by robbery, plunder, pillage and depopulation with fire and sword.

It is no marvel that the most relentless and inhuman spirit of the war found encouragement, if not protection, and expended its force and fury upon the non-combatant and helpless population of Missouri; for this State furnished the bravest men for the armies and the most dastardly cowards for "home protection." While her brave sons fought and fell upon the fields of honor, making the very blood and death of battle illustrious by an unchallenged heroism, the warfare at home presented scenes of outrage and horror unsurpassed by anything in the annals of civilized warfare, if, indeed, there can be such a thing as civilized warfare, for every thing about it is intensely savage.

Between the "Jayhawkers" of Kansas and the "bushwhackers" of Missouri some whole counties were plundered, some were desolated by fire and sword, and some were almost depopulated. Widows' homes were pillaged and burned, delicate mothers and daughters were captured, taken to camp and compelled to cook and wash for ruffian bands of armed men, to say nothing of nameless indignities and the most horrible crimes. Churches and dwellings were seized, converted into barracks for soldiers, stables for horses, and often burned to the ground in wanton destruction.

It was often heard in boast that the track of armies, or more properly predatory bands, should be lighted through entire counties by the glare of burning buildings, and the threat was too often witnessed in all the midnight glare of faithful execution by the pallid and panic-stricken old men, women and children in midwinter. But the heart sickens at the recital, as the enlightened conscience revolted then at the reality. These statements must suffice to recall the scenes which were enacted and the men who educated and then hardened the public conscience for the crimes committed during the war, against God and his chosen ministers and church, and for the subsequent legislative proscription of ministers of the gospel, as a class, and Christianity as an institution.

The attitude of ministers of the gospel in Missouri toward the issues of the war, and how far they participated, on the one side or the other, in its fatal scenes require notice here.

At the first, and, indeed, for two years and more after the war commenced, the sentiment of the State was so equally divided between the contending sections that ministers who did not propose to forsake their high calling and become active participants in the strife were very cautious in their expressions of sympathy. But as the Northern or Southern feeling predominated in any given locality it became so intolerant as to demand from ministers, as well as all others, an unequivocal avowal of sentiment, which always subjected the minister to the severest criticism and the most unsparing censure when he chanced to think differently from the majority. The people of opposite sentiments denied him access to them for good, withdrew their encouragement and support, and thus forced him either into the army or into exile. The people were so prejudiced and intolerant as to believe that a man of opposite political faith was unfitted, by that fact, to minister to them in holy things

—that sectional sympathy disqualified men for the ministry, and that the men who would preach Christ must either dry up the fountains of human sympathy, surrender all the rights of citizenship, or subordinate the message of life and salvation to the *dictum* of the leaders and representatives of the intolerant spirit of anti-Christ that prevailed. In this shape the persecution of ministers of the gospel commenced in Missouri with the first breaking out of the war. Ministers were forced to give up their pulpits and abandon their congregations where the two were not in sympathy upon the issues of the war.

Many an old man who had been settled for years in one pastoral charge, where his children had grown up and some of them had died, and where all the tenderest and dearest associations known to the sacred relation of pastor and people had ripened and matured around the fireside, in the sick room, the funeral scene, the homes and hearts of grief, and around the bridal and sacramental altars, suddenly found himself and his family proscribed, maligned and friendless in the very homes and hearts in which aforetime their pre-eminence was unchallenged. A bitter necessity forced him often to give up his home and his pulpit, leave his flock in the wilderness and seek protection and support either in the army or among strangers. In this way many ministers, old and young, were driven to a course which they did not elect, and forced into a position which was neither of their own choosing nor consistent with their sense of ministerial propriety and ministerial obligation.

And yet for a position forced upon them by the proscriptive intolerance of their former friends they were held responsible, and even severely censured by the public.

Many went into both armies—not willingly, but by constraint—not of choice, but of necessity—not to fight the living with carnal weapons, but to save the dying with the power of salvation, and to fight the battles of the Lord of Hosts with the spiritual weapons that are "mighty through God to the pulling down of strongholds."

Some ministers of the gospel entered the army as soldiers to fight the battles of the country, and no doubt did it conscientiously, believing it to be a high patriotic duty. They claimed nothing on the score of their profession, but accepted in good faith the issues of war and the arbitrament of the sword. Those who survived the war claim no undue credit, and those who sacrificed their lives for a principle and a cause deserve no censure.

Those who entered either army voluntarily, either as chaplains or soldiers, did it understandingly and, perhaps, conscientiously, and accepted the penalty or reward due to such a position only. As a soldier the preacher claimed no exceptional privileges, and as a preacher the soldier claimed no exemption from duty on the field or punishment at home. But it is a notorious fact that preachers who were in the Southern army as soldiers, and who survived the war and returned to their homes in Missouri, no matter how gladly, gracefully and loyally they accepted the situation, have not met the consideration nor received the treatment in all cases meted out to other Confederate soldiers; nor have preachers from the Union army in all instances been treated as other Federal soldiers who returned from the same regiments and to the same counties. Charity at least demands the belief that this is due rather to the instinctive disapprobation in the public mind of ministers bearing arms at all than to any studied maliciousness; and the belief is just as grateful as it is warranted by the facts. But if it should fall out in the subsequent facts to be presented in this book that a studied malice and a methodical madness have done more than the anti-war sentiment, then, however ungrateful, we must accept the facts as the best interpretation of the antichristian spirit which has exhausted itself upon the ministers of the gospel in this State.

Under this kind of pressure many pastors were without churches and many churches without pastors; and, in many parts of the State, the churches were disorganized and broken up, and the flocks scattered in the wilderness, like sheep having no shepherd. It is true, some ministers refused to be driven, but remained faithful to their trust, in the midst of many discouragements, much threatening, much murmuring, and not a little persecution. Such men, pursuing the even tenor of their way, neither turning to the right or left, reviled, but reviling not again, "counting not their lives dear unto themselves," nor "conferring with flesh and blood," deserve the most honorable mention; and with those who know the pressure of sentiment brought to bear upon them they will ever be revered as the finest models of moral heroism and ministerial fidelity. This class of men were not confined to any one church, but have their representatives in all the churches which, by construction, were considered unfriendly to the ruling powers of the State. Many of them were faithful men of God—men of one work—seeking the souls of men, and continuing "steadfast, immovable, always abounding in the work of the Lord," through all the storm and shock of war; and this, too, at no little cost.

It was a time of wide-spread iniquity with almost all classes. Crime, in every conceivable form, reveled without shame, and hesitated at no atrocity. The officers of law and the courts were alike powerless to punish crime and protect innocence; "and because iniquity did abound the love of many waxed cold," and the man of God who could be faithful to the souls of men without fear or favor had nerve, courage, faith.

His home was at the mercy of lawless bands whose nameless crimes his last sermon rebuked, and his head was a target for the assassin's bullet whose cowardly heart felt the sting of conscious guilt under the searchings of God's truth—a guilt, too, of which the minister was wholly ignorant. More than one faithful watchman, during those "times that tried men's souls," went from his pulpit to find his home in ashes, his wife and children shelterless in the storm, and breadless and friendless in the world; and more than one, who did not know that they had an enemy in the world, were called from their beds at midnight to be shot down like dogs, or butchered like hogs in the very presence of their families, without warning, without any known provocation, and without knowing their murderers.

Some of the brightest and purest lights of the Church went out at midnight—suddenly, appallingly—and their "souls were under the altar" many long, weary hours before the news of their murder could pass beyond the family threshold, and often days before it could even reach the family itself. Many of these murders are wholly unaccountable upon any other hypothesis than that intimated above, as the victims hereafter to be named had kept themselves from strife, and had pursued, with "singleness of heart as unto the Lord," their one calling; they had taken neither part nor lot in the war, one way or the other, and, indeed, were not all of one political faith; their sympathies were—some for the Union and some for the South.

The men who stood faithful amid the faithless were not rash and reckless, but prudent and cautious, as it well becomes those who stand up for the truth in the midst of a crooked and perverse generation. Some ministers, by a prudent, consistent course, ministering to all alike, and keeping their political views and sympathies to themselves, conquered, in a measure, the respect and confidence of the leading men of both parties, after so long a time, and they were henceforth pretty secure. But many had to abandon the ministry for the time being and seek a support in other pursuits.

For some reason, no part of the minister's public exercises were looked to with more interest or scrutinized more closely than his extemporaneous prayers. Military officers, partisan leaders, and all men of strong sympathies either way, watched with more vigilance than devotion the objects, the subjects, the language and the sentiment of the extemporaneous prayers of the pulpit. They were supposed to show the drift of the minister's sympathies and reflect his political sentiments, and many people felt much more interested in that than in any supplications he might make for the pardon of guilt and the salvation of the soul. Post Commanders and Provost Marshals would not unfrequently send written orders to the officiating minister whose sympathies were suspected, commanding him to pray for Mr. Lincoln, for the flag, for the success of the army in crushing out the rebellion, or for the destruction of all traitors, or something else of the sort as a test of loyalty. And often a minister's bread, his home, his liberty or his life were suspended upon and determined by the shade of meaning given to a word or phrase in his prayer. The effort was made to force the conscience at the point of the bayonet, and convert the prayer into blasphemy, or get from it a pretext for executing a malicious purpose already formed, and for which there existed neither cause nor occasion.

CHAPTER VIII.

ANOMALOUS CONDITION OF THE STATE—GREAT EXCITEMENT.

Border Slave State—Missouri State Convention—The Last Hope—Virginia Convention—Missouri would not Secede—Rights in the Union—Disappointment—Anomalous Position—Governor Jackson and General Price—Great Excitement—Ministers Embarrassed—One False Step Fatal—The Sword *vs.* Sympathy—Why the Innocent and Helpless Suffered more in Missouri than Elsewhere—Constructive Sympathy—Predatory Bands—Hon. Luther J. Glenn Commissioner from Georgia — The Effect of the Fall of Fort Sumter and President Lincoln's Proclamation—The State Officers, Legislature and Militia Adhere South—Assemble at Neosho, Pass an Act of Secession, Elect Delegates to the Confederate Congress, etc., etc.—Preparations for War—Union *vs.* Price's Army—State Convention Meets Again—Its Acts and Doings—Two State Governments—Sympathy, Property and Plunder—Ministers Again—Their Course—Days of Fasting and Prayer—Conferences—Meeting in St. Charles—Resolutions—Prudence and Prayer—The Press—Anti-Christ Abroad—*Central Christian Advocate* and a few Facts—Rev. Mr. Gardner—"Men and Brethren Help"—State Convention again in October—The First Oath for Ministers.

The people of Missouri contemplated the possibilities of civil war with the peculiar interests of a border State, fearing that when it came the border slaveholding States would be the main theatre of strife. They looked with the deepest solicitude to every plan for the peaceful adjustment of the troubles, and not until the failure of the "Crittenden Compromise" did they consider the result inevitable. The much talked of "Border States Convention" inspired hope in the less informed, but when nothing came of it the last hope perished.

The Missouri Legislature, by an act, "approved January 21, 1861," called a State convention "to consider the then existing relations between the Government of the United States and the people and Government of the several States and the Government and people of Missouri, and to adopt such measures for vindicating the sovereignty of the State and the protection of its institutions as shall appear to them to be demanded."

This convention assembled in Jefferson City February 28, 1861, and organized and proceeded to the work for which it was called.

By the time of its session no less than seven of the Southern States had, by their conventions, adopted ordinances of secession, declaring themselves separated from the Government of the United States, and organized for themselves a distinct national confederation. Other States were in a greatly disturbed condition, had called State conventions, and would inevitably follow their sister Southern States. War was imminent and preparations for it were active—alarming.

Many still clung to the delusion that the national difficulties would be settled without bloodshed, and that the very preparations for war would prevent it.

Virginia, "the mother of Presidents," had a State convention then, either in session or about to assemble, and the deepest anxiety was felt throughout the whole country as to the course that sturdy old State would take. It was believed that the action of Missouri and Virginia would either prevent or precipitate war, by determining the true position of all the border slave States; consequently, every act of these conventions, and every sentiment uttered in them, was watched and weighed with an interest and eagerness never before known in the history of the country.

In Missouri the liveliest interest was taken by all the

people in the debate on the report of the committee on Federal Relations, and not until it became an ordinance of the Convention could the majority of the people in the rural districts believe that the State would not secede from the Federal Union and unite her fortunes with the Southern Confederacy. The simple fact that Missouri was a slaveholding State was sufficient in the minds of many to determine her Federal relations, or at least the policy of secession. Rights in the Union were considered possible by the few; rights out of the Union were considered the only hope by the many.

The fact that the State officers and Legislature, elected just the fall before, were so nearly unanimous in their Southern sympathies that they could, and did, secede in a body without disorganization, and without taking the State with them, shows how strong must have been the Southern feeling at the time of their election. Sectional issues were as clearly and distinctly made in the State as in the Presidential election, and with a unanimity rare in the history of elections the people endorsed the pro-slavery party.

The action of the State convention in February, 1861, put the State in an anomalous condition. The effect was to detach the State government from the State and vacate the several departments of the State government without a vacating ordinance. The representatives in the State Legislature found themselves without a constituency and the people without representatives. It was soon evident that neither Governor C. F. Jackson and his cabinet nor the majority of the General Assembly were in sympathy with the action of the Convention. The President of the Convention, Hon. Sterling Price, and a respectable minority dissented in their feelings from the action of a majority, and conscientiously believed that the true interest of the State was in political and commercial alliance with the Southern Confederacy.

Notwithstanding the majority of the people were loyal to the Federal Government when the delegates to the State Convention were elected, in January, 1861, yet the course pursued by Governor Jackson, General Price, and those high in authority who were associated with them, very greatly unsettled the people of the State in their political faith, and produced such general excitement amongst all classes, that the greatest fears were entertained from the first of an intensity and bitterness of strife in Missouri to which other States would not be subjected.

No one not then residing in the State can fully appreciate the condition of things which this complication of public policy developed. Ministers of the gospel and other non-combatants were not prepared to meet the novel exigencies arising out of such an anomalous state of things, in consequence of which many of them were placed in very embarrassing circumstances, and not a few found themselves forced into positions which their cooler and better judgment afterward condemned. The pride of some kept them in positions where their indiscretion had placed them, and from which their sober judgment would fain extricate them; and in this way many non-combatants were made combatants, and many were forced from their families, their homes, their property and their country. The people were all unused to civil revolutions and inexperienced in the art of adjustment and adaptation. One false step in youth may be fatal to all the objects and aims of life, blast all its hopes and promises, and cause all its plans and purposes to miscarry—may be irretrievably disastrous. So in the first stages of civil revolutions, a mistake may be fatal; and fatal mistakes are common. Men who were not secessionists found themselves fighting for secession, and men who were not Union men were forced by a combination of circumstances to fight for the Union. A man's sword often cut through his sympathies, and his sympathies often formed the scabbard for his sword; while the "aiding and abetting" was as often by constraint and coercion as by choice. Even the regimental colors of opposing armies did not always and faithfully reflect the true sentiment of field and staff, rank and file. Sympathy was too confused and policy too unsettled to admit of either infallible prescience in choice or fidelity in the execution in all cases. Hence many good men suffered for principles not their own, and sacrificed life and all for a cause with which they were not in sympathy.

Popular excitements are never favorable to deliberate prejudgment or right action, and in Missouri more than elsewhere the intensity of excitement at this time dethroned judgment and defeated action. It is believed that much suffering and many of the most shocking features of the war could have been prevented by the party leaders on both sides in Missouri.

It is confidently believed that when a true history of the war is written, it will appear that, in its recklessness of life and wantonness of destruction, and in all its most shameless, and revolting, and nameless crimes perpetrated upon the unoffending, the innocent and the helpless, the non-combatant population of Missouri has suffered more than any other class of people in any State. And much of the sufferings of this class of people is justly chargeable to those into whose hands the conduct of the war in this State was first placed. The just judgment of posterity and the just retributions of eternity will hold to a righteous accountability those who, under whatever pretense, made war upon ministers of the gospel, unoffending old men, and helpless women and children, dragging them to prison and to death, while the pretext for it was found only in the hasty expression of sympathy, or the constructive connection with one side or the other based upon church affiliations.

For instance, Southern Methodists, and Southern Baptists, and Southern Presbyterians were by the Union men and forces constructively identified with secession and rebellion, and put in sympathy with the Southern cause. The first from the beginning, the last two after the virtual disruption of those respective churches.

Under the heat of party passion many innocent victims suffered the spoiling of their goods, and often the loss of life itself, only upon this constructive evidence. The principal portions of the State were always held by the Union forces, and their subordinate officers and independent, predatory bands were either commissioned to make war upon these innocent and defenseless people or they did it without commission. Certain it is that it was done, and done, too, relentlessly and indiscriminately. How far this state of things is due to the converse action of the legitimate State Legislature and the legitimate State Convention—the one elected in November, 1860, and the other elected in January, 1861, and both assuming to reflect the will of the people—and how far it is due to the course pursued subsequently by Governor Jackson, General Price, and the whole State Government, with the legislative branch thrown in, adhering South, may be determined by others. The people of the State, who were not accustomed to a long search after remote causes, were free—and many of them are still free—to attribute these most inhuman features of the war to those who were put in command of the Federal forces in this department, the officers and men of the State militia, and the "Kansas Red-legs," as they were generally called.

The first session of the State Convention did very little more than discuss and determine the Federal relations of the State. The State of Georgia had an accredited commissioner present in the person of Hon. Luther J. Glenn, a distinguished citizen of that State, asking Missouri to secede and join the Southern Confederacy. The Convention heard him respectfully, but, after due deliberation, rejected the proposition, and resolved to remain in and try to preserve the integrity of the Union.

The Convention also appointed a Commission to attend the "Border States Convention," and adjourned to await results.

The people of the State were still in much of a dilemma until after the fall of Fort Sumter, the proclamation of President Lincoln, and the capture of Camp Jackson. Then it was discovered that the State Government, with

Governor Jackson at the head, was in sympathy with the South, and would adhere South in defiance of the Convention. It was also discovered that the "Missouri State Guard," which had been raised, officered, armed and equipped by the Legislature the previous winter, would adhere South, with General Sterling Price in command. These revelations excited and alarmed the people all over the State, and presented new difficulties and embarrassments, which were greatly complicated and enhanced by the simultaneous appearance in different parts of the State of the U. S. forces equipped for war. Indignation and consternation alternated in the public mind, until some definite line of policy was disclosed and the people knew what to expect.

Governor Jackson fled the capital of the State with his officers and army, taking the great seal of State and the official records of the several State Departments with him, as far as it could be done. He convened the Legislature in Neosho, organized and put into operation the several Departments of the State Government. "An Act of Secession" was passed by the General Assembly; delegates were elected to the Confederate Congress; a proclamation was issued to the people of Missouri, and many other things were done to force the State out of the Union and commit her destinies to the fate of the Southern cause. This meant war; and the wisest men abandoned for ever the idea of a peaceful adjustment of the difficulties, and prepared for that which neither the counsels of the prudent nor the prayers of the good could avert.

For the next few months the preparations for war on both sides were active and general. Plows were left standing in the furrows; wheat stood unshocked and ungarnered in the fields; mechanics and artisans closed their shops and exchanged hammers and saws for guns and swords; merchants dismissed their clerks and manufacturers their hands, and all prepared for the war; saddleries, foundries and gunsmiths were pressed out of measure with work, and the country was ransacked for mules and horses for service. The policy was, "He that hath no sword, let him sell his coat and buy one."

President Lincoln's call upon Governor Jackson for the quota of troops from this State to help the Federal Government put down insurrection and rebellion had been promptly and curtly declined by that official, and yet ten times more than the President asked for stood ready to respond to the call in defiance of Governor Jackson.

The cities and towns along the railroad lines especially turned out a heavy surplus population for the Union army, while the river towns and rural districts supplied men and material for "Price's army," as it was familiarly called.

The state of things thus presented made it necessary to convene the State Convention again, which was done by the Committee appointed for that purpose at its first session. In pursuance of the call of a majority of said Committee the State Convention assembled again in Jefferson City, July 22, 1861.

A very different state of things existed now in the State, and the Convention had to meet new questions and provide for new exigencies. The Governor of the State, the president and many members of the Convention, and the Legislature that originated and provided for the Convention, had all cut themselves loose from the Convention and the people represented by the Convention.

The State was virtually without a Governor, and the Governor was without a State. The Convention did not hesitate in meeting these novel exigencies promptly and decidedly. On the seventh day the Convention passed "An Ordinance providing for certain Amendments to the Constitution," which ordinance vacated the offices of Governor, Lieutenant-Governor, Secretary of State and members of the General Assembly, provided for the election of the first three by the Convention immediately, and then ordered a general election the following November. Hon. Hamilton R. Gamble was elected provisional Governor, Hon. Willard P. Hall Lieutenant-Governor, and Hon. Mordecai Oliver Secretary of State. Henceforth the people of the State had two State Governments, and the divisions and strifes were distinct and complete.

The effect of this state of things was to unsettle the people more than ever, and the lines were clearly drawn. The policy of the Federal and State authorities was more positive and decided. "He that is not for us is against us" was not only of frequent utterance, but of dogged application. It was assumed that all men had sympathies for one party or the other, and an expression of them in any way was sure to provoke the hostility of those who assumed the guardianship of human sensibilities. Property belonging to persons of opposing sympathies was confiscated and appropriated to the use of the officers and men taking it; and at this stage of the war the effort was made to force the sympathies of men through their property. Many a well stocked farm was stripped of everything that could be carried off and the dwellings burned to the ground, because it was said the family had Southern sympathies; and many a helpless man and woman, too, had to prove themselves innocent of crimes of which they were assumed to be guilty to save them from an uncoffined grave.

Armed brigands came down from Kansas and Iowa, and over from Illinois, to plunder and rob the rich farmers of Missouri, and many of the poor ones, too, in the name of the Union, and to preserve the Constitution. They carried away wagons, horses, mules and stock of every description, plundered houses of silver plate, jewelry, beds and bedding, carpets, clothing of men, women and children—even the mementoes of ladies and the toys of children—everything that could gratify their cupidity or vex and mortify the original owners. All this for the preservation of the Union, by enriching the houses and pockets of men who cared for no higher distinction.

Ministers of the gospel suffered in common with others, especially those of the Southern Methodist Church, and others who were suspected of disloyal sentiments. Many of them had to "take the spoiling of their goods joyfully," or otherwise, and were wholly broken up and reduced to penury and want, and yet many of them were honestly and earnestly laboring to abate the feverish excitement, allay the bitterness of feeling and promote "on earth peace and good will toward men."

The Annual Conferences of the M. E. Church, South, in the fall of 1860, recommended to all Christian people the observance of a "day of fasting, humiliation and prayer" for the peace of the country and the amicable adjustment of existing difficulties. This had been generally observed throughout the State the week before the Presidential election, and, doubtless, did much good in humbling the Church before God, and in directing the hearts and faith of the people to the only "refuge and strength and present help in time of trouble."

After actual hostilities had been in progress a little more than one month a number of ministers of different churches assembled in St. Charles, Mo., May 21, 1861, and, after prayer and deliberation, adopted the following:

"WHEREAS, In the Providence of God our country is now involved in a civil war, which has already brought upon us many calamities, and still threatens to introduce a state of ill will, discord and desolation utterly inconsistent with our condition as a Christian land; therefore,

"*Resolved*, 1. That we meet together on this day in the fear of God, and with a firm reliance on his divine Providence as a Christian people, communicants of the respective churches in this city, to observe such means as will at least tend to promote good will among ourselves during the continuance of this war.

"2. That we regard all war as a sore calamity, contrary to the spirit and teaching of the gospel, and more especially a civil war, as revolting to our Christian teaching, unnatural, abhorrent to all our Christian instincts, and subversive of the cause of Christ, whose blessed mission was to establish peace on earth.

"3. That, as ministers of the Christian churches, irrespective of our private opinions, we do hereby pledge ourselves, one to another, ministers and people, to abstain as far as possible from all bitter and exciting controversy upon the questions now agitating the public mind, but will, each within the sphere of our influence, endeavor to promote a spirit of brotherly love, and by calm and judicious counsel, animated by the Spirit of Christ, our peaceful Master, suppress every act among ourselves which may have a tendency to increase the present difficulties.

"4. That we call upon the Christians of our land to band together to stay, if possible, the further shedding of fraternal blood, etc., etc.

"5. That we will not forget our best refuge—prayer—and therefore humble ourselves before God and supplicate our Heavenly Father to quell the madness of the people and put away from us all bitterness, and anger, and clamor, and evil speaking, and animate us with the gentle spirit of peace on earth and good will toward men.

"6. That, with trustful resignation and humble faith in the strength of the Lord of Hosts, we do cordially recommend to all Christian churches to set apart Thursday, June 6, 1861, as a day of private and public supplication, with fasting, humiliation and prayer," etc.

Similar meetings were held in other places to avert the calamity of war, or to abate some of its bitterness, and promote peace and good will amongst neighbors and non-combatants.

Very few ministers, comparatively, espoused actively the cause of either party, but pursued with a singleness of purpose their legitimate calling, ministering to all alike, and seeking only to make the gospel the "power of God unto salvation." Individual ministers and ecclesiastical bodies felt deeply the importance of prudence, quietness and ministerial fidelity to the Church of Jesus Christ, over which the Holy Ghost had made them pastors; that the ministry be not blamed, that the cause of the Master be kept above reproach, and that a pure Christianity might always conserve the public peace.

Notwithstanding the good intentions and laudable efforts made by the ministry of Missouri generally to promote the public peace, the press of the State, both secular and religious, did very much to break the force of their well-meant endeavors, and seemed determined either to drag the Church into the most ultra partisan support of the war, or, in case of failure, to place both under the suspicion and surveillance of the military authorities.

The spirit of anti-Christ, which had been increasing and spreading for years in Missouri, now assumed a boldness and a defiance that hesitated not to use the party hatred of religious editors and preachers to make a bold advance upon the doctrines and services of those who represented a pure, non-political, unsecular Christianity. It was not uncommon for the plainest facts to be perverted, if, by so doing, the cry of persecution for loyalty's sake could be raised and the most reckless passions of men could be fired. In this kind of business the Northern Methodist preachers and papers were more expert than others, and the hope of wreaking a mean vengeance on the M. E. Church, South, supplied sufficient motive. Such a declaration should not be made unless demanded and supported by the plainest facts. Unfortunately they are not wanting, and a few only must be selected from the many.

The *Central Christian Advocate*, published in St. Louis for the M. E. Church, North, and edited by Dr. C. Elliott, seized every event that could be tortured into an occasion for an inflammatory article against the ministers and membe s of the M. E. Church, South.

Some time in September, 1860, the Northern Methodists held a camp meeting not far from Utica, in Livingston county, North Missouri. The preacher in charge was one Rev. Mr. Gardner, who had already rendered himself obnoxious to the people by intermeddling with politics, tampering with slaves and unministerial conduct in the social circle. This camp-meeting was broken up on a Monday without service and in great confusion. The cause was no matter of conjecture, nor of its authenticity were the people permitted to doubt.

The Rev. Mr. Gardner had, the night before, been found in the wrong tent, from which he was summarily ejected by the ladies. The public indignation was too intense the next day to allow services to be held, and the crime of the preacher was made too apparent by the separation of a man and wife, the latter of whom had made herself rather conspicuous by her great zeal in the service of Gardner and the Church.

The *Central Christian Advocate* published it as a "great outrage," and made the breaking up of that meeting do good service in the persecution of the ministers of the

M. E. Church by the ministers and members of the M. E. Church, South. The editor of that paper said so much about it that good, honest, reliable men went to the place and investigated the matter. It was afterward ventilated through the public prints, to the infinite humiliation of the profession which the man disgraced and the reproach of the cause which he shamelessly belied.

Many other things of similar character did much good service for the party and the Church during the following winter and spring, doubtless designed to manufacture prejudice against the people of the State, and especially the Southern Methodists.

The *Central*, of May 15, 1861, contained the following:

"MEN AND BRETHREN, HELP!

"One of our preachers, last Sabbath week, some thirteen miles from this city, was struck down, his meeting broken up, and members of the M. E. Church, South, had oversight of the assault, which was conducted under their superintendence. So said Bro. Miller, the preacher, and a member of our Church, a Missourian, whose father and mother were buried in Missouri, and in which he proposes to be buried, whether killed by others or dying in the natural way."

While the editor should be excused for writing a paragraph so awkward and bungling, the real object will not be mistaken. It is only necessary to state that an intelligent gentleman who was present pronounces the whole thing utterly false. The meeting was not broken up, the preacher was not knocked down, and there was but one member of the M E. Church, South, present at the service, and he left before the trouble, which occurred outside of the church after services were closed, and grew out of some insulting language used by the preacher to a gentleman present, which was resented with only one slight blow which scarcely reached the reverend offender. They were separated before any damage was done, and left the *Central* to do all the damage.

In this case, as in the Gardner case, the Southern Methodists were not implicated; but for these and many other things of which they were wholly innocent they had to suffer deeply and grievously, as these pages will show.

During the summer of 1861 a number of ministers in different portions of the State were robbed of all that they possessed of this world's goods, some were driven into exile, and some arrested and put into military prisons. But more of these hereafter.

The State Convention assembled again, October 10, 1861, in St. Louis, passed several vacating ordinances, and provided for the more efficient prosecution of the war and the establishment of a more reliable sympathy between the State and the Federal Administration. Amongst other things it was ordained that all the civil officers of the State should take, subscribe and file with County Court Clerks an oath of allegiance or loyalty to support the Constitution of the United States and of the State of Missouri, and not to take up arms against the Government of the United States or the Provisional Government of this State, nor give aid or comfort to the enemies of either, and maintain and support the Provisional Government established by the State Convention of Missouri. This oath of allegiance was required of *ministers of the gospel, as such.*

CHAPTER IX.

THE PULPIT AND PRESS ON THE SITUATION IN MISSOURI.

Ministers of Peace—Course Pursued by the St. Louis *Christian Advocate*—Rev. Dr. M'Anally its Editor—Candid, Truthful, Honest—The Cause of its Suppression, and the Imprisonment of the Editor—Ministers of the M. E. Church, South, Labor and Pray Earnestly for Peace—Days of Fasting, Humiliation and Prayer—Ministers who became Political Partisans had no use for such days—"Breathing out Threatening and Slaughter"—Spirit of the Northern Methodist Press—False Publications for a Purpose—One Mr. John Stearns and the *Western Advocate*—Glaring Falsehoods—Excitement in St. Louis and Throughout the State—Persecution of Ministers in Kansas and Reign of Terror along the Border—Rev. W. H. Mobly and Rev. John Monroe in Southwest Missouri—Systematic Efforts to Break up the M. E. Church, South, and Disperse her Ministers—Editorial in *St. Louis Advocate*—*The Central Again*—Impressions Abroad—Baptists and Presbyterians Implicated—"Religion in Missouri"—Missouri Conference at Glasgow—St. Louis Conference at Arrow Rock and Waverly—Conference Stampeded by the Rumor of a Gunboat—Author Arrested.

That the ministers of the gospel in Missouri did not commit themselves to the strife of war, but sought to promote peace and good order in the State, may be learned from the frequent counsel given to their congregations to remain at home, and "as much as lay in them live peaceably with all men."

Many a young man was prevented from going to "Price's army," or any other, by the timely advice of these men of God, and many a wife and mother rejoice to-day in the life and love of husband and son *only* through the godly admonition of faithful pastors. Some few ministers, it is true, were led astray by popular excitement, or forced to quit their homes and flocks by causes heretofore mentioned, and then they preached privately what they practiced publicly. But such cases were too rare to involve the whole ministry as a class, even by the weakest implication. Neither were the ministers of the gospel as a whole, nor the ministers of any one Church in Missouri, disloyal to the Government of the United States or the Provisional Government of this State. But the very Churches and ministers that had to suffer the most direful penalties, in the destruction of property, the persecution, imprisonment and murder of ministers in the subsequent years of the war, were now doing more than any other in the State to prevent the war and promote the public peace and tranquillity.

The St. Louis *Christian Advocate*, edited by the Rev. D. R. M'Anally, D. D., contained a series of very able editorials, running through April and a part of May, 1861, on "*The Times*," "*The Duty of Christian Men*," "*The Time for Prayer*," "*To the Ministers and Members of the M. E. Church, South, in Missouri and Kansas*," "*The Times—A Word to our Patrons and Friends*," and kindred topics, in which the people were warned of the character of the danger that threatened, advised to remain at home, cultivate their lands and pursue the avocations of peace and piety in the fear of God, as the best means of promoting good order in the State, and at least mitigating the horrors of war.

That paper was candid and earnest in warning the public of the magnitude of the rebellion and the unprecedented unanimity and courage of the Southern people, and when the Northern press generally represented the boasted strength of the rebellion as too puerile and insignificant to involve the National Government in any serious trouble or protracted war, that paper sought truthfully and conscientiously to disabuse the public mind, and thereby prevent the many disastrous blunders committed by an underestimate of the military resources and strength of the South.

How much of suffering might have been prevented, and how many thousands of valuable lives might have been spared to the country, to say nothing of the millions of treasure, had the advice of that paper been taken and the timely warnings of its honored editor been heeded. But, like all gratuitous counsel that is unpalatable, because truthful, it was contemned, the motive of its author suspected, and the existence of its medium considered dangerous.

Very many of the religious papers of the border States had already been suspended, and the continuance of this one was a doubtful problem for many months before its suppression.

Dr. M'Anally's ideas of right and wrong, of truth and error, of justice and righteousness, were derived from the old standards. He had no patience with the new standards of virtue that grew out of party fanaticism and war expediencies; new fangled notions, dissimulations, prevarication and moral travestie "he could not away with." He had not so learned the responsibilities of public journalism, and hence his simple-hearted appreciation of right led him to expose the wrong wherever it existed. His honesty required him to denounce the wide-spread dishonesty of the times. His simple love of truth caused him to make honest and truthful reports of the "News of the Week" according to the actual facts, without reference to the interest of this party or that party, this army or that, this commanding officer or that. In this his paper presented such a contrast with the press generally that it was sought and read by thousands of both parties, and accepted by the unprejudiced as the most reliable paper then published.

But *because* it was truthful, and honest, and candid, and popular, and reliable, it was pronounced disloyal and dangerous; and because it would not serve the cause of cruelty, confiscation, conflagration, desolation and destruction, and with the venom of a viper hound on the barbarous hordes with fire and sword to the commission of the foulest deeds of war; nor with sanctimonious hypocrisy sanctify the implements and instruments of blood and death, and canonize the vilest thieves, and robbers, and murderers; for these reasons the paper was set down by the enemies of the M. E. Church, South, as in the interest of treason and rebellion, and *by them* the military authorities were induced to suppress the paper and arrest and imprison its editor. Of his arrest and long confinement in the Myrtle Street Military Prison, St. Louis, the reader will be more fully informed hereafter.

That the ministers of the M. E. Church, South, who suffered more than others during the war in Missouri, did not provoke the strife nor enhance its malignity, but, on the contrary, labored earnestly and prayed fervently for the return of peace to our distracted country, take the following from the St. Louis *Christian Advocate*, of June 13, 1861:

"FASTING AND PRAYER.

"*To the Ministers and Members of the M. E. Church, South, in the Missouri and St. Louis Conferences.*

"DEAR BRETHREN AND SISTERS: *Whereas,* our once happy and prosperous country is now involved in the calamities of civil war, which threatens ruin to all our cherished hopes and interests; and whereas, God alone, in the exercise of his sovereign and gracious dispensations, can avert the terrible evil; and as he has promised to be inquired of by those that fear him, and to interpose for those who reverently and submissively supplicate his mercy and seek his Divine interposition, it therefore becomes to every Christian community both a high privilege and a solemn duty, in such times of serious and alarming trials, humbly and reverently to prostrate themselves before the mercy seat and supplicate that aid and deliverance which God only can afford.

"And, as I have been requested by many ministers and laymen of both Conferences (in view of my seniority as a minister) to designate and recommend a day of fasting and prayer, I would, therefore, most respectfully recommend that Wednesday, the third day of July, be set apart and observed for this solemn purpose, and that appropriate religious services be held in all our places of worship; and, in accordance with the expressed wishes of many, and, as I think, in accordance with manifest propriety, I tender most cordially, in behalf of the whole Church, an invitation to all Christian people of the State to unite with us on that day, humbly and devoutly to supplicate, in behalf of our common country, that God, who can turn the hearts of men as the streams in the south, would forgive our sins and in his merciful providence hasten the return of peace to our country—our entire country.

"ANDREW MONROE.

"*Fayette, Mo., June 5, 1861.*

"The undersigned do most cordially approve the above proposition, and earnestly recommend its observance throughout the State.

"JOSEPH BOYLE,
"E. M. MARVIN,
"H. S. WATTS,
"P. M. PINCKARD.

"*St. Louis, Mo., June 12, 1861.*

In compliance with this recommendation the churches of the State were generally well filled with devout worshipers, and the prayers of tens of thousands of earnest Christians ascended to the Lord of Hosts that his anger might be turned away, that "our country—our whole country"—might be spared the further calamities of war, and that "we might lead a quiet and peaceable life in all godliness and honesty."

These public calls to "humiliation, supplication and prayer" were frequent in occurrence and general and fervent in response; and the unpolitical ministry in those days presented a spectacle of touching moral sublimity, in their fidelity to the Church and their unselfish devotion to the cause of peace and righteousness in the midst of universal strife and war, that deserved a higher consideration and a better fate, while it prepared them for the scenes of suffering and the thrones of martyrdom that yet awaited them in the not distant future.

It has not escaped the observant, however, that the ministers who committed themselves and their pulpits to the purposes and prosecution of the war had more days of feasting than fasting; more seasons of glorification than humiliation; more days of thanksgiving than supplication; more banners and bonfires than confessions of sin and prayers for peace. If any of them observed a day of fasting, humiliation and prayer in the proper spirit, during the whole war in Missouri, the fact has wholly escaped the author's mind. Their prayers, for the most part, consisted in "breathing out threatenings and slaughter," and in inflaming the dangerous passions of men by the most unblushing blasphemies and the most envenomed imprecations.

The scenes and services which dishonored the gospel and disgraced the pulpits and those who occupied them in certain quarters during the war can not now be recalled without the most painful sense of humiliation and shame. It would be an outrage upon public decency and taste to reproduce even the best specimens of them in these pages. We have oblivion for the facts and pity for the fanatics; and if a faithful record of the sad history we have made should require any further allusion to such scenes, it will be made with mingled shame and commisseration.

While the ministers in Missouri were striving manfully and humbly to allay the bitterness of strife by frequent calls to public humiliation and prayer, and by wise and godly counsels of peace and quietness, designing men who had left the State, and some even who remained in the State, were at work, through the different media of reaching the public mind, trying to arouse the suspicions and inflame the passions of those in power against the only real "peace-makers" in the State. Specimen extracts have already been given from the *Central Advocate* of Missouri, and it may not be out of place to insert one from the *Western Christian Advocate*, of Cincinnati, of June 12, 1861:

"'METHODIST EPISCOPAL CHURCH, SOUTH,' MISSOURI.

"We had a call from Mr. John Stearns, late a resident of Miller county, Mo. He was formerly of Pennsylvania, but for some years had resided in Missouri, and has been a member of the M. E. Church over thirty-five years. He gave us the names of two of his neighbors who had been hung for their Union sentiments, and for being members of the 'so-called' Northern Methodist Church. The leaders of the mob hanging these men were members of the M. E. Church, South. Mr. Stearns says further that he was informed through a friend that he himself was to be hung Saturday, June 1st, but that he defeated the attempt by escaping the previous night. The man who led on the mob of Jefferson City in riddling the Methodist Episcopal Church there, of which the expatriated Rev. Z. S. Weller was pastor, was the son of Claiborne Jackson, the Governor of Missouri. Mr. Stearns tells us that but for the M. E. Church, South, there would be no secessionism in the State. The preachers and members of that denomination see that the triumph of Unionism is their death knell, and hence the fury and despair which characterize their fight."

It will not be unkind to say now that such stories were manufactured to order and published for effect. The war has come and gone, and passion and prejudice have been measurably displaced by peace and order; and yet, to this day, tho hanging of two of Mr. Stearns' neighbors, in Miller county, Mo., has only come to the knowledge of the people of Missouri through the *Western Christian Advocate*, and upon the authority of one Mr. Stearns, "formerly of Pennsylvania."

But that this assertion is not made without good authority, read the following extracts from two letters, as only a sample of many others on hand:

"PLEASANT MOUNT, Miller Co., Mo., July 4, '61.

"*Mr. Editor:* I see in your issue of June 20th a statement from one Mr. John Stearns, who says he has been a citizen of Miller county for some years, and that two of his neighbors were hung for their Union sentiments, and for being members of the M. E. Church, North; that he himself barely made his escape by starting the night before.

"Now, as to the hanging part, Mr. Stearns has grossly misrepresented the people of Miller county. There has never been any person hung in the bounds of the county, under any pretext whatever, much less for their political or religious creed; and Mr. Stearns knew when he made the statement that it was false. In fact, I doubt whether there has ever been such a man in Miller county, at least I have found no one who has ever known such a man, and I have inquired of the Sheriff of the county, and the Clerk of the County Court, as well as of a number of citizens who have lived here ever since before Miller county was organized, and none of them have ever known such a man as John Stearns; and if it were necessary I could get hundreds of the most reliable men of this county to bear testimony to the truth of the above, &c., &c.

"(Signed) THOMAS J. SMITH."

Another letter, written by Wm. M. Lumpkin, July 2, 1861, says:

"I was born and raised in this (Miller) county, and can safely say there never was a man hung in this county to my knowledge. I have served a good time in this county in the capacity of Deputy Circuit and County Clerk, and County School Commissioner, and I have never heard of such a man before as Mr. John Stearns," &c.

The statements were denied at the time, and means instituted to ascertain their truth or falsity, but up to this time no information of such hanging has come to light. But the article served its purpose, and, like one that appeared a short time before in the New York papers, about the hanging of a Rev. Mr. White near St. Charles, Mo., where no such man had ever been seen, known, or heard of, and many others of a similar style, character and purpose, it passed away much sooner than the prejudices and passions it excited, and which were left to expend their fury upon those who made no "fight," and whose "death knell" was not heard in the triumph of Unionism, except only as it was uttered from the pulpits and pens of "false prophets."

About this time there was intense excitement in St. Louis, especially over the capture of Camp Jackson, the burning of bridges on the Pacific Railroad, and the retreat of Governor Jackson and General Price from Jefferson City. This excitement was greatly increased by the soldiers firing into promiscuous crowds of citizens along the streets, in which a number of citizens, with some women and children, were killed and wounded; and also the battle of Boonville, in which it was reported in the *Missouri State Journal* and other papers that Gen. Lyon's forces had been badly cut to pieces, but which the knowledge of the facts afterward modified to some extent. The small engagement between the Federal and State forces at Rock Creek, near Independence, Mo., about the same time, added somewhat to the general excitement, which by this time had spread throughout the State.

Along the border of Kansas the people of the State were kept in constant alarm by the depredations of what were called at that time "Kansas Jayhawkers." Many families were robbed, houses burned and preachers forced to fly for safety, as the following extract from a letter to the *St. Louis Christian Advocate*, from the Rev. N. Scarritt, a highly esteemed minister and a presiding elder then laboring in Kansas, will show:

"In addition to this, some of our preachers in the southern portion of the Conference have been compelled to quit the field and leave their work for the present, on account of the violence of civil strife so prevalent in that section.

"Our preachers there have taken no part in the political questions that are involving the country in so much trouble. They have been peaceable, law-abiding citizens, leaving politics alone, and devoting themselves exclusively to the peaceable work of preaching the peace-making gospel of the Prince of peace.

"Yet, though this has been their known and acknowledged character, it has not been sufficient to protect them from the rage of fanaticism and outlawed violence. Several of them have had their horses stolen from them by the Jayhawkers. Repeated threats of hanging, shooting, &c., have been made against them by the jay-hawking tribe, though no attempt, so far as we know, has been made in the form of any overt act to execute these threats."

In Southwest Missouri several of the ministers of the M. E. Church, South, were robbed and otherwise mal-treated, amongst them Rev. W. H. Mobley, now gone to rest, and Rev. John Monroe, one of the oldest minis-ters of any Church in Missouri. These occurrences began to attract attention by their frequency and atrocity, and it was soon discovered that a systematic effort was being made to so annoy, and harass, and persecute the Southern Methodist ministers that they would have to abandon the State, and leave their churches and flocks to be seized and absorbed by others.

The following editorial in the St. Louis *Christian Advo-cate*, of July 25th, indicates but too plainly the condi-tion of things then being forced upon us at this early period of the war:

"*Traveling Preachers.*—We are sad, sad indeed, when we think of the privations and sufferings of many of the traveling preachers of our Church in Missouri dur-ing these troublous times. The treatment some of them have received has been severe, not to say cruel. Bad men have sought to implicate them in measures with which they had nothing to do, and have them annoyed and distressed merely that private *piques* and personal animosities might be gratified. A number have literally been driven from their work, either by the malice of their enemies or by pressing want. Some, it may be, have acted imprudently—have become partisans in the strifes now going on, and thus, in part at least, were the authors of their own troubles. We have, at present, only a word to say. We hope that the preachers will remain at their work as generally as possible, that they will devote themselves to their work to the fullest possible extent, reproving, exhorting, comforting, etc., with all long suffering and kindness. In these times we must all suffer, more or less, and let us suffer with our people, and be sure that we suffer for righteousness' sake and not as evil-doers. God rules, and they that serve him in spirit and in truth shall find him a very present help in time of trouble."

The purpose to destroy the M. E. Church, South, in Missouri, was not only formed, but expressed also, and the Northern Methodist papers were then earnestly engaged in the effort to convince those in authority, and to fasten it upon the public mind, that but for the Southern Methodists treason and rebellion could not exist in Missouri. Such declarations as the following, taken from the *Central Christian Advocate*, of August 7, '61, were of weekly publication in the most conspicuous places in their papers, and industriously circulated in the centres of military power:

"*A Ruined Church.*—An excellent brother, for the present a local elder of the M. E. Church, South, in Missouri, under date of July 27th, writes to us as follows: 'I shall endeavor to advance the interests of the *Central;* I have no Christian fellowship with traitors and treason. Dr. M'Anally has ruined the Church in this country, and I hope to see the time when a loyal Church will occupy this entire ground.'"

This, also, may be of a piece with the Gardner, the Miller and the Stearns stories, but it was none the less effective in its object on that account; and the license given to bad men to commit worse crimes by such publications was only equaled by the malicious motive that conceived it, and its influence upon the army, officers and men.

To further show what impressions were made at home and abroad upon the public mind by false publications, let the following item, taken from the Philadelphia *Banner of the Covenant*, of nearly the same date, be noted:

"*Religion in Missouri.*—The Baptists in Missouri, the largest denomination, are about unanimous in favor of secession. The M. E. Church, South, the same, with but few exceptions. The Presbyterians, the third in numbers, are about equally divided. The M. E. Church, North, the fourth in size, are unanimous and earnest in favor of the Union. Half of their membership and one-third of their ministers have been driven from the State."

But for the exceptions in the M. E. Church, South, another paragraph in the same paper would reveal the author of the above information. It is as follows:

"Rev. Mr. Shumate, of Missouri, having been appointed to the chaplaincy of a regiment, asked leave of absence for a few days, made a flying visit to Indiana, and returned with two companies which he had recruited for the regiment."

The papers were filled with statements designed to

prejudice the authorities and the public against the old ministers of Missouri, which had much to do in bringing upon the ministry and Church the peculiar character of persecution which distinguishes the history of those times. Henceforth the Baptist ministers of the State will have to share largely in the persecutions and trials of their less fortunate Southern Methodist brethren, and not a few of the Presbyterian ministers were implicated in the same way, and had to suffer for being in Missouri.

The Missouri Annual Conference, M. E. Church, South, had been appointed to meet in Hannibal, Mo., in September, 1861, but on account of the general excitement in that portion of the State, and the deep prejudices created by false statements against the ministers of that Church throughout the State, it was deemed by them unsafe to attempt to hold the Conference session in Hannibal, and it was removed to Glasgow, on the Missouri river.

This Conference met and transacted its business under circumstances peculiar only to the State of Missouri. It required no small degree of moral courage, but the courageous body attended to its regular minute business, with Rev. W. G. Caples presiding in the absence of a bishop, made the appointments of the preachers and separated to their several fields of labor, all with as much dignity, quietness and decorum as ever characterized a body of consecrated divines. Many of them met in Conference, worshiped and wept together for the last time. Before they could convene again a number of them had ceased at once to suffer and to live, and had gone to mingle with the blood-washed and white-robed beyond the flood.

The parting scenes of the preachers at this Conference were truly touching and solemn. Many of them seemed to be impressed that the trying scenes through which they were yet to pass would not only "try men's souls," but consign many of their bodies to the grave and send their souls "under the altar." What names were on the "death roll" no one could divine, and yet the general fact was scarcely concealed from them, "that in every city bonds and afflictions awaited them."

The St. Louis Annual Conference had been appointed to meet in Warrensburg, but for the same reasons that influenced the Missouri brethren to go to Glasgow the St. Louis Conference session was moved to Arrow Rock, Saline county. The Conference convened September 25, 1861. After organizing, with D. A. Leeper in the Chair and W. M. Prottsman Secretary, and transacting some little committee business, the Conference adjourned to Waverly, believing that more preachers would meet them there, and that they would be less likely to be disturbed in their deliberations. How much the report of a gunboat coming up the Missouri river, or a military transport with reinforcements for the army at Lexington, influenced this movement to Waverly, statements differ. A Methodist Conference stampeded by a rumor, and fleeing for very life across a whole county, scattering Bibles, hymn books and saddle-bags in their flight, was quite a novelty; and whether it occurred or not the report of it was enough for the malicious on the one hand and the mischievous on the other. The very thought of it was so novel and ridiculous that it inspired some youthful poet to immortalize the scene in song, and his failure was due rather to the absence of the genuine muse than to the existence of some basis and a persistent attempt at clever rhyme.

The author himself was spared the novelty and notoriety of the occasion only by the untimely interference of a small detachment of Colonel Nugent's command, then posted at Kansas City.

I had announced on Sabbath to my congregation that I would start to Conference the next day, stating where it would be held, and about how long I expected to be absent.

On Monday morning early, in company with Mr. H. B. Conwell, a brother-in-law and a steward in the Church, I started for Conference. Just as we were passing out of the city on the main road to Independence we discovered a small squad of soldiers riding slowly about half a mile ahead of us. To avoid molestation and detention we took a by-road that would intersect the Westport and Independence road, on reaching which we discovered the soldiers still ahead of us, and began at once to conjecture some designs upon us. They had halted by a peach orchard and were helping themselves when we drove up. They very politely gave us of their peaches and requested us not to go ahead of them.

We traveled on behind them for some distance, when the officer in command stopped to talk with a farmer by the road side who knew me well, and asked when we drove up if I was on my way to Conference.

"What Conference?" asked the officer.

"The Conference of the M. E. Church, South, at Arrow Rock," I replied, quite indifferently.

"What, that secesh concern? I'll see to that. No

such body of traitors can meet in this State." And with the last words he spurred his horse up with his command and detailed four men to put us under arrest and guard us to Independence.

With "two behind and two before" we were ordered to "drive." Thus we traveled until we reached Rock Creek, two miles from Independence, when an orderly was sent back who dismounted and ordered us to "halt."

"I want you men to get out of this," he said.

"For what," I asked, mildly protesting against the proceedings.

"I want to send this buggy and horse back to camp," he replied. "We have use for such things sometimes to ride our wives and children out a little."

"Where is your camp?" was asked by Mr. Conwell, at the same time declaring that the horse and buggy belonged to him. And when informed that their camp was in Kansas City, at Col. Nugent's headquarters, he asked—

"Then why can't you send us back to Kansas City in the buggy, under guard if you like? We live in Kansas City."

"No," said he; "no use talking. If you are loyal men you can afford to walk ten miles for the sake of the Government; and if you are disloyal, we are not round hauling rebels. *Get out!*"

We did not wait for another invitation, but got out; and when we found that it was not *us* but *our's* they wanted we felt somewhat relieved, took a luncheon to stay the appetite, and then the roof of the stage an hour after, which safely landed us back whence we started.

Mr. Conwell soon obtained his horse and buggy, and a message to me, that if I would stay at home and attend to my own business I would not be molested; but it would not be well for me to make another attempt to go to Conference.

The preachers in the city of St. Louis and in Southeast Missouri could not reach the Conference. The session was short, the minute business only receiving attention, and the presiding elders left to make the best disposition of the preachers in their respective districts that the circumstances would allow. The preachers separated to their several homes and fields of labor with about the same feelings and in about the same spirit that characterized the parting scenes at Glasgow two weeks before. Many of them to pass through scenes of trial, persecution, suffering, desolation, blood, and fire, and death, ere another Conference could be held.

Looking back now upon those perilous times, it is "marvelous in our eyes" how that these faithful men of God "endured hardness as good soldiers," "not counting their lives dear unto themselves so that they might finish their course with joy, and the ministry which they had received of the Lord Jesus, to testify the gospel of the grace of God." The history of the Church furnishes few such instances of moral heroism as these men exhibited, even in that early period of the war troubles; and when, afterward, the Baptists, Presbyterians and Catholic priests became our fellow-sufferers, and augmented our moral strength, the moral heroism was complete, sublime. The spirit of consecration to Christ and his cause was equal to the extremest perils of property, health and life.

CHAPTER X.

PILLAGE, PLUNDER, BLACK-MAIL—MURDER OF THE REV. J. FEWEL—3,050 NEW ENGLAND CLERGYMEN.

Indiscriminate Robbery, Pillage, Arson and Murder—Banditti and Revenge—Black-Mail and Espionage—Panic, Depopulation and Plunder—Demoralization—Virtue Sacrificed—Some who Would not Bow the Knee to Moloch—God had an Altar and Israel a Priest—Persecution, Arrest and Imprisonment of Revs. J. Ditzler, J. B. H. Wooldridge and D. J. Marquis—Many others Suffered in Like Manner—Rev. James Fewel Arrested, Cruelly Treated, and Died from the Effects of Inhuman Treatment, aged Seventy-two Years—Many such Victims—The True Office and Work of the Ministry—Its Spirit and Mission—Any Departure Unsettles the Public Mind—A Sad Day for the Country, Church and State—Relations and Dependencies—Three Thousand and Fifty New England Clergymen Before Congress—A Solemn Protest and its Effects—Then and Now—Ecclesiastical Bodies on the "State of the Country"—Ecclesiastical Bummers—A Settled Policy to Drive the Old Ministers out of the State—General Halleck's Order.

The events of 1861 had a very decided moral effect upon the public mind. Several severe battles were fought in the State during the year, and the armies and armed bodies of men were largely recruited. Men who, at the first, had no thought of entering either army found themselves forced, by circumstances, to take up arms in what was, by construction, called self-defense—that is, by constant annoyance from armed men, by harassing fears, from threats and rumors of mischief to person and property, frequent arrests, pillage, plunder, etc., many a peaceable, quiet, orderly citizen was tormented into the necessity of taking up arms.

Armed bands appeared in every part of the State—

some on one side and some on the other, some with authority and some without, but all subsisting as they could, and but few caring how. These bands, many of which were irresponsible brigands and marauders, usually "foraged" on the citizens whose sympathies were on the opposite side. They did not always stop at the necessary supplies for subsistence, but were robbers of houses, and many of them indiscriminate and general thieves, taking horses, mules, cattle, wagons, corn, hay, flour, bacon, fruit, blankets, quilts, feather beds, carpets, clothing of every kind, from elegant silks, furs and shawls to children's shoes and toys; money, watches and jewelry were often taken from the persons of ladies. These highwaymen would often put the torch to dwelling houses at night and take a fiendish pleasure in seeing the awakened inmates make their escape or perish in the flames. Men were shot down by them on the highway, in the fields, the woods and at the doors of their houses as though life was of little value, and its appreciation was about equal to the effect of one bootless, midnight murder upon the great question of Union or division. At all events, after the battle of Lexington, September 21, 1861, and the rapid movements of armies which followed, human life was at the caprice of the armed banditti that multiplied so rapidly over the State.

Many defenseless citizens suffered such indignities and insults from them, in addition to the loss of all they had on earth, that they fled to the army for protection, or to the brush and banded together for revenge. Men, whose houses were destroyed, and whose wives, and daughters, and sisters had been worse than insulted by inhuman ruffians, swore the direst vengeance, and with unsparing recklessness scattered desolation and death in their tortuous track. For their deeds military commanders of posts would hold defenseless communities responsible, levy black-mail upon them, sometimes to the full value of their property, and institute a system of espionage that would put an eavesdropper under nearly every man's window and a detective in every social circle and public assembly. Property and life were thus put at the mercy of unprincipled detectives and spies, selected often from the lowest and most unscrupulous classes of men and women. With such a system of military despotism no man's life was safe, and indeed many men were accused, arrested, imprisoned, tried, convicted and put to death without ever knowing the charges against them.

It is not difficult to conjecture the effect of this state of things upon the public mind. To say that the people in some whole counties along the borders of Iowa and Kansas were seized with panic and consternation is not more than the truth. Men and families broke up, and taking what they could with convenience and safety fled for life and protection, some North, some South, some to Canada, some to California, some to the army, some to the large cities, and some to the brush. Some men ordered and some frightened their neighbors away, and then, to furnish them means to travel, bought their stock and lands at a nominal price—in some instances for a mere song. What a farmer, or mechanic, or merchant left behind in his flight was seized as lawful prey by the first that found it and appropriated to private use. Indeed, in one instance a whole county was depopulated outside of the towns, by military order, and devoted to pillage and plunder, and that the third county of the State in population and wealth.

It was even worse, if possible, in the track of large armies and in those parts of the country upon which they subsisted.

No part of the State suffered more than the Southwest, extending from a line that would strike Rolla, Sedalia and Fort Scott, in Kansas, to the State of Arkansas. Many parts of that section of the State were literally laid waste, and made a desolation by fire and sword. The breath of war, like the simoon, swept over the country, leaving a wide waste of desolation and death, which the benignity of peace and the hand of industry can not reclaim and rebuild for many long years.

To say that public sentiment in the State was demoralized by such scenes before the end of 1861 is an expression too tame to reflect adequately the real fact. The moral forces of society were paralyzed, social restraints were broken down, and even religious character was powerless either for protection or public good. The old standards of virtue, integrity, honesty and right principle were borne down and swept away, and men became reckless of the laws of God and man. In the fury and fire of partisan strife, and amid the familiar scenes of blood and death, men trampled upon right, crucified truth, murdered innocence, loved vengeance, despised virtue, abandoned principle, forgot their loves, left their dead unburied and their buried uncoffined, and hung upon the bloody war path like avenging furies.

In the midst of such fearful and wide-spread demoralization God preserved only a few thousand who would not bow the knee to the bloody Moloch. Israel was not without an altar, and the altar was not without an acceptable sacrifice; but the spirit of anti-Christ seemed the more embittered and enraged by that fact, and the persecution became more general and unrelenting throughout the State.

Many congregations of quiet worshipers were dispersed; many societies were broken up and scattered; many churches were burned, and many ministers arrested, silenced or banished—not in the cities so much as in the country.

Amongst the first arrests was that of the *Rev. J. Ditzler.*

In 1860 and '61 Rev. J. Ditzler was stationed in Jefferson City, in charge of the M. E. Church, South. He was also chaplain to the lower House of the General Assembly.

After Governor Jackson and General Price had evacuated the State capital and the United States forces under General Lyon had taken possession, Mr. Ditzler remained as a non-combatant, supposing that he would not be molested. In this he was mistaken. He was not allowed long to remain in his quiet study at the Ferguson House or to attend to his pastoral duties. An "orderly," with a guard of seven men, called on him at the Ferguson House, arrested and marched him through the city, and put him with others in an old meat (smoke) house. He was taunted and sneered at by his guard—the Dutch—through the cracks of the old log house. Mr. Ditzler talked back at them in German, Italian, Spanish, French, Greek and Hebrew, quoting freely from Schiller, Goethe and other German authors of note, for his own relief and their amusement, until he was reported to Col. Boernstein, Post Commander, and by him unconditionally released, solely upon literary grounds. No charges were preferred against him, nor could he ever find out why he was imprisoned. His father fought at Tippecanoe, in 1812, and his grandfather at Valley Forge, under Washington, and this treatment was not borne without some little indignation.

Brigadier-General Brown succeeded Col. Boernstein, and Mr. Ditzler was apprised of the purpose to re-arrest him. He was advised by his friends to flee, and accordingly took the train late Saturday night for St. Louis; and at noon the next day (Sabbath) a posse of ten armed soldiers entered his church to arrest him, but he was gone. They followed him to St. Louis only to find that he had taken a train on the Ohio and Mississippi Railroad and made his escape.

The Rev. J. B. H. Wooldridge, the Rev. D. J. Marquis, and other ministers, were arrested and imprisoned about the same time, and without cause. Indeed, it became so common for ministers to be arrested that by the last of the year 1861 it ceased to be a matter of surprise to any. The only novelty was in finding a minister out of the army who had not been arrested by one party or the other, and the most that could be hoped was that life and liberty to non-political and non-juring ministers would be exceptional.

If he lived out of the track of large armies, he would not escape the marauding bands; and if his home should be so secluded and retired that he could not be reached by the public highway, or easily found, there were al ways unprincipled men in every neighborhood who, to seek revenge, gain favor with the authorities, or to make an opportunity to pillage and plunder from the sheer love of it, would go to the nearest military post, inform on the quiet "parson," and volunteer their services to guide the ruffian soldiers to the home of the innocent victim. From such causes many an innocent man suffered both in property and person.

When ministers of the gospel happened to fall into the hands of regular army officers or those lawless brigands they were treated with a severity and cruelty that was not often visited upon others, and which indicated with alarming certainty the policy that would be pursued toward the enemies of all unrighteousness.

Amongst the many instances of cruelty to ministers of the gospel who had committed no offense whatever against the peace and dignity of the State, it is sufficient here to mention the case of the *Rev. James Fewel.*

This venerable servant of the regular Baptist Church, who had lived and labored in Henry county, Mo., for many years—known, respected and honored as a peaceable, upright, good and useful citizen—was found and arrested near his own residence and taken off as a political prisoner to Sedalia, thence to St. Louis, where he lay in prison more than a month, and until death came to his relief.

His death was due solely to the cruel treatment he received from his captors and persecutors. He had never taken up arms against his country, had never committed a crime of any sort—not even what irresponsible persons call treason—and had never been engaged in lawless acts of any kind; but, then, he was a minister of the gospel, and the parties who arrested him, and those who afterward guarded him, had commiseration neither for his profession nor gray hairs. He lacked only three days of being seventy-two years old when he died.

He was arrested by Capt. Foster's company of Col. Hubbard's regiment, Missouri State Militia, in the latter part of December, 1861, near his own residence, in Henry county. The weather was cold, and when the old man found that he would be taken off he begged permission to go to his house for more and warmer clothing. This was refused him. He then asked the natural privilege of sending a message to his aged companion, to inform her of his condition and obtain at least a blanket to protect him from the weather. Even this poor boon was denied the old man, and he was torn from his home and hurried away to Sedalia. The weather turned bitterly cold, and the freezing December blasts swept mercilessly across the extended prairie the livelong night, while this old man was kept in an open railroad car, shelterless, bedless, blanketless and comfortless. His very prayers and tears seemed to freeze on the chilly night air as he thought of home and his long years spent in the service of God for the good of his race. But he had to suffer this cruel treatment and trust the God of Elijah to prepare him for what was still in store for him. The morrow came, and with it still further and severer trials. The weather did not moderate, neither did the severity of his persecutors. With others he was placed in a common stock car and sent to St. Louis. With no better protection, no better accommodations, than the horned beasts who had been temporarily displaced by them, and even with insufficient supplies of food, they were kept traveling and stopping all that day and night. Chilled through and through, hungry and half dead, this old man reached St. Louis and was hurried off to the military prison, in which he soon fell a victim to pneumonia, and lingered—without accusation, without trial, and without even permission to be seen by his friends—until February 1, 1862, when death came to his release and found him ready to "depart and be with Christ, which was far better."

If any charges were ever preferred against him they never came to light.

This is only one of the many instances of cruelty that occurred during the latter part of this year, in which ministers of the gospel were persecuted and imprisoned, and some of them died of their treatment, not because they had been in rebellion, or because they were trying to save the Union, but because they were ministers trying to save the souls of men.

We have been accustomed to look upon ministers of the gospel as the divinely commissioned ambassadors of Heaven, sent forth with a dispensation of the gospel of peace, preaching "Jesus and the resurrection," and "praying men in Christ's stead to be reconciled to God;" that their one work was to preach the gospel, build churches, devise ways and means for the furtherance of the kingdom of grace, project schemes for the enlargement of the borders of Zion and for the diffusion of the power and spirit of Christianity; to plant the gospel standard where it is not, and build up the waste places; to do the most possible good to the greatest number, and to do this work of love in the spirit of the divine

Master, by "being an example of the believers, in word, in conversation, in charity, in spirit, in faith, in purity," "by pureness, by knowledge, by long-suffering, by kindness, by the Holy Ghost, by love unfeigned." In this way and in this spirit to spread "scriptural holiness over these lands," and promote "peace on earth and good will to men." These ideas of the spirit and work of the gospel ministry have become so deeply rooted in the hearts of men, and so thoroughly interwoven with their thoughts, that any departure from that work as thus understood creates surprise, suspicion and distrust in the public mind.

When ecclesiastical bodies assemble it is assumed that they meet to deliberate upon the legitimate interests of the Church of Jesus Christ—how that form of it committed to them may be made more efficient in bringing men to a saving knowledge of Christ Jesus, the Head of the Church, and how their plans and polity may be improved and vitalized.

It was a sad day for this country when the gospel ministry first departed from this work and began to legislate upon questions purely secular and political; and if our free government should ever be broken up and our free institutions destroyed—if our religious liberties should ever pass away, and a political and ecclesiastical despotism be established in this land—the philosophic historian of the future, whose melancholy task it will be to chronicle the "decline and fall" of the greatest republic of the world, will linger with painful interest upon that sad event as the beginning of the catastrophe.

The separate but mutually dependent relations of

Church and State, the support of the Church and her ministry by the voluntary contributions of the people, liberty of thought and speech, the freedom of worship and the rights of conscience, are almost peculiar to our country and form of government. In these things our institutions are distinct from, and in contrast with, the Church establishments and ecclesiastical hierarchies of Europe and Asia.

They constitute the soul and centre of our free Republican government. The very genius of our institutions resides in them, and the ægis of liberty shields and protects them. The State may not restrict or control them, and the Church dare not intermeddle with the affairs of State.

The two may exist together, but can never coalesce. They must be distinct and separate in their laws, their government, their administration, their spirit, their agencies and their objects, while they have the same subjects. So long have Church and State existed separately in this country, and so widely different in their spirit, agencies and objects, that it is both natural and philosophical for the public mind to be disturbed and alarmed by every attempt of the one to intermeddle with the legitimate affairs of the other.

Few events in the history of this country caused greater alarm for our peace and safety in the minds of reflecting men than the appearance before the Congress of the United States of three thousand and fifty clergymen of New England in the following protest against the passage of the Kansas-Nebraska bill, in 1854:

"*To the Honorable, the Senate and House of Representatives, in Congress assembled:*

"The undersigned, clergymen of different religious denominations in New England, hereby, in the name of Almighty God and in his presence, do solemnly protest against the passage of what is known as the Nebraska bill, or any repeal or modification of the existing legal prohibitions of slavery in that part of our national domain which it is proposed to organize into the Territories of Nebraska and Kansas. We protest against it as a great moral wrong, as a breach of faith eminently unjust to the moral principles of the community, and subversive of all confidence in national engagements; as a measure full of danger to the peace and even the existence of our beloved Union, and exposing us to the righteous judgments of the Almighty: and your protestants, as in duty bound, will ever pray.

"Boston, Massachusetts, March 1, 1854."

This pretentious protest—"in the name of Almighty God"—was the first open and bold attempt of the clergy in this country to influence national legislation; and while Messrs. Mason, Douglass and others in the United States Senate administered to these officious clergymen a severe rebuke for thus intermeddling with the affairs of the National Government, good men were justly alarmed for the result, and the whole country was appalled by this bold advance of the Church toward the control of the affairs of the State.

Then the finest model of ecclesiastical polity in the world trembled and the wisest frame work of civil government felt the shock. Then the work of our fathers—combining the wisdom of the ages and the religion of the gospel in one grand structure of civil and religious liberty—the glory of Washington, the pride of every American, the dread of tyrants and the admiration of the world, began to reel upon its throne and totter to its fall. Then the deadly virus was injected, and the veins and arteries of national life carried the poison to every part of the body politic, and from that day forth "death was in the pot." Then the axe was laid at the root of the fair tree of liberty, whose roots had been fastened deep in the national heart, and whose branches already spread over a continent and toward heaven, under which the oppressed of every nation found shelter, and the down-trodden of every clime sought repose, peace, liberty and life. Then the religious and political waters mingled, and the whole stream of national life was corrupted and hastened on in turbulent commotion to the "blood, and fire, and vapor of smoke" of '61.

Ministers contented themselves then with a firm and solemn protest; they afterward made imperious demands. They sought then to prevent the enactment of "a measure full of danger to the peace and even the existence of the Union;" they afterward demanded, in the name of Almighty God, the enactment of laws, the conduct of the war, the election of men to office, the success of party measures, manhood suffrage, and any other purely political matter, as though the union of Church and State was an accomplished fact and they were the constituted vice-regents to supervise and control the legislation of the country.

At the beginning of the war, and during its continuance, when ecclesiastical bodies met, about the gravest matter before them for deliberation was the "State of the Country," and how they could deliver themselves so as to effect in any particular direction either the course of Congress, political elections or the movement of armies. This was true in an eminent degreee of the M. E. Church, the Presbyterian Church (Old and New School), Congregational, Unitarian, and some Baptist associations of the Northern and Eastern States.

Nor were these deliverances confined to the larger representative Bodies of these Churches, but the primary church courts, ministers' associations, conventions and Conferences made themselves conspicuous by such unwise interference with matters purely secular and political.

Secret conclaves were held in Missouri by ministers and others professing to be disciples of Christ, in which plans were devised and projected to persecute, by proscription, robbery, arrests, imprisonment and confiscation, if not by means still severer, ministers of the gospel in this State who would not stultify themselves nor disgrace their profession by falling in with them and joining the hue and cry for blood and death.

Consultations were had and schemes devised by which the military authorities could be used to oppress and persecute ministers whose loyalty was questioned by these politico-ecclesiastics, and whose only crime was that they possessed property and stood high in the confidence of the people whom they had served faithfully for many years.

Revolutions never go backward, and it was a part of the forward movement of these scheming adventurers who followed the army to keep out of danger, and who served post and field commanders as volunteer aids for the uses they could make of them in taking possession of churches, persecuting and running off ministers and foisting another ministry on the people.

It was a settled purpose to drive the old ministers out of the State. Those who had planted the Church and grown up with her institutions, and whose long and useful lives were identified with the early and heroic history of the Church, had now to give place to newcomers, whom the people did not want, or yield to the pressure of the new order of things. These ecclesiastical bummers had influence at military headquarters, and could use the officers of the army to accomplish their purpose; and it was doubtless through their influence that so many orders were issued from the Headquarters of the Department of Missouri bearing directly upon ministers as a class. Not enough to affect them as citizens in common with other citizens, but *as ministers.*

The following order may suitably close this chapter:

When Major-General Halleck was in command of the Department of Missouri he caused to be issued an Order, under date of February 3, 1862, called "General Orders No. 29," requiring the "President, Professors, Curators and all other officers of the University of Missouri to take and subscribe the oath of allegiance prescribed by the sixth article of the State Ordinance of October 16, 1861," or failing to do so within thirty days their offices will be considered vacant, and "in order that its funds should not be used to teach treason or to instruct traitors, the authorities of the University should expel from its walls all persons who, by word or deed, assist or abet treason."

The offices of railroad companies, Government contractors, agents, clerks and Government employees, and all military officers were required to take either the same oath or the one prescribed by an act of Congress, approved August 6, 1861.

This long military order closes as follows:

"V. It is recommended that all clergymen, professors and teachers, and all officers of public and private institutions for education, benevolence, business and trade, and who are in favor of the perpetuation of the Union, voluntarily to subscribe and file the oath of allegiance prescribed by the State Ordinance in order that their patriotism may be made known and recognized, and that they may be distinguished from those who wish to encourage rebellion and prevent the Government from restoring peace and prosperity to this city and State."

Or, in other words, "mark them that company not with us."

CHAPTER XI.

SEIZURE OF CHURCHES—CHURCHES IN KANSAS CITY AND INDEPENDENCE.

Church Property—Can the War Revive or Create Titles—Church Property on the Border—Maysville, Kentucky—Legal Rights of Property—Attainder—Honest Inquiry—Eighth Commandment—The Truth of History—*Church in Kansas City*—North Methodists—Faithful Ladies—What was Said at the Time—Some who were with us Went out from us—Their loss our gain—*Church in Independence*—How they Got it and Why they Kept it—The Former Pastor—Why he left—Battle of Independence—"Black Thursday"—A Rev. James' Lee—How he got Possession of the Church—Rev. Mr. DeMott—How he got Possession of the Parsonage—A Poor Widow Turned Out by Military Order—Strategy—Rev. M. M. Pugh Demands the Property—Why Refused—Recourse to the Civil Courts—Statement of the Case by Counsel—Side Scenes—Extracts from the St. Louis *Advocate*—This Property in the Statistics of Northern Methodism—Action of the Missouri and Arkansas Conferences, M. E. Church, on the Subject—Reflections.

The fact has been stated elsewhere that the division of the Methodist Church in 1844 extinguished all right and title to the Church property in this State that inhered in the M. E. Church, North. After the Missouri Conference voted, in the fall of 1845, to adhere South, and by that act became an integral part of the M. E. Church, South, according to the "Plan of Separation," the other wing of the Church became, in fact and in law, dispossessed of all the Church property in the State. By the decree of the Church and of the civil courts the right and title of the M. E. Church, North, to all species of Church property was so effectually extinguished that no claim was ever set up and no effort made by that

Church to gain possession of any church, parsonage, or other property in this State, from the vote of the Missouri Conference in 1845 to the beginning of the war in 1861. That Church accepted the situation, acquiesced in the decision, and yielded her claims to the decree of Missouri Methodism.

If any claim was ever set up to any species or piece of property, or any suit in any civil court was ever instituted to gain possession of any property during this period of seventeen years, the author is to this day ignorant of the fact. A residence in the State of nearly twenty years has failed to bring the fact to his knowledge. It is, therefore, of no minor significance that these facts stand in the records of history, and must enter largely into the consideration of subsequent facts now to be put on record. Let them be duly considered and they will color with deepest significance the acts and doings of that Church during the war.

It may be that the decision of the Church in Missouri was too nearly unanimous, and the force of public opinion was too strong in its endorsement of the Plan of Separation and the vote of the Conference; and, then, it may be that the few scattered preachers and members whose sympathies were with the Church, North, were in themselves too feeble at any given point, or had the sense of justice and right too strong at every point, to encourage any attempt to gain possession of property that rightfully belonged to others. If their complete acquiescence can not be accounted for upon either of the above hypotheses, then it rests with the fact that in other States the rights of property would be settled by the civil courts; and in Missouri they preferred to await the decision of courts in those States where the Northern claimants would not be put at such great disadvantage.

While the property question was in an unsettled state several churches along the border of Kentucky and Virginia were put through the sharpĕst litigation.

Prior to the decision of the Supreme Court of the United States in the great "Church Property Case," appeals were made to the civil courts in several places to decide the rights of property, of which that for the Church in Maysville, Ky., was among the earlier and most noted.

In this Church, out of a membership of two hundred and fifty-six, ninety-seven voted to adhere North. This minority had a preacher sent to them from Ohio and sued for possession of the Church property. The case was carried to the State Court of Appeals, and that distinguished jurist, Chief Justice Marshall, in decreeing that the property rightfully belonged to the M. E. Church, South, among other things, said:

"There are now two distinct Churches in the place of the M. E. Church of the United States—the one the M. E. Church, North, the other the M. E. Church, South—these two differing from the original and from each other only in locality and extent; each possessing in its locality the entire jurisdiction of the original Church."

Wherever the right of property was referred in any given locality to the civil courts the decision was the same as that above, and the Northern Methodists of Missouri acquiesced in the extinguishment of their right to all the property formerly owned by the original

Church, and its legal confirmation to the M. E. Church, South.

Now, it may well and significantly be inquired how the civil war of 1861 could revive the title to property that had been extinguished, in fact and in law, by the will of its legal owners in 1845? Laws may be repealed, altered and amended, but not so as to affect the previous rights of property. Nothing is more sacredly guarded by civil legislation than the rights of property. Laws may change, but justice and equity remain the same; and courts of equity not unfrequently pronounce upon the equity of legislation in respect to the rights of property. Hence the strongest rights are those founded both in law and equity.

If the rights of property were revived by the civil war it must have been done in one of two ways: either by legislation or attainder. It was never claimed to have been revived by legislation, which, to say the least, was a doubtful expedient, and conferred a doubtful right, if any at all. It could not have been done by attainting the blood of the lawful property holders, except by due process of law and for cause. This was never even attempted.

Then we fall back upon the original inquiry, how the civil war revived property rights that had been extinguished nearly twenty years? What virtue in armies, in battles, in fire or blood to resuscitate extinguished titles? What virtue in martial law, in military occupation and orders, or in drum-head courts-martial, to set aside the legal and moral rights of one Church and set up the legal claims of another Church? Was it the right of might, and the might of arms? Could bullets and bayonets set aside or substitute warranty deeds? How could the battle of Springfield, fought August 10, 1861, affect the title of Church property in Springfield secured by deed of conveyance, dated October 11, 1856, to certain gentlemen as trustees of the M. E. Church, South, to hold in trust for the uses of said Church? Or how could the battles of Boonville or Lexington destroy the rights of property in those cities which inhered in the members of the M. E. Church, South?

If the ministers and members of the M. E. Church sought, under cover of military orders and with the support of bayonets, to gain possession of the property of others, was it not *prima facie* evidence that their claims would not be recognized in law or equity? and was it not a confession to the mean purpose of obtaining by force that to which they had no shadow of right in law? If they obtained Church property by unfair and clandestine means, under the covert sanction of the military authorities, wherein do they differ from others who break the eighth commandment? Can military orders suspend Divine commands and confer a moral right to take possession and appropriate the property of others? Let these questions, and all others of a kindred nature which the curious casuist may be disposed to ask, be answered in the light of the foregoing and the forthcoming facts. Put that and this, then and now, together, and let the conscientious verdict of an enlightened public judge between us.

The truth of history requires a record now, and a detailed statement of historical facts, that for the sake of common honesty, the plainest equity, the humblest scale of justice, and the lowest stages of our common Christianity, should forever be buried with the dead past and lie forgotten "as a dream when one awaketh." But truth and justice demand many things which a common charity, and even a common decency, would consign to oblivion. A diluted charity should never make the pen hesitate in the presence of important, though unpalatable, truths. History must be worthy of its theme, and the pen must be equal to the utmost demands of the history. "Naught extenuate, and naught set down in malice."

In 1862 and '63 there was a movement—so general over the State that the conviction that it was concerted and simultaneous can not be escaped—to seize, possess and hold for their own use, by the Northern Methodists, the churches belonging to the M. E. Church, South. Persistent efforts for this purpose were made in almost every county in the State; and if the whole history could be brought to light it would be seen that there was held, at some place or places, a secret conclave of ministers in which the purpose and the plan were agreed upon. It will not be necessary to specify the particulars of every case of church seizure, but the following more prominent cases will be sufficient:

Church in Kansas City.

In the fall of 1862 Rev. M. M. Pugh, then stationed at Kansas City, was forced by persecution to abandon his church and charge and flee for protection to a neighboring military post. Mr. Pugh was watched by enemies and warned by friends. The threat, oft repeated, of arrest and imprisonment did not deter him. But to know that his steps were dogged, that detectives were on his track, that his life was threatened, and to be told by military officers that they could not be responsible for his life any night, and to be advised that there were lyers-in-wait to assassinate him, put his life in too great peril to remain with his people. He fled.

As soon as his absence was known the Northern Methodists took possession of the church and held it under military protection. They organized a society composed of a few Northern fanatics and a few renegade and weak-kneed Southern Methodists. They pronounced the M.E. Church, South, dead and beyond the hope of resurrection, tried to get possession of the church records and declare all the former society of Southern Methodists members, *nolens volens*. When they found that but few would accept the transfer, they pronounced the rest disloyal, and threatened them with confiscation. "But none of these things moved them," and they maintained their fidelity to the Church of their choice notwithstanding all the abuse, and slander, and threatenings, and slaughter, that these religious loyalists could bring to bear upon them.

After the occupancy of the church for some months they became conscious of wrong-doing and of guilt, and in shame and humiliation turned the property over to the rightful owners. They found that military orders did not confer letters of administration. If the Church, South, was dead and buried, what right had they more than others to administer on the estate?

In the *St. Louis Christian Advocate*, of May 31, 1866, a correspondent from Kansas City makes the following statement:

"But the Church. During the war our Church passed through sore trials—had 'fightings without and fears within.' She was 'persecuted, but not forsaken; cast down, but not destroyed.' Rev. M. M. Pugh remained with the Church in Kansas City until the latter part of 1862, attending to his legitimate business in his own quiet way—preaching Christ and his cross to perishing sinners—when the presence of blood-thirsty Northern Methodist preachers and their willing tools, threatening his life on the streets and dogging his steps, hounded him off to safer quarters where he could rely upon the protection of military power. The Northern Methodists then took possession of the church, organized a society, composed in part of a few blinded fanatics and weak-kneed renegades from the M. E. Church, South, who at once imagined themselves possessed of other people's property, began to abuse and traduce Southern Methodists, pronounced the Church dead, and proceeded to administer on the estate.

"But 'military necessity' did not confer upon them letters of administration, and they reckoned without their host. It is true, the General Conference of the M. E. Church, North, enacted a political test of membership for all persons everywhere who seek admission to her pales; and I submit whether or not they make the repeal of the eighth commandment, also, a test of membership for the province of Missouri. For it seems that no sooner do people get into that Church than they proceed to take and to hold, to possess and to use, property for which others have paid, and houses which others have built, supposing that membership in that Church invests them, under the operation of a 'higher law,' with rights and titles above warranty deeds and Supreme Court decisions."

In the same paper, of June 13, 1866, the following statement appears upon the same subject:

"After Brother Pugh was run off the Church was occupied for some time by the Northern Methodists, who assumed that the Church property was theirs, to have and to hold, with all the appurtenances thereto belonging, to them and to their successors forever. They abused Southern Methodists roundly, threatened them much, and with all the prestige of power assaulted the gates of our Zion until they became so offensive that all *true* friends of our Church and of the Government gave them a wide berth and left them alone in their shame.

"Some who in name had been with us, but were not in heart of us, went out from us to take shelter under their political banner, prove their loyalty to the Government, and—as they were told—save their property and their lives, and be fitted, as it proved, to enjoy the product of others' labor and the spoils of pious conquest.

"The faithful of our Church pursued the even tenor of their way, and when refused their own house of worship met in private houses for worship, and when denied this means of grace they kept up the sewing circle and mite society, and in this way the 'faithful women not a few' preserved an organization, a name and a life. While their harps were upon the willows they often sat down together and wept when they remembered their Zion, once so beautiful for situation—the joy of all hearts. They suffered all that the betrayal of Judas and the denial of Peter could inflict upon them. Yet, believing truth and right, though nailed to the cross and buried in the tomb, would, like the divine Redeemer, rise again leading captivity captive and conferring gifts upon men, they waited patiently and hopefully till their change should come. And it did come, and that by a way they knew not. They were, like their Lord, 'despised and rejected of men,' yet their faith failed not. They had confidence in the Church and the pledges of her risen Head. Their faith grew sublime as the darkness increased and the troubles multiplied about them. 'The gates of hell shall not prevail against it,' they heard in the thick darkness, and bowing to the storm they sheltered themselves within the clefts of the everlasting Rock 'until these calamities be overpast.'

"There were some men in authority who loved the right and hated the wrong. There were, also, 'good men and true' in the Church, whose loyalty to the Government was only equaled by their fidelity to the Church, and neither could be shaken by all the libels and slanders of ecclesiastical hirelings. When such men have the adjustment of the rights of property, truth and righteousness will at last prevail, and justice will be reached in the end. To such are we indebted for our Church property in Kansas City."

These extracts show the purpose and the plan of these ministers and members of the M. E. Church. The virtues of superloyalty claimed for themselves, and the cry of disloyalty and treason against Southern Methodists, were not to go unrewarded. It may be uncharitable to suspect the motives of others, but it is not uncharitable to record their acts and doings when the cause of truth and righteousness will be served and the truth of history vindicated thereby.

Church at Independence.

In 1857 the members and friends of the M. E. Church, South, erected, finished, furnished, dedicated and paid for a beautiful Church in the city of Independence. The architecture was half Gothic, and most elegant in its proportions and finish, two stories, with Sunday school, lecture room, pastor's study, class rooms, closets, library and furnace rooms below, and above one of the handsomest audience rooms in the State. The whole cost was over $15,000. A convenient and commodious parsonage in the rear, on the same lot, with ample and tastefully ornamented grounds for both Church and parsonage.

This property was built and paid for by Southern Methodists, and used and occupied by them without molestation till the fall of 1862, when it was left temporarily without a pastor. A covetous eye had been on it, and the pastor for 1861 and '62 had often been warned of personal danger and advised to seek some place of safety. He was several times put under military arrest, and several times informed of plots and purposes to shoot or hang him. The leaders of marauding bands of Kansas "Redlegs" or "Jayhawkers" had often sworn vengeance against him because he was a Southern Methodist preacher. They had hunted diligently for some accusation against him, or some pretext for taking his life, but he had been too prudent and cautious for their purpose; had pursued with singular fidelity his own calling, nor turned to the right or left for any purpose or party; had made many warm friends amongst the best Union men, who demanded that he should be let alone in his work and not molested any way by the authorities. They pronounced him loyal to his Master, his Church, his country, "and to have nothing laid to his charge worthy of death or of bonds." He felt safe in the hands and under the protection of the regular military authorities, even such desperate characters as Lane, Jennison, Anthony, Montgomery, Nugent, etc., within whose military lines he had lived, and preached, and labored without any great annoyance or molestation. But the bands of lawless desperadoes and plunderers who could be used by designing men for any purpose whatever, such as Cleveland and others, from Kansas, were too irresponsible and reckless to trust. Friends had traveled in the night from Kansas City to Independence, a distance of twelve miles, to warn him of threats to hang him made by Cleveland and other outlaws, and through many other sources he was impressed with the fact that to remain would be to sacrifice his life causelessly. His friends advised him to seek safety in flight, even the Union military officers of the post counseled this course and provided the necessary facilities.

While his preparations to leave were being made the battle of Independence was fought, in which the Confederates, under Colonels Hughes, Thompson, Boyd and others, succeeded in taking the city, with its garrison, after a contest of four hours. This occurred on the morning of August 13, 1862, and precipitated the flight of the pastor. After the surrender he spent the day in caring for the wounded and dying, the night in packing up and storing his effects, and the next day at 2 P. M., with his family, his trunks and some few movable effects, in a coverless two-horse wagon, he started for Lexington and St. Louis.

He had not been gone two hours when the city was re-entered by the Federal forces—a much enraged Kansas regiment—and for some cause yet unknown his house and church were searched, and every place of possible concealment in the whole vicinity visited with unsparing vigilance to find him. Enraged soldiers stamped the pavement in bitter disappointment, and swore loudly that if he could be found the first limb would be too good to swing his lifeless carcass for the fowls of the air.

Many a dark day had he shared with his flock, and they rejoiced now in his safety. He will never forget the "Black Thursday," as it was called by sad distinction, when all the men of the city were arrested by Col. Jennison, penned up in the Court House yard, and guarded by a double line of soldiers all around the public square, while the drunken negroes of his command were turned loose upon the city to free the slaves and pillage and plunder the homes of the people to their hearts' content. The insults offered the ladies by those beastly semi-savages, infuriated by bad whisky, and the deeds of horror committed by them, will sufficiently characterize the day as the "Black Thursday," and distinguish the annals of crime without any detailed record here. None can forget the pillage and burning of Porter's elegant residence and the very narrow escape of his sick daughter, who was rescued from the second story only by the efforts of the ladies, in defiance of the threats of the brutal soldiery; nor will that line of burning buildings, the light of which fell on their retreating path all the way back to Kansas City, and made lurid and fervid the evening sky, ever pass from the mind. Many other scenes of similar character had made life and property insecure; and Southern Methodist ministers were the objects of particular displeasure.

During that fall, and before the church had been supplied with another pastor, a Rev. James Lee, of the M. E. Church, North, made his appearance in Independence and demanded possession of the church. He first demanded the key, which the rightful owners refused to give up. He then appealed to the military commander of the post. This officer ordered the trustees of the M. E. Church, South, to report the key to his headquarters under pain of confiscation and banishment. The key was surrendered to him, and he gave it to Mr. Lee with his authority to hold and use the church. After Mr. Lee got possession of the house of worship he, as if to "add insult to injury," went through with a formal dedication service, setting the house apart to the worship of God as though it had been a pagan temple; after which it was used by the Northern Methodists as though it belonged of right to them, and without any seeming compunctions of conscience. The Church, South, had no place of worship, and in some respects the ladies of Independence duplicated the work and re-enacted the scenes of Kansas City.

In 1864 Rev. Mr. DeMott was sent by his Church to hold possession of and use the property. Not content with the church, he demanded the parsonage. He already had the coat and he wanted the cloak also. But the trustees of the M. E. Church, South, had rented the parsonage to a poor widow, Mrs. Brazil by name.

Mr. DeMott asked her to vacate the house, this she declined to do; he demanded the key, she refused to give it up. He then appealed to the Commander of the Post, and returned with the result of this appeal in the form of the following military order:

"HEADQUARTERS 43d INF. MO. VOLUNTEERS,
INDEPENDENCE, MO., March 31, 1865.

"*To Mrs. Brazil, living in Methodist Parsonage, Independence, Mo.:*

"It having been represented to the commanding officer that you occupy the parsonage belonging to the Methodist Episcopal Church, and persist in retaining the possession of the same to the exclusion of the minister of said Church, using in connection with such refusal language defiant of the Federal authorities and treasonable to the United States Government, you are therefore required to move your household goods out of and evacuate said parsonage by the morning of the third of April proximo; at which time, on failure on your part to comply with this order, your goods will be removed by the commander of this station.

"Very respectfully,
"B. R. DAVIS,
"Major 43d Mo. Vols., commanding station."

Now, let it be understood that this property, as well as the church, had been built and paid for by the Southern Methodists, and of the three hundred members of that Church then in Independence, not more than eight or ten united with the M. E. Church, North.

The language of the above order sufficiently indicates the representations made by Mr. DeMott to the military authorities to influence them to move in that direction in their work of saving the Union.

To turn a defenseless and helpless widow with her children and household effects into the streets to make room for a Northern Methodist minister to occupy and hold property that belonged to others was, perhaps, a military movement of great strategic importance to the cause of the Union and the restoration of the Government; but in the light of moral honesty and Christian decency the military manœuvre becomes a pious fraud, which the perpetrators were forced, after using its opportunities for several years, to confess before men.

The church and parsonage were occupied and used by Mr. DeMott, when in the fall of 1865 Rev. M. M. Pugh was appointed by the St. Louis Annual Conference, M. E. Church, South, to the Independence station. On his arrival he made a formal demand of Mr. DeMott for the property. This was just as formally refused; the occupant declaring at the same time that he "had been sent there by his Church to hold that property for the use and benefit of the M. E. Church, and he intended to do it." Recourse was had to the law, and suit for possession was instituted.

This suit was called in the Circuit Court for the spring of 1866, when Mr. DeMott made affidavit that important witnesses were absent and he was not ready for trial—the case was continued. The following fall term of the Court was held, and the defendants again swore that they were not ready for trial. Again the case was continued, but it was apparent that the motive for continuing the case so often was the farther use of the property, of which they knew the law would deprive them. They were never ready for trial, but began to feel the force of public sentiment and the shame of fraudulent dealing, if the sense of shame still remained; and the wiser and abler of them began to fear the penalty, not only of fraud, but of rents and damages, and advised a compromise. In February, 1867, they proposed, through their counsel, one Col. Hines, to surrender the property and pay all costs if the M. E. Church, South, would withdraw the suit. To this Messrs. Sawyer, Chrisman and Hovey, counsel for plaintiffs, agreed. The suit was accordingly withdrawn, the property vacated, and the rightful owners took possession.

The property was much damaged, and involved heavy expense in the necessary repairs. Those who occupied it evidently felt that it did not belong to them, and abused it accordingly.

To show more fully the grounds of the suit and the defense set up by defendants it may not be out of place, as an important part of the history of this affair, to introduce here a statement of the case furnished by Sam'l Sawyer, Esq., of Independence, one of the counsel for plaintiffs. It is as follows:

"The Church property at this place (Independence), as you are aware, was taken possession of by the M. E. Church, North, during the war, and the trustees of the Church, South, were compelled to assume the offensive. At first a suit by forcible entry was instituted before a Justice of the Peace, which was moved to the Circuit Court by *certiorari;* but as the suit, however determined, would not settle the title to the property, it was thought advisable to institute a suit, not only for possession, but also to quiet the title. In this last suit a full history of the church at Independence, as well as of the action of the General Conference in New York in 1844, and the Louisville Convention in 1845, was set up. In the answer filed by defendants they admitted the action of the General Conference of 1844, and the Convention at Louisville, Ky., the following year; also, the action of the Missouri Annual Conference of 1845, but deny their authority to act in the premises, and assert that the property was conveyed for the use of the M. E. Church at Independence Station, that they are the successors of the original trustees named in the deed of conveyance, and as such they assert their title to the property. Within the past few months several passes have been made for a compromise, but nothing definite was proposed until last Saturday, when I received a proposition from the attorney for defendants to surrender the whole property and pay all the costs. This proposition, although not what it should have been, yet, under the circumstances, and in view of the uncertainty hanging on the future, it was deemed best to accept; and on last Monday morning I received the keys, and possession was at once given to the trustees of the M. E. Church, South. This I hope ends the controversy.

"I would be glad to believe that the motive claimed, viz., a disposition to do right, was the governing motive in giving up the property; but my own opinion is, they saw that whenever trial could be had they had no case, and hence concluded to get out of a bad scrape with as much credit as possible. There was a difference of opinion among their members. Those, as usual, who had no pecuniary interests, and no property to answer for the costs and damages that might be recovered, were for fight to the last, while the more moderate and the men of means were determined to yield the possession, and their better counsels prevailed."

Thus ended the case as it exists plainly in the facts of history, but there are some side lights and side scenes in the details without which the affair will not be complete. A few circumstantial details, which are contained in a communication found in the *St. Louis Christian Advocate*, of June 20, 1866, will serve to sample the whole. Take the following extracts:

"And there, too, stands that elegant church, with its stained windows and tall, graceful spire, at once the pride and ornament of the city; but its aisles are trod by other feet, and its cushioned pews are filled or reserved for other worshipers than those who built, or bought, or owned the property. The pulpit and altar, so tastefully fitted and furnished by the young men in 1857, are now served by other hands and other tongues, and I had almost said by another gospel, than those for whom or that for which they were prepared.

"The parsonage, which has housed so many good men of our church and their families, for whom it was built, is now occupied by another; and the spacious yard, once so tastefully ornamented with shade and fruit trees, flowers and evergreens, is laid waste and almost bare—now the common resort of horses, cows, hogs, dogs and dirty children from the streets.

"Sadly I turned away from a scene of wrong and desecration to pity the moral condition of the hearts that could meditate and the hands that could perpetrate such sacrilegious injustice. What right have the Northern Methodists to this property? Did they build it?

buy it? pay for it? or even give one dollar toward paying for it? What claim do they set up? What show of right? If there be a higher law than civil law—if there be another standard of moral justice and right than the inspired gospel which they pretend to preach and practice—then they may have some show of claim; not without.

"For nearly twenty years that property has been held by trustees, regularly appointed, for the use and benefit of the M. E. Church, South, and no one questioned their legal right or sought to disturb their peaceable possession.

"But during the reign of terror, in 1862, '63 and '64, under which so many people in Jackson county lost their lives, and so many more their property, and under the oft-reiterated threats of Northern Methodists and their hirelings, with no inconsiderable military pressure, this property passed out of our hands without the formalities and fogyism of bargain and sale, or legal transfer of title.

"* * * When the war closed, and President Johnson had ordered the return of the property taken from us in the South under the notorious Stanton-Ames order, the trustees of our church made a civil demand for the restoration of this property also, which was refused by these loyal (?) property-lovers.

"The ladies, believing that they had the first and best right to the property, and chagrined at this refusal, entered the church one day with their knitting and sewing, to the number of thirty, and disposed of themselves in a peaceable, quiet, orderly way, to spend the day in the house of worship built and paid for by their husbands, fathers and brothers. The Northern Methodist preacher, soon apprised of the fact, hastened to a civil magistrate and made affidavit that these ladies were 'disturbing the peace,' procured a peace warrant and a constable and proceeded to the church, where he found these orderly ladies 'assembled, neither with multitude or tumult,' and had them arrested and dragged before the civil officer for trial. With all of their 'false witnesses' nothing was found in them 'worthy of prison or of death,' and after binding them over to keep the peace they were released.

"* * * President Johnson was applied to personally for the restoration of this property to its rightful owners, as it had been taken under military authority and order. He referred the matter to General Pope, commanding the Department. Gen. Pope put the case, with instructions, in the hands of a subordinate officer, and he buried it so deep in his pocket that it never came to light afterward."

These are only some of the circumstances that seem necessary to develop the whole transaction, but they must suffice. The case is on record, with many others of like character, to go down to posterity as a part of the history made during those dark days. The Northern Methodist papers have repeatedly denied that their Church ever seized, held or appropriated the property of the M. E. Church, South. One more fact will be a positive confirmation of their appropriation of this property. It is this:

In the official statistics of the "Missouri and Arkansas Annual Conference of the Methodist Episcopal Church for 1865" this church and parsonage are reported and valued, the church at $17,000 and the parsonage at $3,000. The same property is again reported in the statistics for 1866; and then, without any note of explanation, disappears from the annual statistical report of Church property in Missouri.

To show that this action, with all similar efforts to gain possession of the property of others, was encouraged and sanctioned by the Church in Missouri, and was only a part of their programme of Church extension, in the minutes of the "Missouri and Arkansas Annual Conference" for 1865 the following record is made:

"The following resolution was read and referred to the Committee on the State of the Church:

"*Resolved*, That the preachers of the Conference be, and they are hereby, requested to take all necessary steps in order to repossess the Church property belonging to the Methodist Episcopal Church in Missouri."

That the above committee did most fully meet the intent of that resolution the report which was unanimously adopted will show. It is as follows:

"Your committee beg to record our devout gratitude to the great Head of the Church for the rich and glorious manifestations of his power in the extension of his kingdom within the bounds of the Conference. At such a time and in such an age as this every friend of the truth and every lover of extension should be vigilant and hopeful, and more especially as the ministers and members of the ever loyal Methodist Episcopal Church of the United States, to whom are constantly presenting new and extensive fields of extension, labors and usefulness. Advantages of no ordinary character are presented at this time. The action of the Missouri State Convention, by bill of rights, secures to any loyal trustee or trustees the right to control any church or educational property by application to the Circuit Court for the appointment of such other trustees of recognized and established loyalty; and we deem it proper to direct the attention of the ministers of the Conference to the fact that much of such property now held in this State is under the control of the disloyal and treasonable, property which was originally deeded to the Methodist Episcopal Church of the United States, and we advise our ministers that, whenever practicable, immediate steps be taken to possess and retain the same according to the forms of law secured by Bill of Rights. It further appears to your committee as of great importance, in the present state of the Church, that all persons of undoubted and established loyalty and holding the Methodist doctrine should, as far as possible, be in communion with us, that we may strive together for the advancement of our common cause in the earth. In view of these facts it is hereby

"*Resolved*, 1. That a committee of five be appointed whose duty it shall be to draw up a brief address to the ministers and members of the M. E. Church, South, inviting to unite with our Church all who are truly loyal to the Government of the United States, as a common government over all the United States, as recognized in its constitution and laws, and assuring them of an affectionate and hearty welcome to this fold.

"*Resolved* 2, That the ministers of this Conference are hereby requested to take all necessary steps in order to re-obtain possession of the Church property belonging to the Methodist Episcopal Church in Missouri, agreeable to the provisions of the Bill of Rights enacted by the Missouri State Convention."

Let it be observed that the same State Convention that adopted the New Constitution with its notorious "Test Oath" ordained also the "Bill of Rights," over which the Conference indulged such extravagant gratulations.

How many Northern Methodist ministers and members were in that State Convention, and how far that Church influenced the action of the Convention, and how far the said action was *intended* by its authors to restrict the liberty and expose to persecution the persons of Southern Methodist ministers and affect the property of the M. E. Church, South, in this State, others may determine from the facts upon record.

Many things are yet to be revealed upon the subject, and the fact can not be escaped that the plan of persecution was well settled, thoroughly digested, well understood and embraced this church-appropriating or church-stealing business, under military orders and State Convention ordinances.

CHAPTER XII.

CHURCH SEIZURES—CONTINUED.

Church at Lexington—Suit Brought for it by the Methodist Church—Statement of Mr. Sawyer—Suit Dismissed—Salem, Arrow Rock, California and other Churches—*Lagrange Church History*—How the Church North Borrowed and then Seized it—Notice Served—Colonel W. M. Redding the "Faithful Guardian"—Rev. W. C. Stewart—Christian Charity—What a Southern Methodist Says—*Central Advocate*—Mr. Stewart's "Honor" Transmitted—Suit for Possession—Arbitration—*Louisiana Church*—Its History and how it was Seized—Civil Courts and Church Trustees—Names Forged—Counter Petition—Decision of Court of Common Pleas—Supreme Court of Missouri—History of the Case—Opinion of the Supreme Court—S. S. Allen, Esq., on Church and State—Rulings of the Court—The Case Reversed—Efforts to Compromise—Five Years' Possession—Reported in Church Statistics—Supplement—Able Argument of Smith S. Allen, Esq.

CHURCH IN LEXINGTON.

In 1860 the old Methodist Church in Lexington, Mo., was torn down and a new one erected on the same lot. The new edifice was modeled mainly after that at Independence—a little larger, finer and costlier. Up to the time of its completion, in 1862, the Northern Methodists had no permanent organization in the city, except one improvised for the army and other purposes the year before. Since the division of the Church they had never had any hold in that section of the State, and but for the presence and power of the army it is reasonable to suppose that no claim upon that property would have ever been set up. They had a few adherents, and about the last year of the war they instituted suit for the recovery of that Church property. The following statement furnished by Mr. Sawyer, the counsel for the M. E. Church, South, will explain the nature of the suit:

"The suit at Lexington, as you are probably aware, was instituted by certain persons assuming to be the Trustees of the M. E. Church against the Trustees of the M. E. Church, South. It was an action of ejectment for the recovery of the possession on the ground of title. The answer set up the action of the General Conference in New York in 1844, embracing the whole Plan of Separation, as also the action of the Southern Conferences in convention at Louisville in 1845, as well as the action of the Missouri and St. Louis Conferences in reference to the Plan of Separation; all of which action, it was insisted, was in effect a contract between the parties, and valid and binding as such. This was the main ground of defense to the action; and when I went to the court last fall, expecting to try the case, I found the suit had been dismissed and the M. E. Church, South, left in the undisturbed possession of their property."

Finding that they had no shadow of claim to the property, and no pretext even for getting possession by military interference, they withdrew the suit, paid the costs, and turned their attention to other places where they had a better show of success.

Salem Church.

The Northern Methodists took possession of Salem Church, in Pettis county, on the Georgetown circuit, held and used it for several months, and finding that they were not sustained by the citizens, and too remote from military posts, they abandoned it from very shame.

Arrow Rock and other Churches.

The Rev. M. M. Pugh writes:

"They made an unsuccessful effort to appropriate our church in Arrow Rock. The Rev. Mr. Hagerty, one of the most active men in this church-seizing business, made a visit to that place for the purpose of making that church the property of his organization. Our friends watched him closely, and he signally failed.

"They also tried to seize our church in California. I believe they were persuaded to desist in this case. Our church in Warrensburg was burned. I do not know the particulars. So, also, was our church in Miami, but we do not know by whom it was set on fire.

Church in Lagrange.

In 1838 two lots in the town of Lagrange, Lewis county, Mo., were deeded to B. W. Stith, C. S. Skinner, John Lafon, Middleton Smoot and others, trustees, for the use and benefit of the Methodist Episcopal Church, as then constituted. In the following year a small brick house was erected on the lots and used by the Church in an unfinished condition until 1844. It was then finished, and upon the division of the Church passed into the hands and ownership of the M. E. Church, South, The membership in 1845 voted to adhere South, with only three or four dissenting voices, and they acquiesced in the will of the majority and remained in the Southern Church until after the repudiation of the Plan of Separation by the General Conference of 1848. Up to that time the Northern Church attempted no organization in Lagrange. But soon after that event the Church North sent a Rev. Mr. Chivington (the same who made himself notorious a few years ago in the indiscriminate massacre of Indians near Fort Union) to that place. He sought and obtained permission to preach in the church. After sermon he organized a class of seven members, and publicly thanked the members of the M. E. Church, South, for the use of *their* house.

The members of the Church North recognized the validity of the decisions of the courts in the Maysville, Ky., and New York and Cincinnati church property cases, and set up no claim whatever to the property in Lagrange, or elsewhere in Missouri, until after the beginning of the war.

In 1853 the old church was displaced by a new and a more commodious structure, erected and paid for by the members and friends of the M. E. Church, South, at a cost of over $6,000. In this the M. E. Church, North, took no part, paid no money and claimed no interest. In 1863, ten years thereafter, a Rev. Mr. Stewart was sent to Lagrange by the M. E. Church, North. This man professed great friendship for Southern Methodists, and made himself free and easy in their homes. The church was only occupied two Sabbaths in the month, and Mr. Stewart applied for the use of it when it was unoccupied. To this the owners objected at first. Mr. Stewart was offered the use of the German Methodist Church, but it did not suit his purpose, and he urged his application for the Southern Methodist Church. It was objected to by a large number of the members upon the ground that other churches in the State had been seized and possessed by them, some in one way and some in another, and they feared this might be a *ruse de guerre.*

Mr. Stewart finally pledged his honor as a Christian gentleman and minister to return the key every week to the trustees. This he did regularly until January, 1865, when his quarterly meeting was held in the Church, and the Quarterly Conference appointed a board of trustees and authorized them to hold possession of the property. Upon this action Rev. Mr. Stewart went out in town, purchased a lock, employed a carpenter and had it put on in place of the old one. He could then return both lock and key with impunity.

The trustees thus raised and authorized to act for the M. E. Church served the following notice on the trustees of the M. E. Church, South:

"LAGRANGE, LEWIS COUNTY, MO., Feb. 13, 1865.

"*To John Munn, J. C. Goodrich and others, Trustees of of M. E. Church, South:*

"GENTLEMEN: Having a just and legal claim to the property of the Methodist Episcopal Church in Lagrange, as trustees of said church, we hereby notify you that we intend to hold said property for the use and benefit of the ministers and members of the Methodist Episcopal Church in the United States of America, according to the Discipline and Rules of said Church, and the provisions of deed recorded in Book C, page 341, Lewis county Records. We have accordingly taken possession of the herein mentioned property.

"Done by order of the Board of Trustees of Lagrange M. E. Church. W. M. REDDING,

"President Board of Trustees.

"W. C. STEWART, Sect'ry pro tem. and Preacher in charge."

They had either been waiting a suitable opportunity

or a new light had suddenly dawned upon them from some Episcopal, military or other throne of light and power, that they had been using, by gracious privilege and courtesy, property to which they had "a just and legal claim," and they acted accordingly. It may be characterized as at least very cool.

Possession is said to be nine points of the law; and, if the adage is true, the manner of gaining possession will not necessarily raise any curious questions of casuistry. The how will not vitiate the nine points, when a new lock and key with an extra share of loyalty can make up and meet every other point in the legal decalogue. It only remained for them to serve the usual notification, to save the form of the thing, and appoint Col. W. M. Redding President of the Board, and Colonel of a regiment of Lewis county militia—not a member of any church—to hold the property in peaceable possession. This duty he performed faithfully; for which service he received, in the *Central Advocate* of Dec. 20, 1865, the title of "the faithful guardian of the interests of the M. E. Church in LaGrange, Mo."

A member of the LaGrange Quarterly Conference, M. E. Church, South, from whom much of the above information was obtained, writes as follows:

"The next step," after taking possession and serving notice, "was the exhibition of Christian charity (?) to us of the M. E. Church, South, by a polite offer to loan us the use of their (?) house for our religious worship. But we 'had not so learned Christ.' How could we be partakers with thieves and robbers? 'My house shall be called a house of prayer, but ye have made it a den of thieves.'

"Our house had been solemnly dedicated to the worship of Almighty God by Bishop Marvin when there was no name or membership of the M. E. Church, North, in the place; we say, let that consecration abide, and let God defend the right. We can worship there no more until the law, with the whip of justice, shall drive those who trouble us to their own place."

A letter in the *Central Christian Advocate,* of Dec. 20, 1865, from Rev. W. C. Stewart, contains the following paragraph:

"When I was in LaGrange I had the honor to organize a Board of Trustees of the M. E. Church, and by their authority to take possession of the valuable house of worship there, previously in the hands of the Church, South. In this movement Col. W. M. Redding took a most prominent and efficient part. He is still the faithful guardian of our Church property in LaGrange."

This Col. Redding was once a member of the M. E. Church, South, but withdrew some time before this transaction, declaring when he did so that the time would come when a Southern Methodist could not live in that county. He was a prepared instrument of the M. E. Church, North, and well fitted for their special work, as he had once been a negro trader to the South, and had the price of that human chattel in his pocket. A little power makes good Radical leaders and instruments of such men.

Mr. Stewart exults in "the honor of organizing a Board of Trustees, and by their authority taking possession of the valuable house of worship formerly in the hands of the Church, South." The said "honor" is now made permanent and transmitted to posterity.

Some honors burst like the bubble, others are as enduring as marble. "Some men's sins are open beforehand, going before to judgment, and some men they follow after." This same Stewart went over to the Congregationalists.

The trustees of the M. E. Church, South, brought suit for possession in a civil magistrate's court. It was appealed to the Circuit Court for Lewis county by defendants, and then by same party, upon a change of venue, taken to Shelby county. When called in the Circuit Court in Shelbyville they were not ready for trial. But they had brought suit in the same court to test or recover the title, to which a demurrer was filed on the ground that they had not kept up a perpetual Board of Trustees from the date of deed in 1838. They had a Board whose history and authority dated back only to January 30, 1865. To prevent a non-suit they asked a continuance, which was granted. Before the session of the Court in November, 1866, they asked the Church, South, to compromise, by referring the whole case to three men for arbitration. When this was agreed to both parties gave bond in the sum of $500 to abide the decision. February 1, 1867, was set for hearing by the arbitrators. When the case was stated by the Church, South, the other party asked leave to withdraw the bond. To this objections were made, and they wrangled over it till four o'clock P. M. The Church, North, asked a continuance till nine o'clock the next morning. This was granted, and at the appointed time they appeared and revoked their bond, saying that they preferred to have the case tried by the Supreme Court of the United States, and would make it a precedent for

Missouri. Whether this course was intended only for delay their subsequent declaration—that they did not expect to be ready for trial for ten years—is the best interpretation.

Wearied out of all patience with such miserable tergiversation, the trustees of the M. E. Church, South, headed by their pastor, Rev. T. J. Starr, prepared to bring suit again, believing that their only hope was in the civil courts. As soon as Col. Redding and those who acted with him found that they would have to meet the case in the civil courts they proposed a compromise, which, during the absence of the preacher in charge, was accepted. This compromise gave the M. E. Church, South, a quit-claim deed to less than half the two lots with the new church, and the M. E. Church, North, a similar deed to the old church with the rest of the two lots. The old church was just back of the new, and within a few feet of it. To settle the difficulty and have peace, the rightful owners of the whole property had to quit-claim half of it to their enemies, and pay more than half the costs of suits, for the gracious favor of a quit-claim deed to the other half of their own property, and the peaceful possession of their own house of worship in a greatly damaged condition. But, then, our people have so long been inured to privation, wrong and persecution, that they will purchase peace and the privileges of unmolested worship at almost any price but that of honor and integrity. What are houses and lands and earthly possessions to the integrity and purity of the "Kingdom of Heaven" and its unperverted institutions?

In the statistics of the Missouri and Arkansas Conference of the M. E. Church this Church property at LaGrange is returned as the property of that Church, at an estimated value of $12,000.

The Conference session of 1866 adopted the following:

"*Resolved,* That the pastor of LaGrange be authorized to go outside the Conference limits to procure funds to meet the expenses of defending the title to the Church property of the Methodist Episcopal Church at LaGrange.

(Signed) "W. C. STEWART.
"T. B. BRATTON.
"T. J. WILLIAMS."

Comment is unnecessary.

CHURCH IN LOUISIANA.

The history of the Church property case in Louisiana, Missouri, furnishes peculiarities of a nature that will bear a little attention to the details. It is about as follows:

In 1853 a deed to a lot of ground in the city was made by Edward G. McQuie and wife to Edwin Draper, John S. Markley, John W. Allen, Samuel O. Minor, John Shurmur, Joseph Charleville, Ivey Zumwalt, David Watson and Thomas T. Stokes, as trustees of the M. E. Church, South, to hold in trust for the use and benefit of said Church. Consideration, $500. Soon thereafter a commodious church edifice was erected on the lot and dedicated to the worship of God in the name and for the benefit of the M. E. Church, South. It was occupied and used by them unmolested until 1862.

In the meantime vacancies had occurred in the original Board of Trustees by the death of David Watson and the removal from the State of Thos. T. Stokes.

These vacancies had been filled by the regular authority of the Church, and according to law, by the appointment and election of Samuel S. Allen and Wm. A. Gunn, as seen in the records of the Quarterly Conference for Louisiana Station. But this fact did not prevent the tools of the M. E. Church, North, from devising a bold scheme that would put them in possession of the Church property. They could not claim that the property was originally deeded to the M. E. Church and afterward wrested from the rightful owners, as in the cases at Lexington, Independence, LaGrange, Boonville, etc. That plea could not serve them in this case, and to accomplish their purpose they devised another. It was this. An *ex parte* petition was filed in the Louisiana Court of Common Pleas, setting forth the fact of the above mentioned vacancies in the Board of Trustees, and praying the Court to fill the vacancy occasioned by the death of David Watson by the appointment of Charles Hunter, and to appoint Robt. S. Strother to fill the vacancy occasioned by the removal of T. T. Stokes. This petition, as it now stands on the records of the Court, was signed by Edwin Draper, John S. Markley, John W. Allen, Ivey Zumwalt, Samuel O. Minor, Jos. Charleville and John Shurmur, and was granted July 21, 1862.

On the second day thereafter (July 23, '62,) Samuel O. Minor, John W. Allen, Ivey Zumwalt, W. A. Gunn and S. S. Allen filed a petition asking the court to vacate the order appointing Hunter and Strother, and set forth the following facts why the order should be set aside: They admitted the vacancies occasioned by the death of Watson and the removal of Stokes, but set forth from the Church records that on the 21st day of January, 1861, Rev. W. M. Newland, then preacher in charge, nominated, and the Quarterly Conference elected, W. A. Gunn to fill the vacancy occasioned by the death of said Watson, and that the other vacancy was filled by the nomination and election of Samuel S. Allen, April 23, 1862, Rev. W. G. Miller then being preacher in charge. They, therefore, allege that at the time of the appointment by the court of Hunter and Strother no vacancy existed, the same having been filled according to the law of the Church made and provided, and therefore the order of the court ought to be vacated.

They further represented that the names of John W. Allen, Samuel O. Minor and Ivey Zumwalt were used in the original petition without their knowledge or consent, and insisted that the order should be set aside for that reason.

Both the petitioners and community were astonished when the court refused to vacate the order, and the only recourse was an appeal to the Supreme Court of Missouri on a writ of error. It may not be improper to state in this place that Judge Gilchrist Porter, then on the bench of that Judicial District, presided; and Thos. J. C. Fagg, then Judge of the Louisiana Court of Common Pleas, was counsel for the M. E. Church, North, in his own court.

The cause was argued July 24, '62, and the petition overruled. The petitioners filed a bill of exceptions and the case went up to the Supreme Court.

The case was not heard in the Supreme Court until

January 10, 1866, when the judgment of the court below was reversed and the case dismissed upon the ground of irregularity and informality.

As this case may involve several legal points of importance to the Church, it may be proper to transfer so much of the decision and rulings of the court to these pages as will be of general application.

S. S. Allen, Esq., for plaintiffs in error, submitted the following points of law, and the court ruled accordingly:

"1. The Church, by means of its preacher in charge and Quarterly Conference, had full and ample power to fill vacancies in its board of trustees (see 'Doctrines and Discipline of the Methodist Episcopal Church,' p. 254).

"2. Over the Church, as such, the temporal courts of this country most clearly have no jurisdiction, except to protect them, and to protect the civil rights of others, and to preserve the public peace, none of which were necessary in this case (see Baptist Church in Hartford, vs. Wittnell, 3 Paige, Ch. 301; Sawyer vs. Cipperly, 7 Paige, 281 etc.)

"3. There were no vacancies in the board when the court below acted, said vacancies having been duly filled by the preacher and Conference long before the court acted. (See 'Minutes of the Conference.')

"Dyer & Campbell for defendants in error.

"Lovelace, Judge, delivered the opinion of the court."

In this opinion the court holds the following language, after a statement of the case:

"The case is not free from difficulties. The court below seemed to be acting under the statute concerning 'Trusts and Trustees.' But this case does not fall within the statute, for that only provides for appointing trustees in deeds of trust made to secure the payment of a debt or other liability. R. C. 1855, p. 1554, §1.) So in this case, it would seem that the parties must resort to their equitable remedy to prevent the trust from being defeated for want of a trustee.

"There are more informalities than appear upon the record, but they are not alluded to by either party. The question presented by the parties is, whether there are vacancies in the Board of Trustees to be filled. Both parties admit that there have been vacancies, but the defendants contend that the vacancies have been filled by the Church according to the rule and discipline of that Church, and the evidence proves conclusively that the board of trustees for church purposes, under the rules and discipline of the Church, had been filled; but whether, under the peculiarities of this deed, the legal title to the property described in the deed will descend to the trustees thus appointed seems doubtful.

"The uses and purposes for which the property is to be used is not expressed in the deed, but the property is merely deeded to the petitioners, naming them, together with Watson and Stokes, describing them as 'Trustees of the Methodist Episcopal Church, South,' and to them and their successors in office, lawfully appointed, forever, for a consideration of five hundred dollars. It is not stated, except as mentioned in the deed, though it may perhaps be inferred that the petitioners at the time of the conveyance were in fact trustees of the Church, appointed by the Church under its rules and discipline; nor does it appear who furnished the money to purchase the property. If it was furnished by the Church, then, most certainly, the court, upon proper application, would order these plaintiffs to convey it to such person or persons as the Church might name, to hold it for their use and benefit; but if, on the contrary, the money was furnished by these plaintiffs, the naked fact that the grantors in the deed have described them as 'Trustees of the Methodist Episcopal Church, South,' would not of itself operate to destroy their interest in the property. In the former case they would hold the property in trust for the Church, and would be compelled to convey to any persons the Church might nominate to receive it; but this could only be done upon proof of the fact that the Church furnished the money with which the property was purchased.

"3. Upon the face of this deed the property belongs to the grantees in the deed; and to divest them of the title it must be shown *aliunde* that the purchase money was furnished by the Church. The legal title is in the grantees; but in case somebody else furnished the purchase money, then the grantees will be regarded as holding the property for whomsoever furnished the purchase money.

"If, then, the above views be correct, there can be no question of vacancy in the Board of Trustees as respects this property until the question of the title is first settled. If it belongs to the grantees, no trustees are necessary; they can manage it for themselves. If the Church is entitled to it, then the grantees must first be divested of their title, and the title vested in some person or persons for the use of the Church. The proceedings here are irregular and premature. The judgment must be reversed and the cause dismissed. The other judges concur."

Pending this case Mr. Allen, counsel for plaintiffs in error, made a very able argument upon the relation of the Church to the civil government. He took high ground upon the separate and distinct jurisdictions of Church and State, as understood by our fathers and as developed in this country under the genius of our government. He characterized severely the efforts made by partisan fanatics to confound in fact what was distinct in law, and to unite the Church with the State for purposes of ecclesiastical power and political corruption. His argument was well worth preserving.

The decision of the Supreme Court in effect sent the case back for a trial of the rights of property, for which suit was immediately brought in the Circuit Court. But under the operation of the order of the Court of Common Pleas of June 31, 1862, the church property passed out of the possession of the M. E. Church, South, to whom it was originally deeded, and into the possession of the self and court-constituted Board of Trustees, for the use and benefit of the M. E. Church, North. The property was used by them from July 21, 1862, to some time in the spring of 1867. In March, 1867, a letter was addressed by a number of the trustees to the presiding elder and preacher in charge of Louisiana Station, who were supposed to have influence with the authorities of the Church then holding and using the property, asking their kindly offices and services in an honorable and amicable adjustment of the difficulty and the return of the property to the rightful owners.

The following answer was elicited:

"LOUISIANA, Mo., March 21, 1867.

"*Messrs. Sam. S. Allen, W. A. Gunn and others, members of the M. E. Church, South, Louisiana, Mo.:*

"GENTLEMEN: Your communication of the 4th instant

is received and would have been answered sooner but we have not had time since its reception for consultation until yesterday. We would gladly do anything in our power to bring about an honorable adjustment of the matter of which you write, but as the controversy is between you and the trustees of the church, we are wholly without authority in the premises, and therefore have no right to advise the board of trustees how they shall settle the matter. If we had the power to act, our action would fully recognize the asserted rights of the trustees until the proper legal tribunal decides the question. We will not, however, be in the way of any compromise which the parties may be able to make. With assurances of personal regard, we are, gentlemen,

"Yours very truly,

"NAT. SHUMATE.

"J. S. BARWICK."

They declined to interfere in the matter as long as they could hold and use the Church property. But, as in other cases, when they found that they had no shadow of title, and could not even frame another pretext for holding on to the property, they were magnanimous enough to propose or accept a compromise by which the property could go back into the hands of the rightful owners without the humiliation of being forced by law to pay damages and rents, which a common honesty demanded.

The suit for title was stricken from the docket without being heard, and those who bought the lot and built and paid for the church are again in possession of their own; albeit they were kept out of the use of it for nearly five years, and then received it in a condition that required extensive repairs, for which those who had used and damaged it had no disposition to pay a single dollar. Thus one by one the property that was taken from the Church, South, was restored, after being used and abused by "our friends, the enemy."

It does not add any thing to the credit of the Northern Church to record the fact that this church, also, was reported in the statistics of the Conference, valued at $5,000.

To those who have believed the reiterated statements of the Northern Methodist preachers and press, that they never seized, possessed or used any property that belonged to the M. E. Church, South, these facts, furnished by reliable men and taken from official records, are commended. The facts are humiliating enough without the reflections suggested by them.

SUPPLEMENT.

The following able argument in the Louisiana Church property case, before the Supreme Court of the State, made by Smyth S. Allen, Esq., of Hannibal, Mo., counsel for plaintiffs in error, is not only a part of the history of the case, but too valuable and vital to the great questions at issue to be lost. It may very properly supplement this chapter, as its merits demand a more permanent form than the newspaper columns. It will be perused with interest, especially by the legal profession, and will not be without interest and profit to the general reader.

Edwin Draper and others, *ex parte* petitioners and defendants in error.	*Error from the Louisiana Court of Common Pleas.*
Sam'l O. Minor and others, plaintiffs in error.	

If the Court please: The extraordinary conduct of part of the *ex parte* petitioners and defendants in error in this case is perhaps sufficiently disclosed in the written statement of facts filed by plaintiffs, which I have already drawn up and placed on the files of the Court. This part of my subject I will, however, with the indulgence of the Court, consider more fully hereafter.

This case, on the face of the *ex parte* petition, appears to be an application by seven of the trustees of the Methodist Episcopal Church, South, at Louisiana, Missouri, made to the Louisiana Court of Common Pleas, to have two pretended vacancies in that Board of Trustees filled by appointment of that Court. These seven *ex parte* petitioners on the face of the petition are Edwin Draper, John S. Markley, John W. Allen, Samuel O. Minor, John Shurmur, Joseph Charleville and Ivy Zumwalt.

But in fact this is not the application of three of the pretended petitioners, to-wit, Samuel O. Minor, Ivy Zumwalt and John W. Allen; on the contrary, these three gentlemen are indignant at the proceedings. As evidence of this I will here state that they became, and are, parties to the motion to set aside the order of the Court below appointing Strother and Hunter to fill the pretended vacancies. By their affidavit, appended to said motion, they and each of them solemnly swear that said *ex parte* petition was gotten up, and their names used therein as petitioners, without their knowledge or consent and against their will; and that the same was filed and the unjust and illegal action of the Court below had thereon without their knowledge or consent.

These gentlemen must not, therefore, be considered as acting in concert with Draper, Markley and others, but must, in justice to them and to their action in the premises, and to their said affidavits, be regarded as honest and candid objectors to the petition and to the action of the Court thereon.

These three gentlemen stood before the court below on the hearing of the motion to set aside its illegal order and made known these facts and verified them by their affidavits, and asked the court to revoke and set aside its order. And they, with Minor and Gunn, now stand before this court in the person of their counsel and ask that said order may be set aside. And in this they simply ask that that justice may be done to them which was strangely and wrongfully denied by the court below.

Here we have the strange spectacle of three men, on whose petition this order seems to have been made, coming in and disclaiming the whole thing and asking this court to set it aside.

As a legal proposition I maintain: First, that in this country the widest latitude is given by law to religious sentiment; and second, that the temporal courts have no jurisdiction over churches or church judicatories or church members, as such, except simply to protect them, to protect the civil rights of others, and to preserve the public peace.

In the case of the Baptist Church in Hartford vs.

Witherell, in the Court of Chancery in the State of New York, Chancellor Walworth, in delivering the opinion of the court, says:

"Over the Church, as such, the legal or temporal tribunals of this country do not profess to have any jurisdiction whatever, except so far as is necessary to protect the civil rights of others and to preserve the public peace." (See 3 Paige Reports, 301.)

So in the case of Lawyer vs. Cepperly, the same court decides substantially the same thing. (7 Paige Chancery Reports, 281; see also Angel & Ames on Corporations, sec. 58, page 28, note 1, page 29; Stebbins vs. Jennings, 10 Pickering Rep., 172; Gable vs. Miller, 10 Paige Rep., 627.)

I am fully aware that courts of chancery have ample jurisdiction to determine questions touching the legal title to church property, real or personal; and that in order to protect a Church in the enjoyment of its corporate property that court might appoint trustees.

But even this is to be understood with some limitation. Suppose, for example, that a church has full and ample power by its own church laws, church courts and judicatories to protect itself or to put itself in a condition where it will not need the action of the temporal court, *ought the temporal court to interfere? Most clearly not.*

And more particularly the temporal court ought not to interfere in this case, for the following six plain and sufficient reasons: *First,* because there is no contest in this case about property; *second,* because no title is involved; *third,* because no possession is asked for; *fourth,* because no obedience to rightful authority or authority of any kind is sought to be enforced; *fifth,* because no wrong is sought to be prevented; and *sixth,* because no injury to the church is sought to be avoided.

If protection to church property required that Hunter and Strother should be put into this Board of Trustees, the Church, by means of its preacher in charge and Quarterly Conference, had full power to put them there to fill vacancies without action of the court below, *provided vacancies existed.* The church law on the subject of appointing a Board of Church Trustees and filling vacancies therein is found on page 254 of a book entitled "The Doctrines and Discipline of the Methodist Episcopal Church, South." It is a book of universal authority in that Church, as we all know, and was largely referred to by all parties to this contest on the trial in the court below, as is fully shown by the Bill of Exceptions. At page 254 I find the following plain and simple provision:

"In the appointment of Trustees, except where the laws of the State or Territory provide differently, the preacher in charge, or in his absence the Presiding Elder, shall have the right of nomination, subject to the confirmation or rejection of the Quarterly Conference. All vacancies in the Board of Trustees occasioned by death, separation from our Church, or otherwise, shall be filled without delay."

This, then, is full and clear, and confers ample authority upon the preacher in charge and Quarterly Conference to appoint trustees for the Church and to fill vacancies without the aid or interference of the temporal courts. It is the identical same provision of the "discipline" under and by virtue of which Draper, Markley and all the other trustees of that church were themselves appointed. They were appointed under and by force of this provision long before the date of the deed of McQuie and wife to them in trust for the Church. McQuie and wife did not appoint them. They—McQuie and wife—had agreed to convey to the Church at Louisiana certain ground for a certain money consideration paid to them by the Church, and were directed by the Church to convey, and did convey, to its board of trustees then existing. As the ground was purchased from McQuie and wife, and full value received for the same, therefore McQuie and wife had no right to appoint the trustees, as they would have had if they had donated and given the lots. The Church having purchased and paid for this ground, had the sole right to say to whom it should be conveyed. If the Church had the exclusive right then to say who should hold its property in trust for it, surely it has that right now. But the Court below has destroyed that right by placing in the Board of Trustees two men—Hunter and Strother—whom the Church did not select in its appointed way, or in any other way, and by vesting in them the legal title to its property without its consent, and perhaps against its will. Against Messrs. Hunter and Strother I have nothing to say; but there is not the slightest evidence on the record, or anywhere else, to show that the Church at Louisiana is pleased with them or desired their services in the Board.

But the Church, through its preacher in charge and Quarterly Conference, as we have seen, not only had power to appoint trustees and to fill vacancies in the Board when vacancies existed, but I now proceed to show that it actually did fill said vacancies—the identical same vacancies stated in this *ex parte* petition to have existed at the time of the filing thereof—by appointing said William A. Gunn to fill the vacancy created by the death of said Watson, and by appointing said Samuel S. Allen to fill the vacancy created by said Stokes ceasing to be a member of the Church and leaving the State. To prove this fact I beg to be permitted to read to this Court so much of the minutes of said Quarterly Conference as may be necessary, and which was copied into the bill of exceptions from the minutes themselves, and proves the fact beyond all doubt, and is as follows:

"On motion of Brother Newland, preacher in charge of this (Louisiana) Station, Brother W. A. Gunn was nominated and confirmed as trustee in place of Bro. David Watson, deceased."

Immediately following the above evidence in the bill of exceptions I will read further evidence in these words:

"The proceedings of said Quarterly Conference, of which the above is part, was had on the 21st day of January, A. D., 1861, and are signed by B. H. Spencer, presiding elder, and attested by William A. Gunn, secretary."

Surely the minutes of the Quarterly Conference is the best evidence of what it did. The minutes thus authenticated by Spencer and Gunn are as conclusive in fact as they are valid in law, and do show that the Watson vacancy was duly filled by said preacher and Conference just one year, five months and fifteen days before the filing of the *ex parte* petition herein. With this evidence before him can any man believe, or can any court decide, that the Watson vacancy existed in the Board of

Trustees when the petition of Draper & Co. was filed? Surely not. Then what right had the Court below to fill a pretended vacancy that in fact and law did not exist? *Certainly none at all.*

I now proceed to show that the Stokes vacancy was also a mere pretense, and did not exist in the Board when this petition was filed, having been filled by the preacher in charge and Quarterly Conference in like manner long before this petition was filed by Draper and others in the court below. The evidence to prove this fact is equally clear and conclusive. I will read to the court from the Bill of Exceptions, in these words:

"The petitioners also offered and read in evidence another portion of said minutes, proving that on the 23d day of April, A. D. 1862, and at said Conference, the Rev. G. W. Miller, then preacher in charge of said Louisiana Station, nominated Bro. Samuel S. Allen as trustee, to fill the vacancy created by the withdrawal from the church of Thomas T. Stokes; and proving, also, that said nomination was confirmed by said Quarterly Conference on the same day."

Thus the court will readily see that the Stokes vacancy was duly filled on the 23d day of April, A. D. 1862, just two months and twelve days before this petition was filed. To say, therefore, that the Stokes vacancy existed in this Board at the time of the filing of this *ex parte* petition is to make sport of language, and is, in my humble opinion, wholly untrue. To say that the Watson and Stokes vacancies existed in this Board when this petition was filed is to deny that Gunn and Samuel S. Allen were members of it. And to deny that Gunn and said Allen were members at that time, is to deny that the petitioners themselves were members of it; for they were all, as we have already seen, appointed by the same power and in the same way—that, is by the Church, through its preacher and Conference. In short, to deny that Gunn and said Allen were members of said Board when this petition was filed is to deny that the Church had any trustees whatever.

The Board, in fact, when this petition was filed, consisted of nine members, namely, Draper, Markley, the two Allens—John W. and Samuel S.—Minor, Shurmur, Charleville, Zumwalt and Gunn, nine in number, and it could not lawfully contain any greater number. (See Discipline, page 254.) There is, therefore, no room in the Board for Strother and Hunter. Samuel S. Allen and William A. Gunn must first be ejected from it, and this can not be *lawfully* done without first giving them reasonable notice and a chance to be heard in the court below. In this case there was no notice until after the court below had acted; and of course no defense was made. The action of the court below, taken without notice to these parties, is void; and this court ought, for that reason (if for no other), to reverse and set it aside. Draper, Markley, Shurmur and Charleville well knew when they filed this petition that Gunn and Samuel S. Allen had been appointed by the preacher and Conference to fill the only vacancies mentioned in the petition. These gentlemen—Draper & Co.—were both attending and attentive members of the Board. They took a lively interest in whatever affected the welfare of the Church. They had acted in the Board with Gunn and Samuel S. Allen, and knew when they filed this petition that said Gunn and Allen had been appointed to fill said vacancies and claimed to be members of the Board. But why they desired to ignore their authority and purposely avoided disclosing the fact to the court below in their petition, we are left to conjecture.

A few more words and I close. The very aims and objects of the Churches in this country constitute a powerful reason why the courts should refuse to interfere with their affairs. No man can reflect upon these aims and objects for one moment without rejoicing that he lives in a land of Bibles and Churches. These Churches, including the one in question, aim at nothing less than the promulgation of the doctrines of the Gospel among all men; the due administration of scriptural ordinances; the promotion of works of piety and benevolence; the revival and spread of scriptural holiness, and, in short, the conversion of the whole world to the faith and practice of Christianity.

An organization of men and women for these high and holy purposes ought to be permitted to chose its own officers and to manage its own affairs in its own way. Whenever the courts of the country have interfered to settle Church difficulties, they have in almost every instance created new and more serious difficulty in the Church. In this very case the action of the court below has already produced discord and alienation in the Church, which perhaps will never be cured. It has in that way, beyond all question, done the Church ten times more harm than good.

When there were vacancies in the Board the Church filled them, as we have seen, by its own laws and in its own way, and there were no complaints, no law-suits, no alienations, no withdrawals from the Church. But when this petition was filed in the court below, and acted upon by that court without notice to anybody, and the names of trustees used without their consent, a large portion of the Church was uncharitable enough to suppose that advantage was sought and wrong intended. Besides, this court having large experience in the affairs of men will readily see that action by our courts in church cases gives great encouragement to discontented and litigious persons to annoy the Church with fruitless legal proceedings, and thus retard its progress in its great work of mercy and benevolence. Better, far better, is it for all parties, and for the cause of Christianity itself, to leave these difficulties to be settled in the Church where they originate.

Thanking this Court for the patient hearing which it has given me in this case, and hoping your Honors will give to the case that consideration which its importance requires, I now take my leave of it.

CHAPTER XIII.

CHURCH SEIZURES—CONTINUED.

Church in Boonville—One of the Oldest Religious Centers—Rev. J. N. Pierce and his Exploits—"An Honest Looker On" in the St. Louis *Christian Advocate*—Circuit Court vs. County Court and J. N. Pierce—Supreme Court—Howard et al. vs. Pierce—Report and Opinion—Circuit Court Sustained—John N. Pierce et al. Exhibited in no Enviable Light—Legal History of the Case—Decision—Points to be Noted—Moral Travestie—Judgment of Posterity—*Church in Springfield*—How Obtained—How Long Used—How Released—Particulars Reported by a Committee of the St. Louis Conference—*Church in Potosi*—Statement of W. S. Woodard—Plattsburg, Fillmore, Macon, Glasgow and other Churches—Strange Assertion—Statistical Value of Churches Seized over $100,000—How Restored—Property Rights Secured to the M. E. Church, South—Great Moral Courage or "Hard Cheek"—"Making History"—Martyrdom of Principle.

Church in Boonville.

The church in Boonville is one of the oldest and most honored houses of worship in the State. Far back in the history of Methodism in Missouri the Church in Boonville became quite a center of religious influence and power in the rich and fast-filling counties south of the Missouri river and near the geographical center of the State. It was for many years a strong base of operations for the hardy moral pioneers who first penetrated that part of the State, planted the first standard of Christianity and laid broad and deep the foundations of Methodism in the wilderness made famous by the exploits of the illustrious hunter and pioneer, Daniel Boone.

Bishops and other distinguished men of the Church

have stood in its pulpit and preached life and salvation to the multitudes. Conferences have been held, and ministers ordained, and sacraments administered in its sacred walls, and for long years it had been a solid, substantial station, supporting some of the finest talent in the pulpit. No one ever thought of disturbing the rights of property. Before the division in 1844 it belonged to the M. E. Church. After that event, to the M. E. Church, South; and for over twenty years the latter had been in undisturbed possession. If the M. E. Church, North, had an organization in Boonville at all before the war, it was very feeble, and never set up any show of claim to the old church until after the war had come and gone.

In February, 1866, a Rev. J. N. Pierce, of the M. E. Church, North, obtained an order from the County Court of Cooper county putting him in possession of the church in Boonville. The first notice or information the Trustees of the M. E. Church, South, had of the proceedings was a demand upon them for the key of the church by said Pierce, by the authority of the order of the County Court. The trustees promptly refused to give up the key, and denied the jurisdiction of the County Court over such matters. But Mr. Pierce was not to be defeated in that way. He soon obtained skillful and corrupt help, went to the church, forced an entrance, removed the lock, put on a new one and took formal possession in the name of his Church.

The following account of the affair was furnished at the time for the St. Louis *Christian Advocate* by one who subscribed himself "*An Honest Looker-on*," and who was fully endorsed by the editor:

"MR. EDITOR: It affords the people of this community

pleasure to hear from other quarters: perhaps others would be equally interested to hear from us. I write more especially for the Church which I believe your paper represents.

"The pastor of the Southern Methodist Church, appointed by the last session of the Annual Conference, took charge of his congregation a few weeks ago. He had not been here more than two or three weeks before he and his congregation were turned out of doors by the Methodist Episcopal preacher in this city. First, under pretense of an order from the County Court, he demanded the key, with all the authority usually exhibited by his class on such occasions. Failing in this, he secured the co-operation of a few kindred spirits, and having secured the services of one skilled in such matters, proceeded to the church about the going down of the sun, effected an entrance, removed the locks, replaced them with new ones, and took possession in the name of the Lord. It was not the last of the old year, but it is said they kept watch-night, it being, as they supposed, the last of the old church. Whether their devotions kept pace with their watchfulness we are not informed. We are told that they affected an exercise of the sort, at least for a time. Meanwhile, in strict conformity to the Scriptures, they watched, also having their sentries, armed it is supposed, stationed at the door; and, not knowing at what hour the thief would come, they watched, it is said, until the morning. If they expected any interference from the owners and former occupants, they have yet to learn that it will not do in every case to judge others by themselves. No Judas came to betray the Master, with his disciples, into the hands of the chief rulers, for it is said that some of the latter joined that night the worshipers and watchers. For the first time in many years their hearts inclined them to go to the house of prayer.

"The eyes of the community have since regarded some of these with peculiar solicitude, looking for further indications of a continued and growing concern; but the proverb is verified: 'The dog is returned to his vomit again, and the sow that was washed to her wallowing.' Alas for Ephraim! his goodness was transient as the morning cloud and early dew.

"The day of their calamity did not overtake the poor Southern Methodists unprepared. They were found with their lamps trimmed and oil in their vessels. There was a good supply of fuel, also, properly prepared; carpets, Sunday school library, etc. The house itself they found swept and garnished. The ladies, only a day or two before, had given it a thorough cleansing. Poor souls! their labor was not in vain in the Lord. * * * *

"Southern Methodism in this city, though cast down, has not been destroyed. Sister churches felt and manifested sympathy. The Presbyterians kindly offered the use of their church on the following Sabbath, and a gentleman, who makes no pretensions to religion, generously tendered the use of a hall, which at present they occupy. The varied character of the seats—chairs, boxes, rough planks, old sofas, etc., might excite a smile, but, under the circumstances, they are regarded as very comfortable. The attendance on the services of the sanctuary has doubled since this wholesale excommunication. The same is true of the Sabbath School; and on every hand there are manifestations of increasing interest. The Church is said to manifest a very good state of feeling, exhibiting very little of that bitterness and malice which such injuries are apt to engender. They forgive and commit their cause to the Lord, exhibiting much of that 'charity that suffereth long and is kind.'

"A writ prohibiting the interference of the Methodist Episcopal Church with the property and rights of the Southern Methodists was granted by proper authority and sustained by the Circuit Court last week. The former occupants patiently wait for the officers of the law to execute their trusts. When this shall be done you may expect to hear from us again.

"AN HONEST LOOKER ON.

"*Boonville, March 10, 1866.*"

The Circuit Court granted a writ of prohibition, and the defendant, J. N. Pierce, appealed to the Supreme Court, and made a motion by his attorney that all proceedings be stayed till the decision of the Supreme Court could be had, which would leave him in possession of the Church until the slow ploddings of law could be made. The court would not grant his motion, but ordered a writ of restitution to issue *instanter*, to which defendant excepted.

The legal history of the case can better be seen in the "Missouri reports," vol. 38, p. 296, a part of which may well be transferred to these pages.

"This case was commenced in the Cooper Circuit Court by filing a petition praying for a writ of prohibition to issue against the County Court and John N. Pierce, stating that the plaintiffs were trustees of the Methodist Episcopal Church, South, situate in the city of Boonville, on the south half of lot 238 on the plat of said city, and that they, as such trustees, were in the actual and rightful possession of said Church property, and that they and the persons under whom they claim have had the actual and adverse possession of said church for more than twenty years, claiming the same as the property of the Methodist Episcopal Church, South; and that the defendant, John N. Pierce, applied by petition to the County Court of Cooper county at the February term, 1866, and in said petition asked the said court to put him, the said Pierce, in possession of said church; and further stating in said petition that said County Court, or a majority of the members of said court, assumed to act on said petition, and did in fact entertain said petition, and made an order and caused the same to be entered upon its records, declaring in said order who are the owners and entitled to the possession of said church. The petition further stated that said court, in assuming to act on said petition, exceeded its powers; that said court had no jurisdiction over the subject matter in said petition, and praying a writ of prohibition to the said County Court and John N. Pierce to prohibit them from proceeding to enforce said order, &c.

"Upon this petition a writ of prohibition issued, returnable to the Circuit Court on the 19th day of February, 1866, and upon the return thereof the defendants moved to quash the writ of prohibition, which motion was overruled, and judgment was entered by the court making the writ of prohibition absolute, and ordering a return of said Church property to the plaintiffs. The court adjourned till the fourth Monday of May, 1866.

Upon the fourth Monday of May, at a session of the Circuit Court, the defendants, by their attorney, filed and argued a motion to vacate and set aside the judgment. The motion was overruled, to which defendant excepted.

"The defendant, John N. Pierce, at the session of said court made and filed an affidavit and recognizance for an appeal to the Supreme Court, which was approved by said Circuit Court and an appeal allowed. The defendant, Pierce, then made a motion that all proceedings be stayed till the decision of the Supreme Court be had, which was refused by the court, and a writ of restitution was thereupon ordered to issue *instanter*, to which the defendant excepted."

A portion of the opinion of the court throws additional light on the subject, and will be sufficient to place all the material facts in the case before the reader. For the questions of law involving the powers and jurisdiction of the courts respectively the reader is referred to the case as reported in "Missouri Reports," vol. 38, pp. 296–302.—Howard *et al.* vs. Pierce.

"Holmes, Judge, delivered the opinion of the court. This was a writ of prohibition against the defendant, Pierce, and the Justices of the County Court of Cooper county, upon a suggestion, supported by affidavit, but without an exemplification of the record of the proceedings being filed therewith. The suggestion, or petition, contains but a very vague and imperfect statement of the facts, but we are enabled to gather from it that the defendant, Pierce, had filed a petition in the County Court praying to have the plaintiffs ejected from the possession of a lot of ground and a church building situated thereon, in the city of Boonville.

"The plaintiffs do not appear to have been made parties to the proceeding, whatever it may have been, and had no notice thereof; but it appears that the County Court proceeded to entertain jurisdiction of the matter, and made certain orders, the effect of which would be to put the petitioner in possession of the premises in question, ejecting the plaintiffs. This was certainly a very summary process of ejectment. We can only say that it is clear for one thing—that the County Court had not jurisdiction to entertain such proceeding.

"It was said in the argument that the title to the property was vested in the county, and that the defendant's application was only to have the liberty of taking possession of the church; but nothing of all this appears on this record. So far as we can see by the record before us, the prohibition was properly granted.

"It further appears that, in the judgment which was entered, an additional order was made, upon facts made to appear to the court, directing the clerk to issue a writ of restitution to restore to the plaintiffs the possession of the premises which (we may infer) had been taken from them by virtue of the orders which had been made by the County Court in disobedience to the prohibition. We find no warrant in any authority for such a proceeding. The proper remedy for a contempt would seem to be an attachment, to be enforced by fine and imprisonment. The sheriff's execution shows that he had made restitution by putting the plaintiffs in possession of the church from which they had been thus unlawfully ejected. The defendant, Pierce, moved to set aside the judgment, for the reason, among others, that this order of restitution was irregular, and his motion was overruled. The Justices of the County Court appear to have acquiesced in the action of the court below, and refused to join with the defendant, Pierce, in this appeal. * *

"We see no better way than to affirm the judgment, and it is accordingly affirmed.

"Judge Wagner concurs; Judge Lovelace absent."

The following points should be noted in making up the public verdict upon the action of Mr. Pierce and the Church which he represents.

1. Mr. Pierce obtained from the County Court an order putting him in possession of the church upon a false plea—that the property belonged to the county—without notifying the trustees or any other parties, and without making them parties to the proceeding.

2. Mr. Pierce acted as his own sheriff, and executed the unlawful order of the court in an unlawful manner, by forcing an entrance to the church, removing the lock, substituting another, and, with a self-organized posse, guarded the church all night with arms in his hands and the order of the County Court in his pocket.

3. He tried to quash the writ of prohibition issued by the Circuit Court, failing in which he tried to stay its execution by his appeal to the Supreme Court until that decision could be had—to keep possession of the property and use it in the interest of his Church.

4. The M. E. Church, North, of which Mr. Pierce was a minister in good standing, indorsed the proceedings as a part of her policy—announced by her

Conference—to get possession of the property of the M. E. Church, South.

5. The unlawful means used in this case was fully sanctioned, if not instigated, by the Rev. Mr. Haggerty, presiding elder of the district, who was present and aided in nearly all the proceedings in the church and in the courts.

6. The act has never been disavowed, disowned, disclaimed or condemned by any Bishop, Quarterly, Annual or General Conference of that Church; nor was Mr. Pierce's character ever arrested in an Annual Conference for his conduct in this Boonville church affair.

The same may be affirmed of each and every instance of church seizure and appropriation in Missouri.

If they can escape the judgment of Conferences and Courts while party blood is still bounding and burning, they may not escape the just verdict of posterity after the passions have cooled down, and when the names and character of men will be judged by the history they have made and the shadows they have thrown forward upon the world.

Church in Springfield.

Just before the war the members and friends of the M. E. Church, South, erected in the town of Springfield, Green county, Mo., one of the largest and most elegant churches in Missouri outside of St. Louis. It was the religious centre and pride of the southwest. That part of the State was fearfully desolated by the war, and Springfield was an important base of army operations. It was a depot of supplies, and a rallying centre for all the large armies, the scouting parties and marauding bands that operated against the rebels of the South and the citizens of that portion of the State. While the torch was applied to nearly every church in the whole of southwest Missouri it is a little singular that this one should be spared. But so it was.

At what time it passed into the actual possession and use of the Methodist Episcopal Church, and precisely how long it remained in their possession, the subjoined report made to the St. Louis Conference sets forth. Many things are assumed to be of such general knowledge that no particular and definite information is necessary. The authentic information upon the subject is a follows:

1. A copy of a deed of conveyance of a lot or parcel of ground in the city of Springfield, made by Daniel Polk and E. A. Polk, his wife, to Daniel D. Berry, Jas. R. Danforth, Robt. J. McElhany, Warren H. Graves and John S. Waddill, trustees of the M. E. Church, South, for the use and benefit of said Church, to erect thereon a house of worship, &c. Consideration, $350. Dated October 11, 1856.

2. A statement of the debt incurred in the erection of said house of worship, amounting in the aggregate to $4,695.

3. A copy of deed of conveyance of October 22, 1866, made by "Robt. J. McElheny, Warren H. Graves and John S. Waddill, as trustees of the county of Green and State of Missouri," to Richard Gott, John Demitt, J. D. Perkins, James Baker and E. S. Gott, trustees, in trust for the use and benefit of the Methodist Episcopal Church, &c. Consideration, $4,700. One thousand of

which was paid to them in cash, and the balance to go to the creditors of the M. E. Church, South.

Suit was brought by the Church, South, to recover the property upon the ground that the remaining members of the original Board of Trustees had no legal right to sell and convey the property for their own benefit.

The case, like nearly all others, was compromised, and both the church and parsonage were given up and turned over to the trustees of the M. E. Church, South.

The history of the case, as gathered and reported by the committee appointed by the St. Louis Annual Conference, M. E. Church, South, will be found sufficiently full in the following statement of facts and report made by the committee to the Conference in 1868. The reader will appreciate the irony scattered here and there through the report if he can not excuse it. The material facts will be found without the publication of the correspondence to which the report refers. It should not be overlooked that the Northern Methodists took possession of the church at the same time they seized the parsonage, viz., in 1863.

"*To the Bishop and Members of the St. Louis Conference*:

"The committee to whom was referred the subject of your church property at Springfield, Mo., instructed to 'take such measures as they may deem proper to recover the property,' beg leave to submit the following

"REPORT.

"One member of your committee, R. P. Faulkner, residing at Arlington, Mo., and two members in St. Louis, and the property in question and parties holding it being at Springfield, Mo., we have had to labor at considerable disadvantage and loss of time owing to these distances.

"Yet we have endeavored to give the matter all the attention so important a trust deserved; and for the sake of common justice and our sacred Christianity we regret to state that our house of worship at Springfield is not yet in our possession.

"But we are happy to state that we have reason to believe we shall soon regain that which is justly our own.

"A part of your action on this subject at your last session was 'that the Presiding Elder of the Springfield District should see that the Board of Trustees of our property at Springfield be immediately filled according to Discipline.'

"We take pleasure in stating that your instructions in this matter have been complied with by Rev. G. M. Winton, P. E., and the following named gentlemen appointed trustees: Lawson Fulbright, Elisha Headlee, Thomas W. Cunningham, Adam C. Mitchell and William Montgomery.

"*Parsonage Property.*—In the examination of this question we found that the house was taken possession of about the middle of the year 1863 by the authorities of the M. E. Church, under an idea that it would be destroyed as an enemy of the National Government if not protected by them; and subsequently held and used by them under the discovery that it was deeded to the M. E. Church—a Church without representative or existence in that part of Missouri at the date of said deed.

"The facts in regard to the title to this property are best explained by reference to a letter herewith submitted, marked A, from Rev. B. R. Johnson, formerly a member of your Conference, now of California.

"Thus it appears that the title of the M. E. Church to this property is from a clerical mistake and a strong desire to protect our interests from destruction.

"We would further state on this point that our examinations satisfy us that the rental for the use of this property should be at least $25 per month for the whole time—four and one half years—it has been saved from destruction by our friends (?). As will be seen in a subsequent part of this report, a claim, equal to the sum of the rental, is made by those who have possessed and protected this property for 'needed repairs.' We will recur to this subject again in its place.

"*House of Worship.*—We regret exceedingly to have to report a sad disappointment to our friends, the occupants, who were deprived of the use of this house, after great preparations had been made for a fair, festival and feast of fat things, by a thunder storm, whose lightning struck the church and well nigh settled the controversy in regard to it.

"As soon as practicable your committee convened at the St. Nicholas Hotel, St. Louis, and among other things determined that it was necessary for one or more of the committee to visit Springfield.

"Shortly thereafter R. P. Faulkner went to Springfield, and on an inquiry into the matter, elicited from the authorities of the M. E. Church a proposition for settlement, which will be presented presently.

"Just previous to this Wm. C. Jamison, a member of your committee, received the following letter from Judge Baker, of Springfield (marked B).

"We here present the propositions referred to above (marked C), with a letter from R. P. Faulkner to the committee (marked '*one*').

"On receiving this communication your committee convened at Arlington (Wm. C. Jamison absent, being at that time in Wisconsin), and on due consideration of the propositions, made to them the following answer herewith submitted (marked D).

"This, our answer to the committee on the part of the M. E. Church, we enclosed to the Hon. Jno. S. Phelps, of Springfield, with the following letter of instructions (marked E).

"Immediately after closing its session at Arlington your committee received the following letter from Rev. J. J. Bently, P. E. of Springfield District M. E. Church, North, relating to the parsonage (marked F).

"This communication was immediately sent to Hon. Jno. S. Phelps, our counsel.

"Thus we have given you all that we have been able to do in this matter, simply adding our opinion that we will ultimately recover our property.

"The condition of the church at Springfield, as will be seen by reference to the letter of R. P. Faulkner, who examined it, requires immediate attention.

"The damage done to the house on the occasion of the *defeat of the religious fair* is thus reported on by R. P. Faulkner:

"'Though seriously damaged, yet it can be repaired for much less than I had any idea of until I visited it. I had a builder go and examine and make a rough estimate of the cost to repair the damage, including everything but seats, pulpit, &c., who reported to me that, if a thousand dollars would not do it, twelve hundred would.'

"From a careful survey of all the interests of our Church in Springfield, we recommend to the Conference that measures be immediately taken to secure for that station a man of experience, who shall take the charge of the society and the oversight of the repairs of the church. And to this end we submit the following resotions:

"1. *Resolved,* That the Bishop be requested to station one of the most efficient pulpit and business men at Springfield.

"2. That the Missionary Society be requested to make as liberal appropriations as they are able for the support of the preacher stationed at Springfield.

"3. That with the approval of our counsel at Springfield and the recommendation of the Board of Trustees, the preacher in charge be authorized and requested to visit such places as he may see proper to raise means to pay debts and repairs on the Church.

"4. That the whole matter pertaining to the church and parsonage at Springfield be referred to the Presiding Elder of Springfield District, the Preacher in Charge of the Station and the trustees of the church.

"Respectfully submitted,

"W. M. Prottsman,
"W. C. Jamison."

Church in Potosi.

The worthy Presiding Elder of the Potosi District, St. Louis Conference M. E. Church, South, makes the following statement of the attempt to seize and hold the church in Potosi. It furnishes at least an illustration of the fertility of resources possessed by these church seizers, to use a soft term, and the facility with which they could take advantage of circumstances.

"MISSISSIPPI COUNTY, Feb. 6, 1867.

"BRO. M'ANALLY: I send you, for the benefit of your correspondent—a member of the Missouri Conference—some statements of an attempt of 'our brethren, the enemy,' to take, hold and possess our church in Potosi.

"Some time during the year 1865 a Mr. or Major Miller came to Potosi and reported himself a minister of the 'Old Wesleyan Methodist Church;' that he was neither North nor South, but belonged to the good old Mother Church.

"As our people had no pastor, they permitted him to preach in our church, and attended his ministry. He made an earnest effort to proselyte our members, but failed. Rumor said he intended to take possession of our church, but he denied it.

"Early in 1866 Mr. Sorin, his Presiding Elder, announced publicly from the pulpit on the Sabbath that the house belonged to them, and henceforth they intended to hold and possess the same.

"That week Bro. Wallace, one of the trustees of the church, who had been a member for two score years, locked the door, took possession of the key and notified Mr. Miller that he could not preach there any more.

"Mr. Miller then notified Bro. Wallace that he would bring suit for the church. Bro. Wallace assured him that when the law gave him the house he would give him the key.

"In the meantime the Radicals of the town rented a

hall for Mr. Miller, in which they put an organ to help him make music.

"I held a quarterly meeting in Potosi in January, 1867, and while there I learned that the Rev. Major had sold his friends' organ, pocketed the money and gone on a long journey toward the north pole. So Madam Rumor reports.

"Our people are in quiet possession of our church house, have an excellent Sabbath school, an organ to help the children sing, a very gratifying increase in the membership of the Church, and no fears of being disturbed by Messrs. Sorin, Miller and company, unless they do as their confederates did on Castor—burn the church.

"Several of our church houses at other points have been quietly occupied by them, but I believe they have run their race and are not likely to trouble us much more. W. S. WOODARD."

This case, as it exists in the above statement, ought to be sufficient for all the purposes of history.

In Plattsburg, Clinton county, they purchased an old debt and in that way obtained a kind of title to half the church. They also purchased an old debt and got a title to the Plattsburg High School property, and retain it to this day.

The property of the Southern Methodists in nearly every part of the State suffered one way or another, and many houses of worship were seized and used by the Northern Methodists that were not reported in the public prints, adjudicated in the civil courts or published in their Conference statistics.

Amongst the latter may be mentioned the churches

at Plattsburg, Macon City, Fillmore, and a church at Glasgow, built and owned by the Southern Methodists for the use of the colored people. They purchased the other half of the Plattsburg church, gave up the Fillmore church after using it about five years, and never gave up the churches at Macon City and Glasgow.

In the presence of these facts the statement so often made from the pulpit and through the press, that the ministers and members of the M. E. Church never at any time engaged in seizing and appropriating to their use the property of the M. E. Church, South, sounds very strangely in the ears of candid, honest people. They evidently did not foresee the necessity for such a denial, and consequently were not very careful to cover up their tracks. They so far gloried in the history they were making as to report the property they had seized and appropriated in their Church statistics, which they published to the world.

The following list of property is taken from the published Statistics of the Missouri and Arkansas Conference M. E. Church for 1865–6, and which *disappeared* as fast as the suits were decided or the cases compromised:

Independence church	$17,000
Independence parsonage	3,000
Lagrange church	12,000
Springfield church	12,000
Springfield parsonage (not reported)	3,000
Boonville church	10,000
Plattsburg church	5,000
Fillmore church	500
Louisiana church	5,000
Glasgow colored church	3,000
Macon church	2,500
Total	$73,000

To this may be added the churches seized and held by them for a short time only, and given up before they could be reported to the Conference, the property obtained for "less than half its value," by buying up old debts and forcing sales, where that course was necessary, and the furniture and fixtures destroyed and damaged in the use and abuse of the property held by them for so long, and which was assessed upon the lawful owners in the claims of restored decency and comfort, and the grand total would reach over $100,000, to say nothing of rentals, costs of suits, the damage of deprivation, etc.

In the face of all these facts, it must require no ordinary degree of moral courage for men in high position to affirm that the ministers and members of the M. E. Church never stole, seized, pressed, appropriated or possessed themselves of property that did not belong to them. Only the moral abrasion of civil war could produce the requisite "hard cheek."

The civil war has passed away. Missouri is no longer ruled by shoulder straps and bayonets—the civil law is supreme—and even by judges who "neither fear God nor regard man," except of their own party, the M. E. Church, South, has been reinstated and secured in her property rights.

Those who figured conspicuously in this church-seizing business often and loudly proclaimed that they were "making history." True, they made history, and now they should not complain if they stand before the world in the light of the history they have made.

If they could afford to make the history and then boast of it, we can certainly afford to record it, especially when it is a record of the martyrdom of those sacred Christian principles for which a discriminating, righteous charity has no mantle.

CHAPTER XIV.

CHURCH SEIZURES CONTINUED AND MADE GENERAL.

War Claims of Northern Methodists Settled by Ecclesiastical Black-Mail—Military Mitres and Episcopal Shoulder-Straps—The Difference—The "Stanton-Ames Order"—"The Great Episcopal Raid"—"Special Order, No. 15," from Major General Banks—Official Board of Carondelet Street Church, New Orleans, and Bishop Ames—Episcopal Power then and Ecclesiastical Criticism now—Popular Verdict—Abandoned (?) and Embarrassed Churches and Ecclesiastical "Bummers"—Church Extension in the South—Letters and Extracts—Bishop Clark and "Church Extension Meetings"—Does the End Justify the Means, or Success Satisfy the Demands of Modern Ethics?—Property Acquired by the M. E. Church in the South in a few Years—Four Hundred and Eight Churches, Eighteen Parsonages and Eight Literary Institutions in two Years, worth $446,659 00, all in Five Conferences—Opinions of their Leading Men and Journals—Hon. John Hogan, of St. Louis, Scuttles the Episcopal Ram—Order from the War Department, with President Lincoln's Endorsement—Possible Deception—Rev. Dr. Keener, of New Orleans, Sues for the Churches of Louisiana four Months—McKendree Church, Nashville, Vacated, "by Order from Bishop Simpson"—Memorial of the Holston Conference M. E. Church, South, to the Chicago General Conference, and How it was Treated—Action of Chicago General Conference—"Stanton-Ames Order" Duplicated for the Baptists—Conclusion—Sensible Warning from the St. Louis *Anzeiger*.

Both the purpose and plan for the seizure and appropriation of the property of the M. E. Church, South, contemplated a much wider range of territory than the State of Missouri. The M. E. Church, North, had done too much to put down rebellion; had entered too heartily into the struggle, sent too many men to the front, put too many orators on the stump, offered too many prayers from her pulpits and altars for the success of the Union armies and the destruction of all rebels, and had supplied too liberally the moral and material sinews of war, to lose a golden opportunity. The M. E. Church, South, had many fine churches, with costly furniture and garniture, in the chief cities of the South; and were they not rebels—all rebels? What rights have rebels that loyal men are bound to respect? Were not Southern Methodists traitors above all others? The Federal Government, as represented in Generals Grant, Sherman, Butler and Banks, could confiscate, seize and appropriate the property of chief rebels in the South, and especially that which had been, or could be, used in the interest of treason or rebellion; and why could not the Federal Government, as represented in Bishops Simpson, Ames, Clark, Kingsley and the great body of the M. E. Church, confiscate, seize and appropriate the church property that had been, or could be, used in the interest of treason and rebellion? Rebel chaplains might preach in them, rebel soldiers might be quartered in them, rebel hospitals might be made of them, and in them the great rebellion might receive moral support. What reward for loyalty had been specially set apart for the M. E. Church? What the price of her prayers, her sermons, her money, her men? Another, and that the smallest Protestant Church in the land, had the best army and navy chaplains—had the lion's share of appointments. Did not the M. E. Church, South, inaugurate rebellion in 1844? And when the force of the Southern Church is broken by the military arm—when her great centres are broken up and her property confiscated or destroyed, and loyal men preach a loyal gospel from her pulpits, and teach loyalty in her halls and institutions of learning, then may it be hoped that the moral and political heresy will be exterminated with the heretics. Make the M. E. Church a part of the military arm of the Government; invest the Bishops with ecclesiastico-military authority; supply them with transportation, supplies and military escorts; make Department Commanders subject unto them, and if the great rebellion is not put down, the great national Church will be put up, and the property of traitors will be converted to loyal uses. The centres of population and power in the South will be put under loyal training and discipline, and a moral result will be reached which "military necessity" demands. All moral questions down in the presence of a war measure so manifestly right and proper. Military necessity has no conscience in the presence of a gigantic rebellion. What religious difference between a military and an ecclesiastical raid upon the property of rebels? Will the Government and the Church ever quarrel over the spoils of conquest, whether gained by an Episcopal General or a Military Bishop? Episcopal shoulder-straps and military mitres may well lose their distinction in a common cause against a common enemy.

The appropriateness and force of these reflections will appear in the following well authenticated facts.

What has been called, by way of distinction, the "Great Episcopal Raid," had its announcement and authority in the following order, issued from the War Department of the Federal Government, and known as the

"STANTON-AMES ORDER."

"WAR DEPARTMENT,
WASHINGTON, D. C., Nov. 30, 1863.

"*To the Generals Commanding the Military Departments of Mississippi, the Gulf, the South, Virginia, North Carolina, Missouri, etc., etc.:*

"You are hereby directed to place at the disposal of Rev. Bishop Ames all houses of worship belonging to the Methodist Episcopal Church, South, in which a loyal minister who has been appointed by a loyal Bishop of said Church does not officiate. It is a matter of great importance to the Government, in its efforts to restore tranquillity to the community and peace to the nation that Christian ministers should, by precept and example support and foster the loyal sentiments of the people."

"(Signed) E. M. STANTON, *Sec'y of War.*

Thus armed, Bishop Ames started on his Episcopal raid upon the Southern Methodist Churches, taking with him and picking up along the route down the Mississippi a goodly number of "loyal ministers." The details of his exploits in the South, seizing and appropriating to the uses of a "loyal religion" the churches of others would not be appropriate to this work, but will be left to the history of these strange times in their appropriate localities.

In Memphis, Tenn., Vicksburg and Jackson, Miss., Baton Rouge and New Orleans, La., the Episcopal General found and possessed himself of fine and costly churches. In the latter city he called the Official Board of Carondelet street Church together—the largest, finest and wealthiest Southern Methodist church in the city—

and formally demanded the surrender of that and the other Southern Methodist churches in the city to him.

They objected, and in their objection set forth that "Bishop Ames, as an officer of another Church, had no ecclesiastical jurisdiction over them." He replied that he "claimed no ecclesiastical jurisdiction over them any more than over the Catholic or Episcopal Churches, but that he came with an order from the United States Secretary of War, and an order from General Banks, Department Commander at New Orleans, and by that authority he demanded the surrender of the churches."

They replied that, as they "held the property in trust for the use and benefit of the M. E. Church, South, they could not voluntarily give up that trust. If they did so it must be under the stress of a compulsion they had no power, civil or military, to resist—the Bishop would have to compel them."

Whereupon the Bishop obtained a military force, and the churches were taken, just as Memphis, Vicksburg, New Orleans and Richmond were taken.

An extract from the Special Order of Major-General Banks, then commanding the "Department of the Gulf," will show the light in which this church-seizing business was viewed by the military authorities as a moral "war measure."

"HEADQUARTERS DEP'T OF THE GULF,
NEW ORLEANS, Jan. 18, 1864.

"Special Order, No. 15.]

"V. In accordance with instructions contained in a letter from the Secretary of War, under date of Nov. 30, 1863, all houses of worship within this Department belonging to the Methodist Episcopal Church, South, in which a loyal minister, who has been appointed by a loyal Bishop of said Church, does not now officiate, are hereby placed at the disposal of the Rev. Bishop Ames.

"Commanding officers at the various points where such houses of worship may be located are directed to extend to the ministers that may be appointed by Bishop Ames, to conduct divine service in said houses of worship, all the aid, countenance and support practicable in the execution of their mission.

"Officers of the quartermaster's and commissary departments are authorized and directed to furnish Bishop Ames and his clerk with transportation and subsistence, when it can be done without prejudice to the service; and all officers will afford them courtesy, assistance and protection.

"By command of Major-General Banks.

"GEORGE B. DRAKE,
Ass't-Adj't-General."

Under this "Special Order No. 15" the Bishop was put in possession of many churches, his ministers protected, and this general superintendent and representative of the M. E. Church and his clerk were furnished transportation and subsistence by the Government as a "war measure."

This involves more than that Church will admit, now that military protection from the judgment of enlightened Christendom will not avail, and now that ecclesiastical criticism is as unsparing as ecclesiastical presumption was then reckless. The corrollary that the M. E. Church made distinct and aggressive war upon the M. E. Church, South, and hence claimed belligerent rights to capture and hold the property of the enemy in perpetuity, or until formally given up under treaty stipulations, is a very unwelcome and uncomfortable position to those whose religious consciences were not destroyed by a "military necessity." Strenuous efforts are required of the pulpit and press to break the force of the popular verdict of the people upon the religious and ecclesiastical aspects of this "Episcopal Raid."

The authority thus given to Bishop Ames had a much wider and a more general application than his personal operations. This gave the sanction to the church seizures in Missouri, Kentucky, Virginia, East Tennessee, and all through the South. The Bishops of the Methodist Episcopal Church and their ministers penetrated the South in every direction, and were keen on the scent of abandoned (?) churches and other property of the M. E. Church, South. They went to the large cities and railroad centres; got possession of churches by military order or otherwise—"honestly, if they could, but"—*they got them,* and then went out in every direction in search of abandoned, embarrassed and libelled property which they could seize and appropriate to the uses of a "loyal Methodism."

While this plan was being executed in the South the "Church Extension Society" in the Northern States and the "Missionary Society" were furnishing the material aid necessary to support the preachers, buy up old church debts, force sales and bid in the property for the amount of the debt, and thus possess themselves of property for "less than half its value."

To show how the business was carried on, see the following extracts from a letter of one of their missionaries in Alabama—Rev. W. P. Miller—to the Corresponding

Secretary of the Church Extension Society of the M. E. Church, published in the *Western Christian Advocate* of Jan. 1, 1868:

"There are two churches that I could secure with a little ready money. Can you help us in time of need?

"1. A church, 45 by 55, a plain frame, covered with shingles, good floor, with seats and pulpit, but not ceiled; built during the war, but has never been paid for.

"Last year I raised two hundred and fifty dollars, leaving one hundred and fifty unpaid. The man who owns the land and built the house says if we pay him the hundred and fifty dollars he will give us a deed, but we are so prostrated that we can not do it now. If we fail others will do it, and we will be shut out of doors.

"Another church, 40 by 50, in general description like the first. * * * This house was also built during the war and partly paid for. The builder built on his own land, and was to convey the title when paid for. He died in the war, but his widow says she will give us a deed if we will pay her the balance, one hundred dollars. Please help us, if possible, in this case also."

They held "Church Extension" meetings in all the Methodist churches in the Northern States to raise funds to meet just such emergencies. An account of a "Church Extension Meeting," held in Indianapolis, Ind., is given in the *Western Christian Advocate* of February 19, 1868, soon after Mr. Miller's letter appeared. The following is an extract:

"At Asbury chapel Bishop Clarke preached with great power, and in conclusion set forth the claims of the Society. He presented the wants of three Churches in Alabama—one could be *saved* for fifty dollars, another for one hundred, and a third for one hundred and fifty. The Bishop asked the Church to aid these societies of loyal Christians struggling for an existence, and Asbury most cheerfully responded in a contribution of three hundred dollars."

Upon the same subject the *Northwestern Christian Advocate* of March 18, 1868, says:

"When the Church Extension Society was first organized, in commending the new cause to our people, the Bishops in their address said: 'We know of no agency in which the contribution of our people can accomplish a greater amount of good.' At a later date Bishop Clarke, after a careful survey of the field, and especially of the South, put the case in stronger terms, and said: 'I do not know where else a man's money can be used with such certainty of sure and large returns.'"

He then mentions as an illustration the churches reported by Rev. W. P. Miller, and says: "The money was forwarded to Bro. Miller and he has written to the Corresponding Secretary the results, as follows: 'I have invested the means you sent me, and have secured the two churches of which I wrote; title all right. The churches are frame, and are worth here about $1,000.'"

The Missouri and Arkansas Conference, held in Louisiana, Mo., March 7, 1866, adopted the following:

"*Resolved,* That the preachers be urged to exercise personal supervision over such church property not yet secured to trustees, urge the churches to select trustees, and when this can not be done, to petition the County Court to appoint such officers." (Pub. Minutes, p. 36.)

The Louisiana and Boonville Church property cases are in illustration.

All the Bishops and all the Conferences of the M. E. Church endorsed the work of Church Extension in the South, just as it was carried on by Mr. Miller, Mr. Drake, Mr. Pearne, Dr. Newman and their associates, and the plan was successful.

In the philosophy of some men the end justifies the means, and success satisfies all the demands of modern ethics. It will not do to question every wealthy man or wealthy Church too closely as to how their property was acquired during the war. It is enough for the curious to know that they have property, and to hope that they have consciences as well.

That the M. E. Church has property in the Southern States in churches, parsonages and literary institutions is an admitted fact. That nearly all, if not all, of this property has been acquired in a very few years, and years, too, of great poverty and destitution through the South, will not be denied. Now, take the following facts and figures:

The Tennessee Conference was organized Oct. 11, 1866, with thirteen churches valued at $59,100. At its second session it reported thirty houses of worship and one parsonage. The Georgia Conference, at its organization, Oct. 10, 1867, reported forty-nine churches. The Mississippi Conference was organized in 1866 with five churches, and at its session held in December, 1867, reported forty-seven churches, five parsonages and eight institutions of learning. In 1866 the South Carolina Conference reports no churches, but at its session in Charleston, February, 1868, reported forty-nine churches and six parsonages. The Holston Conference was organized by Bishop Clarke in 1865 with 100 churches, valued at $31,250. At its session in October, 1867, just two years after, it reported 203 churches and six parsonages. These five Conferences, with an average existence of two years, report 408 churches, eighteen parsonages and eight institutions of learning, at an estimated aggregate value of $446,659. The increase up to 1868 will reach largely over half a million.

Others may ask where and how they acquired so much property in so short a time, and amongst a people desolated and torn by war and impoverished even to beggary and want by the sword, the torch, the pestilence, the famine, the floods, the drouth, the Bureau and the reconstruction.

The policy of the Methodist Episcopal Church, as announced in their great official organ, the New York *Christian Advocate,* and carried out as far as could be by their emissaries in the South, was to "*disintegrate and absorb the M. E. Church, South.*"

Dr. Newman, editor of the New Orleans *Advocate,* said in the New York *Methodist,* of May 23, 1868:

* * * "And we solemnly hold that it would be of incalculable advantage to the South, and the cause of Christianity therein, if the Methodist Episcopal Church, South, should cease to be."

Upon the reunion of the two Churches, Dr. N. E. Cobleigh, of Athens, Tenn., in an article in the *Northern Christian Advocate,* of April 1, 1868, says:

"The Church property, too, of which we have taken possession in the South, must be given back to them (the M. E. Church, South,) before they will consent to treat upon the subject."

Dr. Daniel Curry, editor of the New York *Christian Advocate,* said before the Preachers' Meeting of New York, in May, 1866:

"Wherever we have taken churches the policy has proved bad. The first act of the Church, South, toward us, after this, was a charge of church stealing—a high crime before the law. We did not mean to do wrong, but it has put us in a bad position."

The New Orleans *Advocate,* of Feb. 10 1866, says:

"We have seen a letter from Bishop Ames, which was dated Baltimore, Md., Jan. 20, 1866, and which contained this glorious news: 'The President has issued an order putting us in possession of 210 churches and 32 parsonages, which the Rebel Methodists in Virginia have occupied during the war.'"

This was "glorious news" to Dr. Newman, himself occupying at the time a church obtained from "Rebel Methodists" by this same Bishop Ames upon an order from Mr. Stanton, Secretary of War. These Bishops had a summary way of getting possession of other people's property. The cry of "Rebel Methodists" and treason against the Government from them and their tools could always move the Government officials to issue such orders as would put them in possession of the property of rebels. But whether the rebels themselves were crushed out or made better by the transaction, are matters about which little was said.

There is yet another aspect of this general question worthy of note. While Bishop Ames was in the South prosecuting under War Department orders his great scheme of ecclesiastical piracy, and the many smaller ecclesiastics were similarly engaged in other portions of the conquered provinces, steps were being taken to forestall the Bishop when his ecclesiastical ram should be directed against the "Rebel Methodists" of St. Louis. Hon. John Hogan, member of Congress from St. Louis. went to Washington and made representations to the President of the facts in the case, and when the good Bishop reached St. Louis he was met by an order from the War Department, with an endorsement from the President of the United States, repealing his Stanton order and putting an estoppel upon his proceedings, especially in Missouri.

The following order was obtained by Mr. Hogan from the War Department, with President Lincoln's endorsement exempting the churches of Missouri from seizure under Mr. Stanton's order:

"WAR DEPARTMENT, ADJUTANT-GENERAL'S OFFICE,
"WASHINGTON, February 13, 1864.

Order.]

"*Major General Rosecrans, U. S. Volunteers, Commanding Department of the Missouri, St. Louis, Mo.:*

"SIR: I am directed by the Secretary of War to say that the orders from the Department placing at the disposal of the constituted Church authorities in the Northern States houses of worship in other States is designed to apply only to such States as are designated by the President's Proclamation as being in rebellion, and is not designed to operate in loyal States, nor in cases where loyal congregations in rebel States shall be organized and worship upon the terms prescribed by the President's Amnesty Proclamation.

"I am, sir, very respectfully,

Your obedient servant,

"JAS. A. HARDIE,

"Assistant Adjutant-General."

This order bears the following endorsement in Mr. Lincoln's own proper hand:

"As you see within, the Secretary of War modifies his order so as to exempt Missouri from it. Kentucky was never within it; nor, as I learn from the Secretary, was it ever intended for any more than a means of rallying the Methodist people in favor of the Union in localities where the rebellion had disorganized and scattered them. Even in that view I fear it is liable to some abuses; but it is not quite easy to withdraw it entirely, and at once. A. LINCOLN.

"February 13, 1864."

That is a damaging disclosure. Were Mr. Stanton, Secretary of War, and Mr. Lincoln, President of the United States, imposed upon and deceived by these high Church dignitaries? The famous Stanton-Ames order "never intended for any more than a means of rallying the Methodist people in favor of the Union in localities where the rebellion had disorganized and scattered them!" Was it ever used for other purposes? How about the Churches seized and appropriated by authority of this same order in cities and communities where the Methodist people had never been disorganized and scattered, and where "the Methodist people" intended to be "rallied" had never been organized—never even had an existence?

It did not require Mr. Lincoln's sagacity to see that such an order was "liable to some abuse," but it does require a good deal of effort to believe that even Northern Methodist Bishops could deceive the Government, and then pervert and "abuse" an order from the War Department. But we are forced to accept the facts in the case.

The action of Mr. Hogan and his success in defeating the purposes of Bishop Ames gave hope and courage to others, and in June, 1865, Dr. Keener, of New Orleans, went to Washington and made a formal and most earnest application to the President and Secretary of War for the restoration of the churches in Louisiana to their rightful owners.

He remained in Washington prosecuting his almost hopeless mission for four long, weary months. After this wearisome prosecution of what seemed to be a forlorn hope, the President (Mr. Johnson) gave the order and restored the property, which the Northern Bishops could have restored with the stroke of a pen. This gracious favor was obtained from the President much upon the principle of the widow and the unjust judge: "And there was a widow in that city; and she came unto him and said, avenge me of mine adversary. And he would not for awhile; but afterward he said within himself, though I fear not God, nor regard man, yet, because this widow troubleth me, I will avenge her, lest by her continual coming she weary me."

So it was the Churches, at least some of them, were restored. "And will not God avenge his own elect which cry day and night unto him? I tell you, he will avenge them speedily."

Enboldened by success, others made application to the President for the restoration of their churches. Upon such application the churches in Vicksburg, Miss., Memphis and Nashville, Tenn., were given up.

In regard to the latter a Nashville (Tenn.) correspondent of a Northern Methodist paper says:

"Things are moving slowly, as far as our church is concerned. Upon an order from Bishop Simpson, we vacated McKendree last week, and are now holding services in Masonic Hall. Our congregations are small, but we hope for better times. * * * * Our dear Southern brethren of the Methodist Episcopal Church, South, persuasion are flocking back to their old haunts, and hold up their heads as if they were not guilty of the blood and suffering of the past four years."

"Upon an order from Bishop Simpson" they vacated McKendree, after they had been put into it and occupied it so long upon an order from Bishop or General somebody else. But who "ordered" Bishop Simpson? Why did he require his brethren to "vacate McKendree?" For the same reason that Dr. Newman vacated Carondelet street Church, New Orleans, and the churches in Memphis, Vicksburg and other places were vacated.

Others may detail the "pious fraud" upon the churches at Knoxville, and Athens, and other places in Tennessee, while the general subject only requires here a notice of the Memorial of the Holston Conference, M. E. Church, South, to the General Conference of the M. E. Church at Chicago, in the spring of 1868, and the notice taken of it by that General Conference. The following is the

MEMORIAL OF THE HOLSTON CONFERENCE METHODIST EPISCOPAL CHURCH, SOUTH.

"*To the Bishops and Members of the General Conference of the Methodist Episcopal Church, at Chicago, Ills., May, 1868:*

"The undersigned were appointed a committee at the session of the Holston Conference of the M. E. Church, South, held at Cleveland, East Tennessee, in October last, to memorialize your reverend body, and to set forth distinctly the wrongs which we are suffering at the hands of agents of the M. E. Church within our bounds; and also to entreat you to devise some means by which an end may be made to these outrages, for the honor of Methodism and for the sake of our common Christianity.

"Our churches have been seized by ministers and members of the M. E. Church, and are still held and used by them as houses of worship.

"To give the semblance of legality to these acts and of right to this property, trustees have been appointed by the authorities of the M. E. Church; and these churches are annually reported by your ministers in their Conference statistics.

"From these churches our ministers are either excluded and driven, or allowed only a joint occupancy with your ministers. From some of them our ministers in their regular rounds of district and circuit work are excluded by locks and bars, or by armed men meeting them at the doors; from others they are driven by mobs, and threatened with death should they attempt a return; at one a presiding elder and a preacher in charge of the circuit, at a quarterly meeting appointment, were arrested and marched fifteen miles amidst indignities and insults; at another, an aged and godly minister was ridden upon a rail; at another, the same man found at the door bundles of rods and nails, and also a written notice prohibiting him from preaching at the risk of torture; at another, a notice was handed to our preacher, signed by a class leader in the M. E. Church, in which was the following language: 'If you come back here again we will handle you;' and, true to the threat, on a subsequent round, not two miles from the place, this worthy minister, as he was passing to his appointment on the second Sabbath in February last, was taken from his horse, struck a severe blow upon the head, blindfolded, tied to a tree, scourged to laceration, and then ordered to lie with his face to the ground until his scourgers should withdraw, with the threat of death for disobedience. All this he was told, too, was for traveling that circuit and preaching the gospel as a Southern Methodist preacher; from another, the children and teachers of our Sabbath School were ejected while in session by a company of men, who were led by a minister of the M. E. Church.

"Our parsonages, also, have been seized and occupied by ministers of the M. E. Church, no rent having been paid to us for their use.

"Thirty-six hundred dollars, appropriated upon our application to the United States Government for damages done to our church at Knoxville during the war, were, by some sleight-of-hand movement, passed into the hands of a minister of the M. E. Church. This money is still held from us.

"In other cases, school and church property of our's

on which debts were resting has been forced upon the market by agents in your interests, and thereby wrested from our poverty and added to your abundance.

"Members of the M. E. Church constitute, in part, the mobs that insult and maltreat our preachers, while ministers of the same Church, by words and acts, either countenance or encourage our persecutors. In no instance, so far as we are advised, has any one for such conduct been arraigned, or censured even, by those administering the discipline of your Church.

"We could specify the name of each of these churches, and the locality, were it necessary, in which our ministers and people are either permitted sometimes to worship, or from which they are excluded and driven by locks, threats, mobs and bloody persecutions. Their names are in our possession, and at your disposal. About one hundred church edifices are held in one or another of these ways, with a value of not less than seventy-five thousand dollars.

"Of this property, it should be added, some was deeded to the M. E. Church before 1844, and the rest, since that time, to the M. E. Church, South. That it is all claimed by the M. E. Church in East Tennessee we suppose to be true, or it would not be reported and received in their Annual Conference statistics. That it belongs to the M. E. Church, South, we suppose also to be true, inasmuch as all deeds since 1844 have been made to us, and all the remainder were granted to us by the decision of the Supreme Court of the United States in the Church suit; unless the ground be assumed by your reverend body that when Lee surrendered to Grant the M. E. Church, South, surrendered also to the M. E.

Church all her property rights. Surely if the United States Government does not confiscate the property of those who are called rebels, the M. E. Church, in her highest legislative assembly, will hardly set a precedent by claiming the property of their Southern brethren.

"But it may, perhaps, be said that we have been sinners, rebels, traitors, touching our civil and political relations to the Government. If this be so, we are unable to comprehend by what authority we are to be punished by the M. E. Church, since for our moral obliquities we are responsible alone to God, and for our political crimes only to the United States Government.

"It may also be asked, what jurisdiction has your General Conference over these deeds of injustice? No civil jurisdiction, we are aware; but your reverend body does possess a moral power of such weight that, if brought to bear in East Tennessee, there would be an end to these acts of oppression and cruelty. A word of disapproval, even, from your Board of Bishops, or the publication in your Church papers of some of the above cited facts, with editorial condemnation, would have done much to mitigate, if not entirely to remove, the cause of our complaints; but we have neither heard the one nor seen the other. Why this has not been done is believed by us to be a want of knowledge of these facts, of which we now put you in possession. Familiar as we are with the condition of things in East Tennessee, and with the workings of the two Methodisms there, we are satisfied that your body could, by judicious action, remove most, if not all, of the causes which now occasion strife, degrade Methodism, and scandalize our holy religion. We, therefore, ask—

"1st. That you will ascertain the grounds upon which the M. E. Church claims and holds the property in church buildings and parsonages within her bounds in East Tennessee, as reported in her Holston Mission Conference statistics.

"2d. If in the investigation any property so reported shall be adjudged by you to belong of right to the M. E. Church, South, that you will designate what that property is, and where; and also instruct your ministers and people to relinquish their claims upon the same, repossess us, and leave us in the undisturbed occupancy thereof.

"3d. Inasmuch as your words of wisdom and of justice will be words of power, that you earnestly advise all your ministers laboring in this field to abstain from every word and act the tendency of which would be the subversion of good order and peace in the communities in which they move.

"In conclusion, allow us to add, that in presenting this memorial to your reverend body we are moved thereto by no other spirit than that of ardent desire to promote the interests of our common Redeemer by 'spreading scriptural holiness over these lands.'

"E. E. WILEY,
"W. G. E. CUNNYNGHAM,
"WM. ROBESON,
"B. ARBOGAST,
"C. LONG,
"J. M. McTEER,
"GEORGE STEWART,

"Members of the Holston Conference of the M. E. Church, South.

"*April, 1868.*"

This memorial, so respectful and dignified, and upon so grave a matter, was referred, without being read or printed, to a select committee of seven. And though presented and referred early in the session, no further notice was taken of it, and the committee did not bring in a report until the very last day of the session and just before the final adjournment. The report of the select committee was read amid great confusion, and passed without debate by a very small vote, but few of the members of the General Conference feeling interested enough either to listen or vote.

The *Daily Advocate,* of June 3, 1868, contains the following account of the affair, with the report of the special committee as adopted :

"The report of the committee on the memorial of the Holston Conference was presented and read, and, on motion, adopted.

"The report, as adopted, is as follows:

"Your committee have had before them a memorial from a committee of seven appointed by the Holston Conference, of the M. E. Church, South, stating that our ministers and people within that region have seized the churches and parsonages belonging to said Church, South, and maltreated their ministers. The statements of the paper are all indefinite, both as to places, times and persons, and no one has appeared to explain or defend the charges. On the contrary, we have also before us, referred to our consideration, numerous affidavits from ministers and members of our Church, in various parts of this country, evidently designed to refute any charges that might be presented by this committee of seven. It seems from these papers that as soon as the federal power was re-established in East Tennessee whole congregations came over to the M. E. Church, bringing with them their churches and parsonages, that they might continue to use them for worship. It also seems that much of the property in question is deeded to the M. E. Church, it being so held before the secession of the Church, South. We have no proof that any in contest is held otherwise. The General Conference possesses no power, if it would, to divest the occupants of this property of the use or ownership of it, paid for by their means, and would be guilty of great impropriety in interfering at all at this time when test cases are already before the courts. If, however, we should proceed so to do, with the evidence before us largely *ex parte*, it is true, but all that we have, the presentation of the memorialists can not be sustained. By personal examinations we have endeavored in vain to ascertain what foundation there is for the affirmation that our ministers and people encourage violence toward the ministers of the M. E. Church, South. We believe and trust there is no foundation for the charge, for if true, it could but meet our unqualified disapprobation. Our own ministers and people in the South suffer severely in this way, and sometimes, we apprehend, at the hands of our Southern brethren, but neither the spirit of our Master, the genius of our people, nor our denominational interest could allow us to approbate in any parties the practice. We are glad to know that our brethren laboring in that region had their attention early called to these matters, and we content ourself with repeating the sentiments of their address to the people. It was in effect as published in the Knoxville *Whig*, by authority of at least four presiding elders, and several other members of the Holston Conference, as well as often stated from our pulpits in the South, and through our Church papers in the North, that violence toward the preachers and people of the Church, South, is unwise, unchristian and dangerous. Our preachers and people in the South, so far as we are apprised and believe, have all and ever held this position on the subject. We recommend the following:

"*Resolved,* That all the papers connected with this matter be referred to the Holston Conference, believing as we do that this Conference, in the future as in the past, will be careful to do justly, and, as much as lieth in them, to live peaceably with all men.

"Your committee have also had before them a letter, published in various Southern journals, and signed by S. F. Waldro, being dated from Chicago, and presuming to state the objects and intentions of the Methodist Episcopal Conference in the prosecution of its Southern work. We are also informed that several similar letters have been published in the South. No effort that we have been able to make has enabled us to discover any such person in this city. Certainly no such person has a right to speak in our behalf or declare our purposes, much less does he declare them correctly. We recommend that the paper be dismissed as anonymous and unworthy of our further consideration.

"L. Hitchcock, Chairman.

"J. M. Reid, Secretary."

The War Department at Washington issued an order similar to the "Stanton-Ames Order," in the interests of the "American Baptist Home Mission Society," requiring all houses of worship belonging to the Baptists in the military departments of the South, in which a loyal minister did not officiate, to be turned over to the agents or officers of the American Baptist Home Mission Society, and ordering Government transportation and subsistence to be furnished such agents and their clerks. Dated Jan. 14, 1864.

This was a new mode of warfare, and will ever stand upon the historic page as humiliating to enlightened Christian sentiment, as it is forever damaging to the spirit and genius of American institutions and the true interests of Messiah's kingdom on earth.

While American citizens are generally unwilling to be instructed in the higher civil and religious interests of this country by foreigners, yet it will not be denied that many of the finest, shrewdest and wisest journalists of the country are from foreign lands.

As a befitting close to this part of the subject, and a wise warning to the politico-religious fanatics who think little of the effect of their reckless disregard of the sacred relations of Church and State, an extract from the St. Louis *Anzeiger,* a German paper of much character and influence, will be appropriate.

It is upon the general subject of the Administration running the Churches, as developed in the order from the War Department creating Bishop Ames Bishop of a Military Department, and authorizing him to take possession of the Methodist churches of Missouri, Tennessee and the Gulf States. It says:

"Here we have, in *optima forma,* the commencement of Federal interference with religious affairs; and this interference occurs in cities and districts where war has ceased, and even in States, like Missouri, which have never joined the secession movement.

"Doubtless the Federal Government has the right to exercise the utmost rigor of the law against rebel clergymen, as well as against all other criminal citizens; nay, it may even close churches in districts under military law when these churches are abused for political purposes; but this is the utmost limit to which military power may go. Every step beyond this is an arbitrary attack upon the constitutionally guaranteed right of religious freedom, and upon the fundamental law of the American Republican Government—separation of Church and State. The violation of the Constitution committed in the appointment of a Military Bishop—one would be forced to laugh if the affair were not so serious in principle—is so much the more outrageous and wicked, as it is attempted in States which, like Missouri, have never separated from the Union, and in which all the departments of civil administration are in regular activity.

"This order of the War Department is the commencement of State and Federal interference in the affairs of the Churches. It is not a single military suspension or banishment order, which might be exceptional and for a temporary purpose. It is not the act of a General who, sword in hand, commands the priest to pray for him, as we read of in times long ago. It is far more. It is an administrative decree of the Federal Government, appropriating Church property, regulating Church communities, and installing Bishops. A similar order has been issued for the Baptist Church of the South.

"If this is the commencement, where will the end be?

The pretense that it is merely a proceeding against disloyal clergymen will deceive nobody. Bad actions have never wanted good pretenses. With the same right with which the Secretary of War makes Bishop Ames chief of a Church in the South he may also interfere in the affairs of all other Churches, or even dissolve any Church at pleasure. We ask again, Where is the end to be? and what principle of American constitutional law will remain if freedom of religion and of conscience is at the mercy of any commander of a military post?"

CHAPTER XV.

MARTYRDOM — REVS. J. M. PROCTOR, M. ARRINGTON, J. M'GLOTHLIN AND JAMES PENN.

Philosophy of Martyrdom — Living Martyrs — Names Made Immortal by Persecution — Martyrs of Missouri — Difference Between Martyrs for the Testimony of Jesus, only Questions of Time and Place—The Spirit the Same Everywhere—Causes — Explanatory Remarks — *Rev. James M. Proctor* Arrested Coming out of the Pulpit—Connection with the M. E. Church, South, his only Offense—Kept in Prison for Weeks, then Released —*Rev. Marcus Arrington*—Chaplain—Insulted—Kept in Alton Prison—*Rev. John McGlothlin*—Petty Persecution and Tyranny —*Rev. James Penn*—Meeting Broken Up—Driven from His own Churches by a Northern Methodist Preacher Leading an Armed Mob—Persecution—Prayer.

Men die, but truth is immortal. The workmen are buried, but the work goes on. Institutions pass away, but the principles of which they were the incarnation live forever. The Way, the Truth and the Life "was manifested in the flesh, justified in the spirit, seen of angels, preached unto the Gentiles, believed on in the world, received up into glory."

Incarnate Innocence was "despised and rejected of men." The Manger, the Garden, the Cross, are but different aspects of the life and light of men, and illustrate the history of the "Man of Sorrows." The disciple is not above his Lord, nor the servant better than his Master, and if such things were done in the green tree, what hope is there for the dry?

There are many living martyrs. Death is not a necessary condition of martyrdom. The souls of many martyrs have not yet reached their resting place "under the altar." They have met the conditions of martyrdom in the garden of agony without reaching the cross. Some men, who still live, have suffered more for Christ and his Church than many who have ended their sufferings with their lives. Not the nature but the cause of suffering imparts to it the moral quality and the virtues of martyrdom. "Blessed are they which are persecuted for *righteousness' sake,* for theirs is the kingdom of heaven." Many suffer and die, but not "for righteousness' sake," and very many "are persecuted for righteousness' sake" who still live. The grave does not limit the roll of martyrs. Robinson and Headlee, and Glanville and Wollard may have suffered less for righteousness' sake than Cleavland, Breeding, M'Anally, Penn, Duvall, Spencer, Rush and many others who still live to bear witness to the truth. True, it is something to sacrifice life for a principle and a cause—to seal the testimony with the blood. Moral heroism can reach no higher form, nor express itself in a more exalted type. Its purest fire goes out and its sublimest consecration culminates in the life blood of the martyr. Many a noble spirit has been offered up in the sacrifice and service of faith, and, like Isaac, bound hand and foot upon the altar, with the fatal knife glittering and gleaming in the upraised hand of the executioner, yet has been rescued by the interposing voice, when perfect faith stood vindicated in the complete consecration. "Was not Abraham, our father, justified by works when he had offered Isaac, his son, upon the altar?" As much so as if the knife had been driven to his heart and the fires had consumed his body. Yet Abraham's faith was vindicated by his works, and Isaac lived to perpetuate the story of his offering. St. Paul says: "For thy sake we are killed all the day long; we are accounted as sheep for the slaughter." And again: "I protest by your rejoicing which I have in Christ Jesus our Lord, *I die daily.*" He was a living martyr, and many Apostles and righteous men have, like him, been "killed all the day long" and "die daily."

Historical facts in support of the position taken are neither wanting nor few, and the roll of living and dead martyrs in Missouri, now to be recorded in these pages, will vindicate the position and illustrate the annals of religious persecution with a chapter but little removed from the horrors of the Spanish Inquisition, and the persecutions of the Vaudois Christians and Waldenses under Francis I., Henry II., Catherine De Medicis and other notable instruments of power in France, which culminated in the Massacre of St. Bartholomew.

Many names have been given a fame as enduring as the virtues they were made to illustrate, by the force and fire and fact of persecution, which otherwise would have perished from the earth. And the cause for which they were persecuted has been given a sanctity in the hearts and a power over the lives of men which otherwise it could not have received. A name however obscure, and a character however humble, become illustrious despite of history when associated with persecution, suffering and death, for a principle and a cause which invest humanity with the purer and higher types of intellectual, moral and religious life. Around such names the divinest principles crystallize, and by such characters the deepest and purest fountains of humanity are touched. Hampden, and Russell, and Howard, and Sidney, and

Eliot, and Brainard, and Wilberforce, and Martin, and others who sacrificed all for the political, mental and moral enfranchisement of their race, have made themselves immortal, as their names are enshrined in the deepest heart of our nature. They will live forever in the cause for which they suffered. So, too, many of less note have been given a fame as enduring as columns of brass, and they will be handed down to posterity without the factitious aid of monuments of marble or pyramids of granite.

Profane history, philosophy and poetry may treat the martyr for the truth cavalierly or ignore his claims altogether, while they panegyrize his executioner. Yet he will live in the hearts of men, ennoble the virtues of men, illustrate the heroism of men, and thrill the purest souls of men with life and immortality after the names of those who despised and rejected him have perished in eternal forgetfulness.

The sweet-spirited-Cowper has anticipated this fact and put his more than poetic conception into the most expressive and poetic language:

> "A patriot's blood may earn indeed,
> And for a time insure to his loved land
> The sweets of liberty and equal laws;
> But martyrs struggle for a brighter prize,
> And win it with more pain. Their blood is shed
> In confirmation of the noblest claim—
> Our claim to feed upon immortal truth,
> To walk with God, to be divinely free,
> To soar and to anticipate the skies."

The martyrs of Missouri, though unknown to fame and unambitious of distinction, have, in their humble, unostentatious, quiet way, suffered as keenly and as severely as any others. They have taken the spoiling of their goods as joyfully, "counted all things but loss for the excellency of the knowledge of Christ Jesus the Lord," "counted not their lives dear unto themselves so that they might finish their course with joy and the ministry which they have received of the Lord Jesus to testify the gospel of the grace of God," and in all their sufferings for righteousness' sake have entered as fully into the spirit of the Master, even in sealing their testimony with their blood, as did John Calos, Nicholas Burton, Paul Clement, John Huss, Jerome of Prague, Bishops Latimer and Ridley, Archbishop Cramner, or any other of the long roll of distinguished martyrs.

The martyrs of Missouri may not occupy a place as high as others on the scrolls of fame, yet it is only a difference of time and country. It is the meridian of the ninteenth, instead of the fifteenth, sixteenth or seventeenth century. We are in Missouri, one of the United States of America, instead of Madrid, the valleys of Piedmont and Savoy, or Paris, or Italy, or Bohemia, or Turin, or London, or any other country or place where the blood of the martyrs has been shed for the testimony of Jesus. The spirit of persecution is the same, and the high sense of consecration to God and fidelity to Jesus that led the old martyrs to the rack and the stake have not been wanting in the ministers of the gospel in Missouri. The spirit, the heroism, the faith, the zeal, the devotion, were all here; and but for the remaining sense of enlightened Christianity that had been so long fostered by the genius of our free institutions, and the power it still exercised upon the public mind, the rack, the stake and all the horrible fires of the Inquisition would have been here also. The absence of these and other instruments of torture from the history of martyrdom in Missouri is due to other causes than the spirit and design of the authors and agents of religious persecution. The spirit was willing, but the cause and the occasion were wanting. Mobocracy sometimes invented a cause and made an occasion. The victim was found and offered without an altar. In such cases brutal cruelty was scarcely softened by religious refinement.

Some suffered for intermeddling with party politics; some for declining to take the oath of loyalty to the Government, as ministers; others for refusing to preach under a flag; others because they did not pray for the destruction of all rebels; others for expressing sympathy for one side or the other; others because they were born and brought up in the South; others, still, for declining to sanction the wrongs and outrages committed upon defenseless citizens, and helpless women and children, and still others because they were ministers and belonged to a certain ecclesiastical body.

How far these various considerations were only pretexts or occasions can not now be determined, other than by the analysis of the state of society heretofore given and the real *animus* of these persecutions.

The following instances of persecution are furnished, in substance, as they came into the hands of the author. Nothing is added, and nothing material to the facts is omitted. In some instances the phraseology is a little changed, more to secure a uniform tone and spirit throughout the work than to alter the sense; but material facts are nowhere sacrificed in the narratives of others, even to the author's taste. Where it can be done, the language of each one's own history is retained; but where only the facts and dates have been furnished, they are put up with the strictest regard for truth and consistency. The reader will see from the narratives themselves that it is impossible to observe chronological order. And, indeed, the classification of subjects makes it necessary to break the narrative of individual persecutions where it can be done, that each individual may illustrate the several stages of this remarkable history. For instance, some men were persecuted during the continuance of the war, and then again under the application of the "test oath" of the new Constitution. These, it is true, are but different aspects and stages of the same system of proscription and persecution, yet the nature and bearing of events require separate treatment where it can be done. The purposes of history can only be served by proper classifications and distinctions. The following narratives of persecution are fully authenticated by official records and responsible names.

The trials and persecutions of ministers of the gospel varied somewhat with the locality. In some parts of the State ministers were partially exempt from the influence and power of lawless men, while in other sections property, liberty and life were all at the mercy of irresponsible mobs.

The following statement is furnished by the minister himself. He has long been a faithful, earnest, exemplary member of the St. Louis Annual Conference, M. E. Church, South. Few men have stood higher in the ranks of the itinerant ministry in Missouri or done more faithful service than

THE REV. JAMES M. PROCTOR.

He says: "I was arrested by W. Hall, at Draby's chapel, on Sabbath, July 6, 1862. Hall, with his company, reached the chapel before me, and had the 'stars and stripes' placed just above the church door. He said that he had been informed that I would not preach under the Union flag. After preaching, and just as I was coming out at the door, near which he had taken his position, he accosted me and said, 'You are my prisoner.' He trembled like an aspen leaf. I said to him, 'Why this emotion, sir? Show yourself a man, and do your duty.' He replied, 'I hate to arrest you, but I am bound to do my duty.' He said I must go with him to his father's then, and the following morning he would take me to headquarters at Cape Girardeau. I could not well go with him that night, as I had been caught in the rain that morning, and had to borrow a dry suit on the road, which I was under obligations to return that evening.

"After some parley, he granted me permission to report at the Cape in a few days, which I did promptly, to Col. Ogden, then Provost-Marshal. Col. Ogden paroled me to report at his headquarters every two or three weeks. On the 29th of September, 1862, I reported to him the fifth and last time, when I was tongue-lashed at a fearful rate by Lieut.-Col. Peckham of the 29th Mo. regiment, and by him sent to the guard-house.

"I asked this irate Colonel if the front of my offending was not my connection with the M. E. Church, South. He replied, 'Yes, sir; and the man who will belong to that Church, after she has done the way she has, ought to be in prison during the war; and I will imprison you, sir, during the war.' 'It is a hard sentence for such an offense,' I said. He replied, 'I can't help it, sir; all such men as you are must be confined so that they can do no harm.'

"I remained in the guard-house at the Cape until Thursday, October 2, 1862, when—in company with thirteen other prisoners, three of whom died in a few weeks—I was sent to Gratiot street military prison, St. Louis. In this prison I met several very worthy ministers of different denominations, and also Brother J. S. Boogher and two of his brothers, nobler men than whom I have not found any where in the world.

"October 20, 1862, I was released on parole, there being no crime alleged against me. The little man who first arrested me was a Northern Methodist. He wrote out and preferred two charges against me, which were so frivolous that the officers in St. Louis would not investigate them. I furnish them here as items of curiosity, as follows:

"'1. He, the said J. M. Proctor, threatened to hang Mr. Lincoln.

"'2. He said that the Federal soldiers were horse thieves.'

"After my release from Gratiot street prison, St. Louis, I went to the town of Jackson, where I was again arrested at the special instigation of a Northern Methodist preacher named Liming. I continued to preach during and after my imprisonment. When the notorious test oath was inaugurated I continued to preach, and was indicted three times before Judge Albert Jackson, of Cape Girardeau county. Revs. D. H.

Murphy and A. Munson were also indicted for the same offense.

"I never took the test oath, nor any oath of allegiance during the war. It was plain to all that the Northern Methodists were our worst enemies during that long and cruel war."

It is only necessary to add that Mr. Proctor remained at home when permitted, attending to his legitimate calling during the war as a minister, and was no partisan in the strife—a peaceable, law-abiding citizen, and an humble, inoffensive minister of the gospel. As he was informed, "the front of his offending was his connection with the M. E. Church, South," while it seems that both the instigators and instruments of his arrest and imprisonment were members of the M. E. Church, North. Proscription and persecution do not always hesitate in the presence of opportunity.

Rev. Marcus Arrington.

It is sad to record the following details of suffering inflicted upon one of the oldest, most useful and honored members of the St. Louis Conference, M. E. Church, South; a man who for many years has been an humble, exemplary and influential member of the Conference, who occupied a high position in the confidence of the Church, and has been intrusted with high and responsible positions in her courts and councils. No man, perhaps, of any Church has stood higher in the esteem of all men of all Churches in Southwest Missouri, where he has so long lived and labored, than Marcus Arrington. Let him tell in his own way the story of his sufferings:

"When the troubles commenced, in the spring of 1861,

I was traveling the Springfield Circuit, St. Louis Conference. I was very particular not to say anything, either publicly or privately, that would indicate that I was a partisan in the strife. I tried to attend to my legitimate work as a traveling preacher.

"But after the war commenced, because I did not advocate the policy of the party in power, I was reported as a secessionist, and in the midst of the public excitement it was vain to attempt to counteract the report.

"At the earnest solicitation of divers persons, I took the oath of loyalty to the Government. This, it was thought, would be sufficient. But we were mistaken.

"Soon after this, my life was threatened by those who were in the employ of the Federal Government. But they were, as I verily believe, providentially prevented from executing their threat.

"After the battle of Oak Hills, or Wilson's Creek, July 10, 1861, it became my duty to do all I could for the relief of the sick and wounded, and because I did this I was assured that I had violated my oath of allegiance. I was advised by Union men, so-called, that it would be unsafe for me to fall into the hands of Federal soldiers. Believing this to be true, when General Fremont came to Springfield, I went to Arkansas, as I think almost any man would have done under the circumstances.

"While in Arkansas, I met Bro. W. G. Caples, who was acting Chaplain to General Price. He requested me to take a chaplaincy in the army, informing me at the time that, by an agreement between Generals Fremont and Price, all men who had taken the oath of loyalty as I did were released from its obligations.

"In December, 1861, I was appointed by Gen. McBride Chaplain of the 7th Brigade, Missouri State Guard. In this capacity I remained with the army until the battle of Pea Ridge, March 7 and 8, 1862. On the second day of this battle, while in the discharge of my duty as Chaplain, I was taken prisoner. Several Chaplains taken at the same time were released on the field, but I was retained. I was made to walk to Springfield, a distance of 80 miles. We remained in Springfield one day and two nights, and whilst many prisoners who had previously taken the oath as I had were paroled to visit their families, I was denied the privilege.

"We were then started off to Rolla, and although I had been assured that I would be furnished transportation, it was a sad mistake, and I had to walk until I literally gave out. What I suffered on that trip I can not describe. When we reached Rolla I was publicly insulted by the Commander of the Post.

"From Rolla we were sent to St. Louis on the cars, lodged one night in the old McDowell College, and the next day sent to Alton, Ill.

"Whilst I was in Alton prison a correspondent of the *Republican*, writing over the name of 'Leon,' represented me as a 'thief and a perjured villain!'

"I was kept in Alton prison until Aug. 2, 1862, when I was released by a General Order for the release of all Chaplains.

"I then went to St. Louis, and thence South, by way of Memphis, Tenn., into exile. I would have returned to Missouri after the war closed but for the restrictions put upon ministers of the gospel by the new Constitution.

"Eternity alone will reveal what I have suffered in

exile. The St. Louis Conference is properly my home, and her preachers have a warm place in my affections. They are very near my heart. May they ever be successful."

Rev. Mr. Arrington pines for his old home and friends, and few men have a deeper hold upon the hearts of the people in Missouri. Thousands would welcome him to warm hearts and homes after these calamities are overpast.

Rev. John McGlothlin.

As a specimen of petty local persecution the case of Rev. J. McGlothlin, a worthy local preacher of the M. E. Church, South, who has long stood high in that part of the State where he resides, will be sufficient for this place.

It was with some reluctance that he yielded to the demands of history enough to furnish the following facts. He is a modest man and shrinks from notoriety.

In 1862 he was residing in Ray county, Mo., when Major Biggers, the Commander of the Post at Richmond, issued an order that no minister of the gospel should preach who did not carry with him the Union flag. A few days after the order came out Mr. McGlothlin was called upon to go to Knoxville, Caldwell county, to procure suitable burial clothing for a Mrs. Tilford, a widow, who died in his neighborhood, as he was the only man available for that service. After the purchases were made and he was ready to return, a Captain Tiffin, of Knoxville, stepped up and asked if he had "reported." He answered in the negative, and convinced the Captain that there was no order requiring him to report, as he had license to preach. The officer then asked him if he had a "flag." He told him he had not. "Will you get one?" "No," said he, "I will recognize no State or military authority to prescribe qualifications for the work of the ministry." The officer at once arrested him. Mr. McGlothlin acquainted Capt. Tiffin at once with the peculiar character of his business in Knoxville, and the necessity of his speedy return, offering at the same time his parole of honor to report to him at any time and place he might designate. This he promptly refused, and the officer said that he would ride out a part of the way with him. When they arrived within a few miles of the house where the dead lay waiting interment, the officer pressed a boy into service and sent the burial clothes to their destination, after detaining them three or four hours on the way.

The minister was not released, even to attend the funeral service, but was kept in close confinement, dinnerless, supperless, bedless and comfortless.

The next day, with over twenty others, he was taken to Richmond and confined in the Fair Grounds and in the old College building for five weeks, and then unconditionally released. The only charge they could bring against him was that he would not take the oath of allegiance, give bond in the sum of $1,000 for his good behavior, and buy a flag to carry about with him as an evidence of his loyalty and a symbol of authority to preach the gospel of Jesus Christ.

Few instances of petty persecution in the exercise of a little brief authority can surpass this. It needs no comment, except to add that the minister who was thus made a victim of the narrowest and meanest spitefulness was a high-toned gentleman of unblemished character, against whom even the petty military officers and their spies could never raise an accusation.

Rev. James Penn.

This venerable minister and member of the Missouri Annual Conference, M. E. Church, South, was the subject of a peculiar class of trials during the war. Mr. Penn is one of the oldest and one of the best men in the itinerant ministry in Missouri.

He has furnished to the ministry four sons, all of whom are worthy and useful men. While the father has given his life and his children to the work of the ministry, it is peculiarly gratifying to the Church and their co-laborers of the Missouri Conference that, up to this time, no moral taint has ever rested upon a single member of the family.

So long known and so highly esteemed by the people of the State generally, it was hoped—vainly hoped—that at least he would escape the fiery ordeal. No one at all acquainted with his spirit and character can ever believe aught against him of harm to any human government or human being. During a long, eventful life he has been a man eminently pure in spirit, and singularly devoted to his one work. In that work he has had no divided heart, or head, or life.

His sons follow in his footsteps—worthy sons of an honored sire—and as such it is not altogether an unmeaning pun which has so generally designated them "Gold Penns."

But it is still true that "they that would live godly in Christ Jesus shall suffer persecution." It would be wrong not to let this honored servant of God tell his own story.

"First. I was arrested in August, 1862, and carried to Keokuk, Iowa, and there detained for about a week. There being no well founded charges against me I was released.

"Second. In August, 1863, I held a meeting in Williamstown, Mo. There was present at that meeting a minister of the M. E. Church, whose name I believe was Moody. On Sunday morning, during prayer meeting, this man, while we were kneeling in prayer, arose and began to read in a very loud tone of voice. The people got off their knees. The man who had thus disturbed an unoffending company of praying men and women was armed, as were some fifteen others whom he had brought with him. I walked toward the door and the people followed me and took a position in the street. I then preached to a large concourse of people, the armed minister and his valiant company retaining possession of the house. I continued the meeting until the next Sabbath, when this preacher with his armed band came again and drove us out of the house the second time. I preached out of doors, as on the preceding Sabbath. The meeting resulted in much good, there being about forty accessions to the M. E. Church, South.

"On another occasion flags were brought and placed on and around the pulpit, and a company of armed men sat near to prevent any one from taking them down. Seeing that this would not deter us from a discharge of Christian duty, a lot of wicked women raised a fight and fought like savages, so we were compelled to leave the house and ceased to preach at that place. Moody was asked why he did so, and his reply was: "Because I can." He is now, I believe, a minister in good standing in the M. E. Church, but many responsible people regard him as a very bad man.

"At Winchester, Mo., we had a very good house of worship, but they ran us out, as they did at Williamstown, until our own people were unwilling to attend divine service in the town. Then the house was almost destroyed, so that there we had no place in which to worship.

"They seized our house at Lagrange, a Mr. Stewart and others of the M. E. Church being the chief actors in this matter. After three years they relinquished their hold upon this splendid house.

"In addition to all this, I have suffered personal wrongs, in various ways, at the hands of these people. But I have tried to keep a conscience void of offense toward God and men. Their wrong-doing is upon themselves. I leave them to be judged by him who is too wise to err and too good to do wrong. May he forgive the wrong done."

This simple narrative speaks volumes, and needs neither note nor comment. The Rev. Colonel Moody, who figured so conspicuously in the persecutions above detailed, it is said, read on the occasion of the first disturbance of Mr. Penn's prayer meeting from Gal. iii. 1: "O foolish Galatians, who hath bewitched you, that ye should not obey the truth?" &c.

It is a singular fact that the ministers of the M. E. Church, North, were conspicuous from first to last in the persecutions of the ministers of the M. E. Church,

South; and, indeed, all other ministers who were under the ban of the Federal authorities. There was not only a bold scheme devised by Bishops Simpson and Ames to possess themselves of the property of the M. E. Church, South, through military authority, as the rightful booty of Northern Methodist conquest," but every minister and member who had position and power in the army, or who could evoke the military power, seemed to consider themselves specially commissioned to seize the property and exterminate the very existence of Southern Methodism.

CHAPTER XVI.

REVS. W. CLEAVELAND AND JESSE BIRD.

Ministers of other Churches in the Fellowship of Suffering and on the Rolls of Martyrdom—*Rev. Wm. Cleaveland* Arrested for Preaching in a Rebel Camp—Imprisoned and Insulted—Made to Pray for Mr. Lincoln on a Loyal Cannon—Rev. Captain Cox, a Northern Methodist Preacher, his Persecutor—Other Indignities—Indicted, Arrested and Arraigned as a Common Felon for Preaching without taking the "Test Oath"—*Rev. Jesse Bird* Arrested, Silenced and Banished—Losses, Exposure and Hardships of his Family—Returns—Arrested and put in Jail for Preaching without taking the "Test Oath"—Public Indignation—The Most Virulent Persecutors Subsequently Elevated to the Highest Civil Offices.

The ministers of the M. E. Church, South, were not the only sufferers. Persecution may sometimes be exclusive and exceptional, but oftener it is indiscriminate. The class of persons marked, or "spotted," for proscription and persecution was not confined to any one Church. Religious creeds were not so much involved as sectarian domination and sectional hatred. To exterminate, or expel from the State, that class of men who had not received their tone and type from New England, or had not fallen in heartily with the loyal religion and the religious loyalty, seemed to be a settled purpose.

It will be conceded that the ministers of the Methodist Church, South, were the greater sufferers, for reasons heretofore given; but to deny others who sacrificed and suffered nobly in the same cause a conspicuous place in the history of these stirring times would be both ungenerous and unjust. Many of the noblest martyrs of this period were connected with other Churches, and heroically and grandly sustained the moral heroism of the Missouri ministry. Common sufferings have sanctified the common fellowship and softened the asperities of sectarian feeling. It has measurably fused the religious heart and diffused the religious charity. Such men as Cleaveland, Duval, McPheeters, Wollard and others, are welcomed to the fellowship of suffering and the rolls of martyrdom.

The following statement is inserted as written. The language might be softened and the spirit toned down to advantage, but a prohibition only secures the facts; they can not be left out.

Case of the Rev. Wm. Cleaveland, a Missionary Baptist.

"I write as a witness for God and his Church, without fee or reward, to vindicate truth and to furnish a correct history of facts concerning myself and my acts which can neither be denied nor gainsaid.

> "'Nothing shall I extenuate,
> Nor aught set down in malice.'

"I am a minister of the gospel of the Missionary Baptist order, and pastor of the churches at Emerson, in Marion county, and Monticello and Mount Gilead, in Lewis county, Missouri; and nearly sixty years of age. In 1862, whilst attending as a member of an Association of the Baptist churches of ———, Col. Martin A. Green, commanding a detachment of Missouri troops in sympathy with the Southern cause, encamped a mile or two off, and despatched a messenger requesting the Association to appoint a minister to hold religious services and preach to his regiment on the Sabbath day. I was assigned to this duty by the Association, and performed it to the best of my humble ability. Perfect order prevailed, much feeling was exhibited, and I received compliments and other expressions of gratitude above measure.

"Returning to my home from the Association, after its close, I was arrested in the presence of my family by an armed force commanded by an officer in Federal uniform, marched off hurriedly to 'headquarters' in the city of Hannibal, and there confined a close prisoner in a filthy, cheerless hovel denominated a 'guard-house,' without fire to warm me, a bed to lie upon, or food to sustain nature, until my masters chose to permit my friends to furnish me supplies. Repeated efforts were made by my relations, brethren of the Church and others, to communicate with me and furnish me necessaries, but all in vain. The subalterns dressed in uniform, who, in the character of sentinels, haunted me like spectres, appeared much gratified to have jurisdiction around, and haughtily domineered, ridiculed, sneered and blustered as if to torture me into submission and humble me as in the dust. Meantime I put my trust in God, and continued 'instant in prayer.' Somehow I felt an extraordinary assurance that He whose right arm brought deliverance to Daniel, and to Paul and Silas, would rescue me from the snare of the enemy. About nine o'clock on the succeeding Monday morning a Northern Methodist preacher calling himself 'Captain Cox,' with a squad of armed men, entered my miserable and filthy prison, and, with an air of much authority, commanded me to march forthwith into the presence of Col. David Moore, who demanded that I immediately appear before him as commander of the garrison.

"Glad of any change in my gloomy situation, I arose and started, closely followed by my reverend persecutor, 'Captain Cox,' and his insolent myrmidons, until ordered to 'halt' in front of the quarters of the commanding officer. Being ushered in, I found Colonel Moore surrounded by an ill-mannered, ruffian-like multitude, who stared and sneered as if I were a curiosity on exhibition. The salutation of the commander was, 'Are you a rebel?' I answered that I had rebelled against the empire of Satan many years before and intended to continue in that warfare while life should last. 'The hell and damnation you have!' exclaimed the gentlemanly commander, in a loud tone of voice. I then said, 'I am a minister of the gospel, sir, and it is my business to make war against the kingdom of Satan. This, and this alone, is my occupation and my daily employment, and this alone I expect to do.' 'Are you a Southern man?' asked he. 'I was born in the South, raised and educated there, and my sympathies irresistibly lead me in that direction. Custom, tradition, my construction of the teachings of the Bible and ancient and modern history convinced me and established my belief to the effect that the institutions of the South were morally, socially, politically and religiously right, and I could not conscientiously say that I was not a Southern man.' 'Other men control their sympathies,' said he, 'why can you not do the same and harmonize with the North as well as the South?' I frankly replied that I would not believe the man that would tell me so. Habit and education made a man's opinions, and the convictions of a lifetime of three score years could not be changed in an hour. 'How do you like old Abe?' said he. 'In some respects well enough; in others not so well. On the whole, I don't indorse him as a President.' 'The hell you don't!' said he, whilst his surrounding admirers screamed with laughter. 'Did you pray for *them* rebels?' said he. 'Yes, sir.' 'Did you preach to them?' 'Yes, sir.' 'How long were you in Green's camp?' 'Two or three hours, perhaps.' 'Why did you go there and pray and preach to *them* damned rebels?' said he. 'Colonel Green sent a request to our Association, then in session near his camping ground, for a minister to be sent to preach to his men on the Sabbath day, and the Association deputized me to the task, all of which facts would appear in our published proceedings.' 'Damned glad you were to go, no doubt; and since you love praying for rebels so well, I will make you do a little *loyal* praying.' 'As to *loyal* or *disloyal* praying, I have no knowledge, but being commanded to pray for all men I endeavor to do so everywhere, lifting up holy hands without wrath and doubting.' I then demanded to know why I was there a prisoner; what was my offense, and who was my accuser. He answered in a violent and spiteful manner, that 'for preaching and praying for rebels in a rebel camp he had ordered my arrest, and that as a punishment for treason I should remain in the guard house a prisoner, on coarse fare, for nine days, and should offer each day a public prayer for Old Abe.' Having grown impatient at the abuse and insults of which I had been the subject so long, I replied: 'Col. Moore, I am told you have a praying wife; and I thank

God this day that I am counted worthy to be punished for preaching the gospel of Jesus Christ and praying for sinners. Sir, I esteem it a privilege and an honor, and shall not only pray, as my penance requires, for 'Mr. Lincoln,' but shall pray with all my heart for all other sinners, especially such as are associated in authority with him.' Springing suddenly to his feet, 'take him,' said he, and with much coarse abuse added, 'convey him under guard back to the guard house, imprison him, give him prisoner's rations, keep sentinels around him; and Captain Cox, I shall look to you to see this order executed.' Hurried back to the stench and filth of my prison house, accompanied by my armed guard, I remained until the next morning, when I was summoned to march out, and followed by several armed men with fixed bayonets and was conducted to a spot where the cannon were stationed. The regiment had been drawn up and formed into an irregular hollow square, in mockery. Many of the officers slunk away, while others stood and incited the men to giggle and perform antics to make the scene ludicrous and mortifying. As my divine Master, like a lamb before its shearers, was dumb, so I opened not my mouth. In an exultant and authoritative manner, the Rev. Capt. Cox, my loving Christian brother, a preacher of the Northern Methodist Church, as before stated, commanded me to 'mount that cannon and offer prayer for Mr. Lincoln, in obedience to orders, as a penance for praying in a rebel camp.'

"Being an old man, and weighing between two and three hundred pounds; having had scarcely an hour's rest for several days and nights; having had no change of clothing and no privilege of ablutions of any kind, I felt very badly, and with difficulty climbed to the top of the cannon-carriage, and there lifted up my heart and hands and voice to Jehovah in humble, fervent prayer. I felt greatly lifted up, much revived and encouraged, and my faith seemed as it were to grasp the very horns of the altar. The glory of the Lord shone forth, the Shekinah appeared to come down and rest upon the camp, and fear came upon the men. The pious rejoiced, the wicked were ashamed, and astonishment pervaded the scene. At the conclusion of my prayer, still standing in the ridiculous attitude I was made to occupy upon the cannon, I opened my eyes and looking around upon what had been my fun-making and pleasure-seeking audience of soldiers and citizens, I discovered many weeping, others hurrying away in disorder, and even the blasphemous Colonel Moore was said to have shed tears. Knowing I had committed no offense against the laws of God or man, and that my blessed Master had been stoned, spit upon, whipped with cords, dressed in mock royalty, crowned with thorns and driven through the public streets in derision for the sport of the mob, I took courage and hoped for the best. 'If they did those things in the green tree, what might they not do in the dry?' The weapons of my warfare were not carnal. Yet these wicked men, actuated by the same malignant spirit which prompted their prototypes to lay violent hands on the Son of God, seized me, an humble and obscure preacher of righteousness, guilty of no offense, and to gratify their malignity, dragged me around, followed by soldiers with muskets and bayonets, exposed me to ridicule and attempted to force me to make a mockery of religion, and thus (as they hoped) bring the Church into dishonor and disgrace. 'But the ways of the Lord are marvelous in our eyes,' for

"'Deep in unfathomable mines
Of never failing skill,
He treasures up his bright designs
And works his sovereign will.'

"Hastened from this scene by the peremptory order of my Rev. Brother, Capt. Cox, I was conducted by an armed guard back to the filth and stench of the guard-house, and there remained, each day going through the same blasphemous exhibition, except that I was allowed to stand on the ground instead of the cannon to offer up my prayer. Many of the soldiers professed repentance, and whilst stationed as sentinels around me tendered me their sympathies, extended many kindnesses, and pledged me that, dying in battle, or when or where they might, they would try to meet me in heaven. Verily and of a truth 'the Lord maketh the wrath of man to praise him.'

"Shortly after these events Col. Moore and his command were ordered South, where they participated in the battle of Shiloh, or Pittsburg Landing, as it is sometimes called. The regiment was cut to pieces, Colonel Moore lost a leg by a *shot from a cannon,* and his Major, Barnabas King, to whose instigation my friends attributed much of my suffering, was killed. The Rev. 'Captain Cox' seems to have kept out of harm's way on that fearful day, for—now that our homes are made a ruin, our land shrouded in mourning, and our dwellings sad and sorrowful on account of the absence of the loved ones who were cruelly murdered in the presence and amid the cries and shrieks of wives, mothers and babes, as well as the brave who fell in battle—he comes again. Not bedecked with the tinsel and trappings of authority, to shut up old gray-headed men in loathsome prisons, march them around surrounded by bayonets, and force them to mount cannons and pray for the amusement and sport of the soldiery and the mob for preaching the gospel to sinners. Lo! he comes again in the lowly habiliments of Christianity, commissioned by the Bishops of the Northern Methodist Church, as an accredited minister of that Church, to teach religion and preach the gospel amongst us, for which purpose the *Rev. 'Captain'* is now perambulating Marion and adjoining counties. 'Vengeance is mine, I will repay, saith the Lord.'

"One would suppose that malignity had exhausted itself in the deeds of the foregoing recital. Not so. While on business in Hannibal one day, after the foregoing had occurred, word came that Col. McDaniel and his battalion of the advance guard of the Confederate army under General Price was marching in that direction; and, having left my wife and daughter at home alone, I called upon Col. J. T. K. Hayward, then in command of the post, for a permit to pass out of the city and go to my family, who would necessarily be much alarmed, and explained my situation. Being a member of the Church, a Presbyterian elder, I expected, of course, Christianlike courtesy. But, to my surprise, I was insolently repelled, vindictively insulted, and peremptorily ordered to remain where I was. Stung with disappointment and burning with indignation, I submitted as patiently as I could, and implored commiseration in the name of my unprotected family.

Remorseless as a bloodhound and pitiless as a hyena, he was inexorable, and forced me to remain until McDaniel retired and his scare subsided. At the solicitation of leading citizens, he then granted me a permit to go, but accompanied the paper with a gruff intimation that the issues of life and death were in his grasp, and by the nod of his head he 'could have me shot.' Perhaps this violence of feeling may have resulted from the fact that the brave Colonel Hayward had, at a recent period, been captured by a Confederate officer, relieved of his watch, his spurs, his purse, his pistols, sword, epaulets, horse and equipments, and paroled on his oath and pledge of honor, both of which he had violated, and was again in arms wreaking vengeance on unarmed and innocent persons. I make no mention of the particulars of the murder of a friendless stranger, laboring under *delirium tremens,* who had just landed from a steamer, and was by his order shot to death upon the wharf at the city of Hannibal.

"Circumstances indicated that my life and my property were eager objects of the pursuit of this class of men. By day or by night, at all hours, and in different ways, my family were often disturbed and interrupted by them. My wife and daughter were made to perform menial service for any number who chose to demand it; whilst the filthy vagabonds, in the uniform of Federal soldiers, would ransack the premises and deface, destroy and steal anything of value they could find in the house or out of it. One night myself and family were aroused about twelve o'clock by the heavy tread of swift-moving horses, and a loud yell at the door informed us that soldiers—two of whom, calling themselves

'Tabor and Watson, of Capt. John D. Meredith's company of the 39th Missouri regiment,' (which Meredith is now sheriff of Marion county)—had come with orders from their superiors to demand my horse and saddle. They said they were in rapid pursuit of the noted Confederate scout, Bill Anderson, and his command; were directed to press into service whatever they needed; must have my horse, and intended to give no quarter until the last officer and man of the enemy were slain. When this was accomplished they should next turn their attention to those who sympathized with the rebels, and would clean out every man, woman and child, until they had made their lands a desolation and their homes a solitude. Intermingling these threats with vulgar epithets and bitter denunciation, they dashed off; and, as their receding forms faded away in the darkness carrying off my fine young horse, my only means of reaching my appointments at the different churches to preach and perform other ministerial duties, a strange and fearful sensation crept over me, as if sad events lay buried in the future. The curtain was soon lifted. A few days brought the mournful intelligence that 'Johnson's battalion had encountered the foe and was annihilated.' On the plain, and in full view of the city of Centralia, in Boone county, the conflict transpired, and of all the 'bloody 39th,' as its commander boastfully called it, who entered the field that day, not a platoon of officers, horses and men escaped death, including my poor horse, which, being ridden by a subaltern officer, is said to have sunk down with his rider in the midst of the battle to rise no more.

"In the order of divine providence friends came to my

relief, and I was enabled, with some difficulty, to pursue my work, although much harassed, sorely vexed and often cast down by fears without and cares within, for my life was often threatened.

"In common with other brethren who feared God rather than Cæsar, I was in due time indicted by the grand jury of Marion county for preaching the gospel to lost sinners without first committing perjury by taking a false oath. Arraigned as a felon on my blessed Lord's account, I felt honored, for the servant is not above his master. I stood at the bar of justice, as he stood before Pontius Pilate; and, although surrounded by murderers, burglars, horse-thieves and others of the baser sort, I there remained, attending their calls from court to court, until for very shame the disgraceful and blasphemous scene was closed by the prosecuting lawyer, Walter M. Boulware, Esq., dismissing the suit; and the Hon. William P. Harrison, now acting as Judge of the Court, discharged me and released my securities, who had entered into bond for a large amount to keep me out of jail. Glory be to God! I am still alive; and, unless sooner taken hence, I feel that there are still some years of service in me, which shall be given with a willing heart to that cause for which I have suffered, and am still willing, if need be, to suffer on.

"'God moves in a mysterious way,
His wonders to perform;
He plants his footsteps in the sea,
And rides upon the storm.'

"WILLIAM CLEAVELAND.

"Marion County, Mo., May 3, 1869."

The Rev. Mr. Cleaveland has for many years stood

high in the part of Missouri where he resides, as an orderly, quiet, earnest minister of the gospel, and now looks back on the scene of his persecutions with feelings that he can scarcely control. His only offense—that he preached in a camp of rebel soldiers in obedience to the authority of the Association; and for this he was not only arrested and imprisoned, but grossly insulted and rudely maligned by the permission and authority of one who styled himself a minister of the gospel. But he told his own story, and it is better without note or comment.

Rev. Jesse Bird.

This able and useful minister of the gospel has long been a member of the Missouri Annual Conference, M. E. Church, South. Few men have stood higher in the estimation of his brethren in the ministry or the communities where his labors have been bestowed. The positions filled by him in the pastoral, educational and judicial departments of the Church for many years, and the ability and fidelity with which he met every responsibility, attest the confidence of the Church and the high appreciation of the Conference of which he is an honored member. The spirit that will prompt men to the exercise of such petty tyranny as that detailed in Mr. Cleaveland's case, and now to be narrated by Mr. Bird, must be the spirit of Antichrist. Neither of the gentlemen was guilty of any civil, political, military or moral offense. But hear him:

"Dear Brother—I see in the *Advocate* a notice requesting persons to give information of the persecutions of ministers of the gospel in Missouri. I send you the following very concise statement of facts in my own case.

"In the fall of 1861 I was appointed by the President of the Missouri Conference to the St. Joseph District. On my first round I went to my Quarterly Meeting for Rockport Circuit, at Spencer's Chapel, in Atchison county. Arriving at the chapel at 11 o'clock Nov. 9, I found a pole had been raised by the door with a rope fastened to it for the purpose of hoisting a flag. There was no one present. I waited a little and saw two men approaching. They informed me that a burial was going on in the neighborhood, and the preaching was postponed till 3 o'clock.

"In the evening I returned to the church in company with a few persons. As we approached the house I saw two men hoisting a flag in great haste. Fastening the rope as quickly as possible, they ran and hid themselves inside a field. Coming up to the house and seeing what had been done, I declined going in, stating that I would preach under no political flag; that I should not mix my religion with politics. I was invited to preach at a private house and did so. I was not interrupted again until on my second round.

"On the 6th of Feb., 1862, I commenced a Quarterly Meeting at Oregon, Holt county. The meeting went on quietly and prosperously until Monday morning, when the flag was hoisted over the door of the church. I again declined going in for the same reasons. In the course of two or three hours I was arrested, cursed and abused in various ways and threatened by some men who styled themselves solders. I was then sent in charge of two young men to Forest City and requested to 'take the oath,' which I also declined. But in order to get off and out of the hands of the law, I agreed to go before a magistrate and take a civil oath to observe the Constitution and laws. From Oregon I returned home and found a notice in my postoffice at Rochester from Ben. Loan, the commander at St. Joseph, requiring me to appear before him immediately. I went down and inquired for what purpose he had sent for me, when he replied: 'You are not to preach any more in this district.' 'Is this all?' I inquired. 'You must go and take the oath,' he replied. I informed him that I should not take the oath; that he could put me in prison or banish me from the State, as he had done others. He immediately made out an order for me to leave the State within thirty days. This was done in the city of St. Joseph, Feb. 14, 1862. I was not restricted to any particular bounds. The ground was then covered with snow and ice to the depth of six or eight inches. I had no money to bear expenses, save about fifty dollars. I gave about two prices for a wagon, put what I could in it, and leaving my house and crop of corn in the prairie, I started on a cold, stormy day (the 20th day of Feb., 1862,) with my wife in feeble health, to go-I knew not whither, and that for no other reason than that I was a Southern Methodist preacher and would not swear falsely.

"This move made it necessary to sacrifice the grain and stock my little boys had worked for, together with our furniture and a good portion of my library. I was accompanied by my daughter and two little sons, and also by Benjamin Bird, his wife and two young children. We started South and traveled four days, reaching the river opposite Lexington, and finding the ice giving way, and there being no boat, we turned up the river to Camden, Ray county, stopping at Brother Menefee's, a most excellent family, where we remained some three or four days. Leaving Camden we went up the bottom to a point opposite Napoleon, in Lafayette county, where we remained in camp two or three days, when, the ice clearing away, we crossed the Missouri river and proceeded through cold and storm until we had passed the town of Clinton, in Henry county.

"Here we met some men who told us, as others had the day before, that we could not proceed beyond the Osage. The Jayhawkers and Home Guards were robbing all who attempted to go through. We turned round and came back to Lafayette county, and finding an empty house near Greenton, stopped and spent the spring and summer there.

"In a few days I went down to Lexington, saw the commander of that post and got a sound cursing for my trouble. Returning to my family and finding the people of the neighhorhood very kind and generous, we remained until the last of August, when we returned to our home in Andrew county.

"I will say nothing of my trials from that time till the close of the war, except that I preached but little. A part of this time I was nominally the Presiding Elder of St. Joseph District.

"About Christmas, 1865, I was employed by the Presiding Elder, H. H. Hedgepeth, to take charge of the Savannah Circuit. I commenced my work immediately, and continued preaching regularly until my last appointment at Savannah, in August, 1866. I had been threatened at different times during the summer by mobs, and sometimes I thought it quite likely I should be put to death by the lawless rabble, but I was left unmolested until I was about to finish my work on the circuit. On Sunday the people expected an interruption while I was preaching, but all continued quiet till night. While in the pulpit I noticed some men come in and whisper to each other and go out, and presently return. When the services closed I heard a lady say: 'They are at the door.' I quietly walked out and went to my room, nobody disturbing me. Next morning I was told they were preparing to arrest me.

"After I had adjusted my affairs, about 10 o'clock, I went home. Having proceeded about two hundred yards I saw the Deputy Sheriff coming at full speed after me. Knowing what it meant, I stopped till he came up. He said he was authorized to arrest me. I was taken before a justice of the peace, who had issued the warrant for my arrest upon the affidavit of one of the party that came into the church on Sunday night. The said justice inquired if I pleaded *guilty or not guilty to the crime of preaching the gospel to the people, in violation of the Fundamental Law of the State of Missouri.* I pleaded *guilty*. Whereupon the said officer required me to give bond for my appearance at the next session of the court, which I declined; consequently I was taken by the Sheriff of Andrew county and lodged in the jail of Buchanan county, in the city of St. Joseph, there being no jail in Andrew county. This was done the 27th of August, 1866. I remained in prison about three hours, when the Sheriff of Buchanan county, accompa nied by Judge Woodson and others of St. Joseph, cam and opened the door of the jail and let me out. On Monday following the Circuit Court of Buchanan county came on, and the judge declining to try the case I gave bond for my appearance at the next term of the Circuit Court for Andrew county, at which time and place I was indicted for preaching the gospel. I took a change of venue to Buchanan county, and before the sitting of the court the decision of the Supreme Court of the United States had set aside the Test Oath, and that ended the matter with me.

"You can make what use of these statements you please in the forthcoming history of the persecution in Missouri. I should have given names, but I have forgotten most of them.

"Yours, very truly, JESSE BIRD.

"*Plattsburg, Mo., Feb. 3, 1869.*"

The account of Mr. Bird's arrest and imprisonment, and subsequent indictment for preaching the gospel without taking the oath prescribed in the New Constitution, could not well be separated from the narrative of his other persecutions.

The author was in St. Joseph when he was brought down from Andrew county and lodged in the jail with common felons. He had many friends in the community, and to see him through the heavy iron grates, classed with horse thieves, burglars, murderers and other criminals, caused no little popular indignation. Men hurried to and fro after attorneys, judges, officers and friends, and stood on the corners in animated conversation until the public excitement boded no peace. The Sheriff of Buchanan county acted prudently and wisely in releasing him on his verbal parole. No other course would have appeased the public indignation or allayed the ever-widening and deepening excitement. No threats of violence were heard, and yet the indications in the public mind could not be mistaken.

Mr. Bird and the Church will ever be under obligations to Hon. Silas Woodson, of St. Joseph, for his prompt and efficient attention to the case. He made an earnest but ineffectual effort to get the case before Judge Heron, then on the Circuit Court bench, on a writ of *habeas corpus.* But the Judge was a little weak-kneed and did not wish to damage his prospects for a seat in the U. S. Congress, and refused informally to grant a writ or have anything to do with the case.

More will be said on this subject at another time and in another connection.

It may as well be stated here, however, as a noteworthy fact, that the military officers and others who were the most officious and efficient in the persecution of ministers of the gospel, during the war and since, have subsequently been elevated to the most honorable and lucrative offices in the gift of the people. While the people have professed the strongest disapprobation of these persecutions, it can not be denied that for some reasons the perpetrators of the grossest outrages upon ministers of the gospel have filled and are now filling the highest civil offices.

CHAPTER XVII.

ELDERS J. DUVAL, ISAAC ODELL AND ALLEN SISK.

Elder James Duval—His Own Statement—Endorsement—Minister of the Regular Baptist Church—Arrested at Midnight—Suffered Much—Passes and Permits—Assessment for Military Purposes—Arrest of Elder G. W. Stout—Elder Duval again Arrested—Sent to Chillicothe—Charge, Trial and Acquittal—Making History—Re-arrested at New Garden—Heavy Bond—In Court for not Taking the Oath—Met others in the Same Condemnation—*Isaac Odell* and *Allen Sisk* under Indictment with Elder Duval—Estebb, the Prosecuting Attorney—Dunn & Garver for the Defense—Baptist Church at New Garden—Trial of their Pastor, Elder Isaac Odell, for not taking the Oath—Acquitted-Then Convicted—Division of the Church—Troubles—Non-Fellowship.

ELDER JAMES DUVAL.

The following sketch, furnished by this venerable servant of God, will be read with thrilling interest by the people of the State where he has been so long and so favorably known. It is unnecessary to present, for the people of Missouri, any endorsement of his character, but for the benefit of others, and because his statement, herewith submitted in his own style, involves the names and details the persecutions of others, it may not be out of place to insert here the following paper:

"RICHMOND, RAY CO., MO., May 22, 1869.

"Elder James Duval, of this county, is a minister of the gospel of the regular Baptist Church, and bears an unblemished character as a preacher and a Christian gentleman.

(Signed) "GEORGE W. DUNN,
"AUSTIN A. KING,
"A. W. DONIPHAN."

These gentlemen are all widely known, even beyond the State, and their endorsement is sufficient to give force to every word of the following statement. The author does not feel at liberty to either divide or abridge the document, lest the peculiar force of the narrative, told in his own language and style, should be marred, and the characteristics of the persecution should be deprived of their richness of detail. Besides, a variety of style is always pleasing to the reader.

"RICHMOND, RAY CO., MO., May, 1869.

"REV. P. M. PINCKARD: *Dear Sir*—You have asked through the *Advocate* for information concerning the 'persecution of ministers of the gospel in Missouri,' and being myself one of the unfortunately proscribed ones by the 'powers that be,' I thought it just and proper that I should contribute my mite of information, which I shall do partly from memory and partly from records.

"I will just here state that I have now been in constant connection with the old regular Baptist Church more than forty-five years. I joined that people upon a profession of faith in Christ, and was baptized, April 18th, 1824, into the fellowship of the Gourdvine church, Culpepper county, Va., by Elder James Garnet, who was then pastor of that church. From Hardy county, Va., in the fall of 1848, I moved and settled in Ray county, near Richmond, Mo., where I now reside, as all the old settlers know. Since then my acts and deeds, both private and public, as a citizen and a minister of Christ's word, are before the public.

"I will here endeavor to give a brief detail of the troubles and perplexities I have had with the Federal authorities.

"About the 15th of February, 1862, Captain Kelsaw, then commanding a company of men at Knoxville, Ray county, sent a squad of soldiers at twelve o'clock at night—as cold a night as well could be, heavy snow on the ground—and had me arrested and taken that night to Knoxville. These men also took from me a wagon and a pair of mules, and afterward two good horses; still later the Federals took loads of corn and hay, for which I have received no compensation. I arrived in Knoxville some time before day, very much chilled, almost frozen, and had to lie the rest of the night on the counter of an old store-room which the soldiers occupied. The next morning, with a guard at my heels, I was allowed the privilege of calling on a friend (Mrs. Mary Stone), when I was kindly furnished with my breakfast.

"I was then put in charge of J. N. Henry, who was acting in some military capacity, who safely, but in a rude and domineering manner, conducted me to Cameron, Col. Catherwood's headquarters. I was then held there as a prisoner, as you will presently see, for near two weeks. It is true that I had the privilege of boarding at the hotel and paying my bill.

"I inquired of Colonel Catherwood what were the charges against me. He never exhibited any. But he finally told me that I would have to give bond to keep the peace, or something to that effect. He then allowed me a certain number of days to return home and get security, which I did in the given time.

"I then got my friend and neighbor, Christopher Trigg, who went with me to Cameron, and entered into bond with me in the sum of two thousand dollars to do certain things therein specified. Upon which I received the following:

"'HEADQUARTERS AT CAMERON,
February 27th, 1862.

"'This is to certify that James Duval has this day subscribed to oath of allegiance to the United States, and filed a bond, as prescribed by the Commanding General. E. C. CATHERWOOD,

"'Col. Commanding M. S. M.'

"'HEADQUARTERS AT CAMERON,
February 27th, 1862.

"'This is to certify that James Duval has been released by giving bond and taking the oath of allegiance to the United States of America, and is entitled to citizenship and protection as such by all United States forces, so long as he regards the same. By order.

"'M. L. JAMES, Major Com'dg.

"I afterward obtained the following passes:

"'RICHMOND, May 1st, 1862.

"'Mr. James Duval has permission to go to Caldwell county to fill an appointment of the gospel, and to Lafayette for the same purpose. ABRAHAM ALLEN,

"'Capt. and Provost-Marshal at Richmond, Mo.'

"'OFFICE PROVOST-MARSHAL,
RICHMOND, Mo., September 30th, 1862.

"'Permission is hereby granted to James Duval to go to Clinton and Caldwell counties, Mo. He being exempt from military duty. Federal soldiers will respect this pass. W. ELLIOTT,

"'By E. G. LOWE, Dept. Provost-Marshal.'

"Some short time after this I was assessed by a committee appointed for that purpose a tax of eighty-eight dollars. Upon what basis or principle this tax was levied I never learned. I failed to pay in time, and I had a notice served on me to pay within five days or property double the amount would be taken to satisfy this claim. This notice I failed to save, or can not just now put my hand on it. However, I paid thirty dollars, and have the following to show for it:

"'RAY COUNTY, Mo., Dec. 22, 1862.

"'Received thirty dollars and — cents of James Duval, for the use of the Ray county Enrolled Militia. Same being *in part* the amount assessed against him for that purpose by the committee appointed under Special Order No. 30, dated Oct. 27, A. D. 1862, Headquarters Ray county E. M. M.

"'D. P. WHITMER,
"'E. RIGGS,
"'A. K. REYBURN,
"'Collecting Committee.'

"Thus you see some of the unjust restrictions laid on the ministers of Christ. When Christ says, 'Go ye into all the world and preach the gospel to every creature,' the party in power say, first obtain leave of us. Judge ye whether it is right to obey *man* or *God.*

"Do you not think that we have great need of faithful gospel ministers, who will cry aloud and spare not; shew Israel his sins and Jacob his transgression? Are not these living evidences in this day of boasted light and knowledge of man's blindness and corruption?

"I will here notice another evidence of blinded Christianity that came under my personal observation. In September, 1862, when our Association met at Crooked river, Ray county, the introductory sermon was preached, by previous appointment, by Elder G. W. Stout, a man of most exemplary Christian character, and held as such by his brethren, and even the world itself honors him as such; and after the Association had transacted its business and finally adjourned, and Elder Stout was on his horse for home, at somebody's instance Capt. John Hawkins arrested Elder Stout for traveling and preaching without first obtaining a *pass*.

"Elder Stout's *friends* interfered in his behalf and vouched for him that he would report himself to Col. J. H. Moss, in command at Liberty, which he did; and I reported the case back to Captain Hawkins. Colonel Moss gave Elder Stout a permit to go to Nodaway Association, and where his business called him.

"Who of Elder Stout's former brethren and friends stood by and witnessed this thing but did not interfere? You who were present and in the confidence of Captain Hawkins answer: 'We ought to lay down our lives *for* our brethren,' but not arrest them and put them in jail.

"In February, 1864, I was reported to Captain Tiffin, then holding the post at Richmond. There being no Provost-Marshal there then, I was sent to Chillicothe, and kept there a prisoner for near two weeks.

"I was placed in the hands of Baker Wilson and two others as a guard to take me to Chillicothe. Baker Wilson treated me kindly and respectfully—very different from J. N. Henry.

"He took me to Mr. Herrick, the Provost-Marshal, who placed me in the hands of John Gant, with directions to go to the jail and get my breakfast, which I did, and then report at his office. I then made a plain statement of facts as they had occurred in this matter, and told him I could prove my assertions if he would allow me time to take a few depositions, which he kindly did. The Marshal then gave me the limits of the town for my boundary.

"I was now kindly invited to the house of Charles H. Mansur, who, with his kind lady, did all in his power to make my situation as comfortable as possible under the circumstances, for which I feel under lasting obligations. I formed some other acquaintances who seemed deeply to sympathize with me, but were actually afraid to let it be known. I occasionally, as directed, reported to the Marshal, who, when not engaged in busiuess, was free and frank to talk, and I think is a just man. He said he was there to punish the guilty, not innocent men. I asked him with what I was charged in this case. He at first refused to tell me. I then told him what Captain Tiffin had told me. He then showed me the affidavit of Mrs. Herod, stating that I had passed her house piloting bushwhackers, and that she heard me say some things to Mr. Jeremiah McDonald. I satisfied the Marshal that these men, who had taken me that day and compelled me to pilot them a few miles, were not bushwhackers, but some of Shelby's men, under Col. Lewis Bohanon, who the day before had taken Carrollton.

"The conversation said to have been had with Mr. McDonald was all satisfactorily settled by his deposition and a few letters from gentlemen at Richmond. So, when the day of trial arrived, there were no other charges against me and I was acquitted. I felt humiliated and mortified to think that I, as a minister of Christ's Word, should bring disgrace on the cause of my Master. But what could I do. All this was forced upon me, without my consent in any wise. It has caused me a great deal of sober reflection and deep searching of heart to know whether I was in fault.

"But upon more mature reflection, considering the excitement of the times and the apparent hue and cry against every man that would not join in the fanaticisms of the day, Paul, the Apostle, in the 2 Timothy iii. 12, came to my relief: 'Yea, and all that will live godly in Christ Jesus *shall* suffer persecution.'

"These statements I have made, and they are well known to be strictly true by many citizens now living in this community; and as we are now making history for the generations who shall live after us, let us pen them down for the benefit of those who may survive us, so that all may clearly see that men are now, as in other days, wicked, and that nothing short of the love of God shed abroad in their *hearts* will make men either love or fear God aright.

"I will now mention some of the troubles that I have had with the State authorities.

"The first trouble, as a minister of Jesus Christ, that I ever had with the State authorities occurred at New Garden church, Ray county, on the third day of November, 1865. I will detail, as near as I can, exactly what happened on this occasion.

"Elder Joseph Warder had an appointment to preach at New Garden on Thursday, the third day of November, 1865, and I promised to meet him there on our way to Little Shoal, Clay county. Elder Warder failed to come, so I had to occupy the pulpit, and tried to preach to the people then assembled from the Acts of the Apostles, v. 38: 'Refrain from these men and let them alone: for if this counsel, or this work be of men, it will come to nought; but if it be of God, ye can not overthrow it, lest haply ye be found even to fight against God.'

"Nothing unusual took place during the services. After the congregation was dismissed, I came out of the house and went where my horse was hitched. There I was pursued by Charles Perkins, with pistols buckled on him, and he told me that he was authorized to arrest me. I asked him for what? He then presented me a paper, which I read, which stated in substance, if not *verbatim*, that, upon information furnished by Andrew Cleavinger, Joseph Warder and James Duval had, on this 3d day of November, 1865, preached at New Garden meeting house without first having taken the oath of loyalty.

"Upon this charge Charles Perkins was commanded to forthwith arrest the said Joseph Warder and James Duval, and bring them before Hiram Enlow, a Justice of the Peace, to answer the aforesaid charges. And this you shall in no wise omit, &c., &c. Signed, Hiram Enlow, J. P.

"Elder Warder was not present, notwithstanding the aforesaid affidavit. I was taken in custody by the said Charles Perkins, who was deputized for the purpose, Allan Sisk, the legal constable of the township, refusing to serve this process.

"So I was held in custody by Charles Perkins, and that evening taken before his honor, Hiram Enlow, J. P., and there bound in a bond of one thousand dollars to again appear before said Enlow on the 17th inst. John Welton was my security for my appearance. I was then released for the present, and went on to Little Shoal, Clay county, to attend my regular appointments.

"While in the 'Squire's custody, I asked him if he believed in the Christian religion? He said he did, and that he liked to hear the gospel preached. I then asked him if he went to New Garden *to-day* to hear the gospel preached? He made no reply.

"On the 17th of November I again appeared before his honor, Hiram Enlow, J. P. Several neighbors and friends were now present.

"B. J. Waters, the present Radical representative from Ray county, was present, acting as prosecuting attorney. When called up for trial, I asked leave to examine the papers, and found they were not the same papers on which I was arrested, and told them so. Elder Warder's name was not on these papers at all. The 'Squire told me that I must answer to the charges on the papers before me. I told the 'Squire that this was all a new business to me, and I did not know exactly how to proceed. I asked him what provisions the law made for me under these circumstances? He told me I could swear that I could not get justice in his court; and that I could appeal to the Circuit Court. I told him that was the thing exactly. I appealed to the Circuit Court. B. J. Waters then asked him for what amount he should take the bond. I replied to him, 'Sir, remember you are not bonding a felon.' The 'Squire said, fill the bond for two thousand dollars. John Cleavinger and John Welton entered as bondsmen for my appearance at the next Circuit Court, the first Monday in March following, where I again appeared.

"At Court I met Elder Isaac Odell and Allan Sisk,

regular Baptist ministers; Rev. Samuel Alexander, D. M. Proctor and Dr. Moses F. Rainwater, Methodist ministers, and Rev. Hardy Holman, Kellyite Methodist —all charged with violating the law, because we could not, and would not, allow them to be conscience keepers for us, in taking an oath that made us bow to their god. By so doing we would acknowledge that men have rights over their fellow-men to make them worship God after a prescribed form of law. We read that 'God is a Spirit; and they that worship him must worship him in spirit and in truth.'—John iv. 24.

"After the convention oath came in force, prohibiting ministers from solemnizing marriages, I acknowledged their right to prohibit in this case; so I did not, while the law was in force, attempt to marry any one. But preaching the gospel to sinners was another thing. Christ said, 'My kingdom is not of this world;' therefore men are not authorized to make laws to govern his kingdom. Christ has given us all necessary laws to govern his kingdom. Let all his followers obey them.

"At the March term of the Court we had no trial, but were all severally bound again to appear at the next term of the Court; Jacob Seek vouching for me in this case in the sum of *four hundred* dollars. Judge Walter King presiding.

"At that March Court two indictments were found against me for preaching the gospel without first taking the oath of loyalty. Simon E. Odell was summoned before the following grand jury and gave information, viz.: George W. Sargeant, foreman, George W. Foster, John Bogart, H. E. Owens, James T. Lamar, David Conner, Charles B. Bacon, Holland Vanderpool, Jeremiah Campbell, Wm. Vanbebber, James Hughes, Joseph Gossage, Daniel Cramer, Edwin Odell, Sam'l Clevinger, John Query, Daniel Parker and Isaiah Mansur.

"I will now relate another case that came under my notice.

"About the first of February, 1866, Aaron Cleavinger gave information to Elisha Riggs, Esq., that Elder Isaac Odell had preached without first having taken the oath of loyalty. About the same time Aaron Cleavinger gave information to Elisha Riggs, Esq., that Allan Sisk had also violated the law by 'performing the functions' of a minister in like manner. Wherefore, the said Elisha Riggs, Justice of the Peace, did authorize and require one Charles Perkins to arrest the said Isaac Odell and Allan Sisk, and bring them before him, the said Elisha Riggs, J. P., which he did about the 11th or 12th of February; and because they refused to give bail in the case, did actually send them to Richmond and put them in the county jail.

"Friends interfered, and Judge Walter King granted a *habeas corpus*, and had them brought before him in Judge Bannister's office. Allan Sisk was now bound in the sum of two thousand dollars to appear at the next Circuit Court; Lawson Sisk, John Seek and Simon E. Odell, securities. Elder Isaac Odell was bound in the sum of two thousand dollars to appear at the next Circuit Court; Lawson Sisk, John Seek and S. E. Odell, securities.

"These bonds and fetters, and this species of tyranny and persecution, did not yet satisfy the enemies of the cross of Christ; their malicious hatred and fiendish propensities were not yet satisfied; they must show the spirit of their master yet a little farther—'Ye are of your father the devil, and the lust of your father ye will do.—John viii. 44. So about the last of May or the first of June, 1866, Nathan W. Perkins informed Elisha Riggs, J. P., that James Duval had again, at some place, or at some time (for the information did not state when nor where the misdemeanor was done), violate the law by preaching without first having taken the oath of loyalty.

"Near about the same time, Alfred Nelson informed Elisha Riggs, J. P., that Elder Isaac Odell had violated the law by preaching without first having taken the oath of loyalty. But he, too, like Nathan W. Perkins, failed to set forth the time or place.

"The warrants to arrest and bring before him or some *other* justice of the peace the said Duval and Odell were placed in Constable Sisk's hands to execute, so he deputized Joshua Smart to execute them. Deputy Smart arrested Elder Odell, and came to my house June 12th and arrested me in like manner, and took us to Richmond, before D. H. Quesenberry, J. P. Here we were, like criminals, arraigned in open court to answer the charge—*for preaching*.

Mr. E. F. Estebb, Prosecuting Attorney, appeared against us. Our mutual friends, Hon. G. W. Dunn and C. F. Garner, Esq., appeared in our behalf before the court without charge. We had quite a contest over the case. Several speeches for and against were made, but as the charges were not very criminal and the information very indefinite upon the allegation—a poor thing at best—the prosecuting attorney failed to convict us, and the unfortunate informers had the costs to pay.

"After the decision of the 'Cummings case we were all discharged from custody, and are still engaged in trying to preach Christ—the Way, the Truth, the Life—to sinners. 'But if our gospel be hid, it is hid to them that are lost.'

"Only think of the age of the world in which we live, with all the teaching and preaching, and laws to restrain men from doing violence and wrong to their fellow men. Yet if men are so wicked and demoralized, and are living in our midst, is it not right and just to hold them to strict responsibility for what they have done? 'Let us not be weary in well doing, for in due season we shall reap if we faint not.'

"Before I close I will mention one other case that took place under these stringent laws of the State that required ministers of the gospel to take a prescribed conventional oath, or they could not perform their ministerial functions without laying themselves liable to law.

"In the county of Ray there is a regular Baptist Church called New Garden. This Church had erected a comfortable building for a place of worship. There were, and had been for some time, political differences of opinion among the brethren, and finally, in the summer of 1866, the Radical or law-abiding party, as they styled themselves, arraigned their pastor, Elder Isaac Odell, a man of exemplary Christian character, as they themselves then admitted, before the Church for 'violating the new Constitution.' Elder Odell denied the charge. This was at their June meeting for business. The case was now brought before the Church, Judge Joseph Thorp, Moderator. The case was argued before the Church for some time, both for and against the charge, and finally the Moderator put the question to the Church, and the Church sustained their pastor.

"The Church considered the question now settled and were remiss in prompt attention at the next monthly meeting; so those who brought the charge took advantage of the absentees and again raised the question, and, having the majority then present, moved to *rescind* what was done at the last Church meeting.

"The Church assumed the right and jurisdiction of a court, and sat in the capacity of a jury, and found, in their way of deciding things, Elder Odell *guilty* of the charge, and excluded him from their pulpit.

"The opposite party, or those who remained with the Association, tried to convince the complainers that this was a political offense, and that they should have nothing to do with it until the courts of the State, which alone had jurisdiction of the case, had convicted Elder Odell of a misdemeanor, and then it would be time enough for them to take cognizance of the case.

"These complainers admitted to the Church while the case was pending that they had no charges whatever against Elder Odell; that his practice was good as a Christian, his faith correct, he observed their Church rules properly, but he must obey the laws of his State.

"Elder Odell, with others, as I have already stated, was at that time, upon information furnished, under an indictment by the grand jury for preaching without first taking the oath prescribed. But these Radical friends would not wait until a conviction was had in open court, but must now execute judgment, which they did, with the following consequences:

"The Church now divided upon the propriety and legality of such procedure, and each party appealed to the Association by sending letters and messengers. The party that remained with the Association sent up the following question: 'Is it wise or scriptural to arraign a brother and exercise Church discipline when the offense is purely political?' To which the Association answered negatively—'neither wise nor scriptural.' So the Radical party was now dropped from the fellowship of the Church and the Association. The former clerk went with the Radicals and kept, by force, the Church records.

"The Radicals locked the church doors and still keep it, and unkindly refuse to allow their former brethren a day in the house, although the latter had paid most in building the house. Each party remains separate and has no Christian fellowship or intercourse whatever, religiously, with each other.

"The indictment against Elder Odell in court failed, consequently the charge was false; and now who is to acknowledge the wrong done in the case?

"I have here stated that this division was political, and not religious, for there was no question concerning the faith ever involved in the controversy. As proof in the case, every Radical member that cried, 'obey the law,' left the Church proper and went with the disaffected ones. Every Conservative member remained with the Church. It is, therefore, apparent to all that this division was on a political question—a thing heretofore not known in our Churches.

"The Regular Baptists have never introduced in their Churches any political tests as terms of membership or Christian communion. Not so with some who have separated from us; 'they went out from us because they were not of us; for if they had been of us they would, no doubt, have continued with us; but they went out that they might be made manifest that they were not all of us.' 1 John ii. 19.

"We allow our brethren to hold whatever political opinions they may think are right and just, provided they do not introduce them into the Church, to the annoyance and disturbance of the peace and fellowship of the brethren. We have always, as a religious body of people, carefully avoided the mixing of Church and State together in our religious devotions.

"Christ says, 'My kingdom is not of this world.' We consider that Christ has given us in his Word a sufficient code of laws to govern us here in this world: 'If ye love me keep my commandments.' And whensoever we disregard the written Word of God and attempt to supply *supposed* deficiencies by the legislation of men, we greatly err to our own hurt. This is a reflection upon the wisdom of God and denies the doctrine of inspiration; from which may God deliver his people.

"I have written these sketches mostly from memory, but I know in the main they are true, and submit them to your discretion and farther disposal, hoping that whatever may be done may tend to the glory of God and the instruction of his people in establishing them in the truth.

"Respectfully, I hope, your brother in gospel bonds for the truth's sake, JAMES DUVAL."

CHAPTER XVIII.

WOOLDRIDGE, MARQUIS, PUGH AND BREEDING.

Exceptional Distinction—*Revs. J. B. H. Wooldrige, D. J. Marquis* and *Geo. W. Johnson* Arrested, Abused and Imprisoned for Associating Together—*Rev. M. M. Pugh* Arrested and Imprisoned—Arrested Three Times—Indicted—Northern Methodists Implicated in his Persecutions—Flags over Pulpits by Military Orders—Efforts to Force the Consciences of Ministers—A Caustic Note—"Der Union Vlag on Der Secesh Church"—A Minister's Wife Ordered to Make a Shroud for a Dead Union Soldier—Keen Retort—An Old Minister in a Rebel Camp—How he "Went Dead" and "Saved his Bacon" and Potatoes—*Rev. J. M. Breeding*—Armed Men Visit him at Midnight—Order him to Leave the Country in Six Days because he was a Southern Methodist Preacher—Arrested at Church by Lieutenant Combs—A Parley—Men said if They were not Permitted to Shoot They would Egg Him—Waylaid by Soldiers to Assassinate Him—Providential Escape—Waylaid the Second Time, and Providential Escape—Move to Macon County—Further Troubles—Reflections.

If to suffer for righteousness' sake entitles men to exclusive privileges in the kingdom of heaven, the ministers of Missouri will have pre-eminence among those who suffer for the word of God and the testimony of Jesus. Exceptional honors among the sanctified will distinguish many of the humblest ministers of this State. And if the instigators of persecution are to be put in the category of the excluded, some of the most notorious ministers of the State will, in the final award, be rejected, disowned and dishonored.

Rev. Geo. W. Johnson, Rev. D. J. Marquis and Rev. J. B. H. Wooldridge.

Among the first to feel the crushing power of the persecutor were Revs. D. J. Marquis and J. B. H.

Wooldridge, of the St. Louis Conference, M. E. Church, South, and Rev. George W. Johnson, of the Baptist Church.

The first two have for many years been zealous, earnest and successful itinerant ministers, and Mr. Johnson is a Baptist minister of high standing and unblemished character, and Principal of the Tipton High School.

In 1861, soon after the occupation of Jefferson City by the Federal forces, these three men were arrested by Col. Boernstein's order, or by his officers, at Tipton, in Moniteau county, taken to Jefferson City, abused by the officers, kept in the dungeon under the State Capitol over twenty-four hours without a mouthful of food, taken out, abused, put on board a steamer and sent up to Boonville. They fell into the hands of Col. Stevenson, who had them closely guarded in the fair grounds for ten days, and then sent to St. Louis. Here they were kept for two days in the guard-house, in the old arsenal, and then released unconditionally, by order of Major-General Fremont.

The only charge against Marquis was that he was a minister of the Southern Methodist Church, and kept company with Wooldridge. They charged Wooldridge with keeping company with Southern Methodist Ministers who were known to be disloyal; and Johnson had associated with Marquis and Wooldridge, and had even aided them in a protracted meeting.

The old adage, that "evil communications corrupt good manners," is scarcely a criminal law, and the associations of ministers of the gospel in their legitimate work can hardly be considered a criminal offense involving the safety of the Federal Government. And yet these humble ministers were subjected to arrest, insult, imprisonment, hunger, abuse and various tortures of mind and body, for no other reason than their ecclesiastical connection and ministerial association.

While Mr. Marquis was attending the Warrensburg-Arrow Rock-Waverly Conference, in the fall of 1861, his home was taken and used for a hospital, and literally stripped of everything of any value—even the clothing of himself and family—leaving not a single change of raiment for any of them. A suit of thin summer cloth which Mr. Marquis had on at the time was everything he had to wear, and with which to start again in life. This act of plunder and robbery was done by General Fremont's men, upon the charge that Marquis was a Southern Methodist minister and had no rights.

Believing that his life was not safe in Moniteau, he removed to Jefferson county, where he was still subject to persecution during the war, and where he had the honor of an indictment from the grand jury, after the war closed, for preaching the gospel without taking the oath prescribed by the new Constitution of the State.

Rev. M. M. Pugh.

The St. Louis Conference of the M. E. Church, South, has few better men than the Rev. M. M. Pugh, at this time (1869) Presiding Elder of the Boonville district. He is a faithful, zealous, able minister of the gospel, and well reported of in all the Churches for his amiable spirit, ardent zeal, self-denying consecration to his work, and successful labors in the pulpit.

In 1861 the Conference appointed him to Kansas City station. The war had then been raging fiercely along the Missouri-Kansas border for several months, and the ministers of the M. E. Church, South, had come in for a large share of persecution, and a number of them had already fled for safety. Mr. Pugh was placed by this appointment in the lines of some of the meanest men who wore the Federal uniform during the war. He had but a few years before left the Northern Methodist Church for the Southern, and he appreciated fully the delicacy of the situation and the danger of the surroundings. He was prudent, cautious and circumspect in the pulpit and out of it; gave utterance to no sentiment that would afford even a pretext for his arrest and punishment. He could not approve of the outrages committed in the name of the Union on the innocent and defenseless, but kept his disapprobation to himself. His extreme caution, however, did not long exempt him from annoyance and trouble. He modestly writes:

"I was first arrested in Kansas City, in the latter part of 1861, at the instance of a Northern Methodist, and confined in Fort Union for a short time, perhaps not more than one hour, then released on parole and granted city limits.

"In the summer of 1862 I was greatly annoyed and frequently threatened by a Northern Methodist preacher who had command of a company in Kansas City at that time.

"To avoid the relentless opposition and persecution of this man, I left home two or three weeks. He said his Church was largely represented in the Federal army, and to a considerable extent influenced the U. S. forces, and that Southern Methodist preachers should be hunted and punished. I mention this to show that we were not persecuted for evil-doing, but simply because we were Southern Methodists. This, in their eyes, was a crime of the greatest magnitude.

"In the fall of 1862 I was ordered to pray for the President of the United States by name, for the U. S. Congress, and for the success of the Union army, 'so-called.' This I refused to do; and said, among other things, that no man, or class of men, should dictate my prayers.

"In the winter of 1863 I was assessed as a Southern sympathizer. I refused to pay the unjust assessment. For this refusal I was arrested and put in the guard-house in Kansas City. Here I was kept in close confinement about twenty-four hours, when, in company with nine others imprisoned for the same offense, I was sent to Independence in a greasy wagon guarded by twenty men and lodged in an exceedingly filthy prison. Col. W. R. Penick, then in command, refused to let us have our meals from the hotel or from our friends. We were kept in this filthy place about twenty-four hours, when we were unconditionally released by order of Governor Gamble.

"Believing that I could do no good, opposed as we were, and that cruel men were seeking my life, I left Kansas City in April, 1863. Soon after I left the Northern Methodists took possession of our church.

"In March, 1866, I was indicted in Independence for preaching without taking the oath of the new Constitution.

"I was arrested by the Deputy Sheriff, a man who before the war would not have been thought of in connection with that office. I gave bond for my appearance at the next term of the court. W. L. Bone and J. B. Henry, Esqs., went on my bond. Judge Tutt was on the bench, and Mr. —— Johnson, State's Attorney.

"In the fall I appeared in court, when the case was continued. The next spring, the U. S. Supreme Court having decided the so-called 'test oath' unconstitutional my case was dismissed.

"I was an ordained Elder in the Church, and had been preaching ten years when I went to Kansas City."

Before Mr. Pugh left Kansas City he was not only informed that his life was in danger, but the Northern Methodist preacher, of whom he speaks, informed him and others that such was the feeling of his men toward Mr. Pugh that he feared assassination every night—that Mr. Pugh could not walk the streets any time, day or night, in safety.

It was no uncommon thing for military commanders to send special orders to ministers of the Southern Methodist Church, ordering prayers for specific persons or things, and requiring flags to be displayed from the pulpit or church door.

It will answer the purposes of history merely to sample these orders. Petty tyranny no where surpasses it:

"[Special Orders, No. 10.]

"HEADQUARTERS, WESTPORT, MO.,
"January 31, 1863.

"I. It being proper that in all our supplications for the blessings of Deity the condition of our beloved but distracted country should not be overlooked; therefore, it is ordered—to the end that should any prove forgetful they may be reminded that they have a government to pray for—that during the quarterly meeting of the Methodist Episcopal Church, South, now in session in this city, the Stars and Stripes be conspicuously displayed in front of the pulpit of the church where said meeting is held.

"II. The pastor of said church will cause this order to be published from the pulpit of his church.

"By order of W. C. Ransom, Major, commanding U. S. forces at Westport, Mo."

Rev. John A. Murphy was pastor, and Messrs. H. Houck and A. P. Warfield "executed the order to save the property."

The following note explains the following order. The order gave rise to many reflections, doubtless, that are not in the note. The note is given *verbatim:*

"BRO. P.—On the opposite page you will observe an item of history which *may* be worthy a place in your forthcoming book. The *occasion* of this order was the anniversary of the 'Camp Jackson Victory,' which was celebrated *hugely* by the St. Charles 'Loilists,' especially by the *Teutonic* portion of them.

"Ours was the only Church in the city honored (?) by Colonel Emmons with an official order to display the National colors. The order was obeyed, of course; and on the return of our '*Super Stupid Union Savers*' from their day of bacchanalian revelry in the suburbs of the city, our church was again honored (?) by a *halt* in front of it, and 'three cheers for *der yunion* flag on der *Secesh Church.*'

"Col. Emmons and his 'Home Guards' ought to be immortalized. Could you not help it on? They will certainly *live* while St. Charles Methodism can *remember*

"Truly, ——— ———."

The order is as follows:

"HEADQUARTERS, ST. CHARLES, MO.,
"May 9, 1863.

"Messrs. Dennis McDonald, Benjamin R. Shores, Dr. Evans and John S. McDowell, Trustees M. E. Church, South, at St. Charles, Mo., will cause the National Flag to be raised over their church in this city without delay.

"BEN. EMMONS, JR.,
"Colonel and Provost-Marshal."

At Kansas City, St. Joseph, Jefferson City and many other places similar orders were issued, and in some instances orders were sent up to the pulpit commanding special and public prayers to be offered for specific persons and things, either to test the loyalty of ministers, or, more truthfully, to trifle with the consciences of men in the solemn matters of divine worship.

In some instances military commanders would order the strongest Southern sympathizers to make Union flags, or shrouds for dead Union soldiers. Not a few amusing incidents occurred from this cause, only one of which must suffice now, as it occurred with a minister's wife, and is a fine specimen of ready retort and genuine wit upon a solemn subject.

In the winter of 1862 Major Oliver, in command of about four companies of U. S. troops, entered Independence, Mo., and established his winter quarters in the Female College buildings. When his command had approached within two miles of the city they were fired on from the brush by Quantrell's "bushwhackers." One man was killed and several severely wounded.

Major Oliver was much exasperated, and made many threats that were never carried into execution. Amongst other things he made inquiry for the strongest female secessionist, or as he termed it, "she-rebel," in the city, vowing that he would order her to make a shroud for the dead soldier. Several ladies were mentioned whose sympathies with the South were very strong, and, amongst the number, Mrs. Wallace, the wife of the Rev. T. Wallace, a Southern Methodist preacher. The fact that she was a minister's wife gave her Southern proclivities pre-eminence in his mind, and he sent his orderly with the goods and about the following message: "Madam, Major Oliver, commanding this post, has learned that you are the strongest secesh woman in this city, and has sent me with these goods and an order that you make forthwith a shroud for a Union soldier killed by the bushwhackers this morning. He hopes that you will in this way compensate, in part, for the work of your bushwhacker friends."

This last sentence was uttered in a tone and with an emphasis that did not permit her to doubt its import. She instantly and politely replied:

"Present my respects to Major Oliver, and tell him the shroud will be ready in two hours; and say to him that it would afford me the greatest pleasure to make shrouds for his whole command."

It is needless to say that Mrs. Wallace was not troubled with any more shroud making for Maj. Oliver's command.

During this same winter, and while Major Oliver was in command at Independence, in the many skirmishes and fights between the Federal soldiers and "Quantrell's bushwhackers," as they were called, many rich incidents occurred, amongst them the following, in which one of the oldest ministers in the State was the hero:

Rev. S. S. Colburn, for many long years a traveling preacher in the itinerant ranks of the M. E. Church, South, and then living in Cass county, in a superannuated condition, had been so much annoyed, so often robbed, and his life so repeatedly threatened, that he concluded to leave his home and place himself under the protection of friendly bayonets as his only means of safety. He happened one day upon the camp of Quantrell and his men, some of whom he knew very well as his "neighbor boys." They prevailed on him to remain with them a few days and they would protect him. He was too old to bear arms and do the kind of fighting they had to do, but he could keep camp for them and stay with his old friends sometimes at night. They offered the best they had, with their most vigilant protection, which the old man concluded to accept for a few days.

He had not been long with them when their supplies were about to give out, and a consultation was had as to the best method of replenishing the stock. It was soon agreed that Mr. Colburn should go to the house of an old friend not far off, stay all night, and bring in a sack of potatoes the next morning. With this intent he left the camp late in the evening, and soon found himself in the comfortable home of his friend, and in the most agreeable family intercourse around a cheerful fire. Old times were talked over and present events canvassed till a late hour, when the "family Bible," the worship, the good night and the downy bed closed the scene. A refreshing sleep brought the old man to an early start, and the friendship of other years filled his sack with fine potatoes; and, as the sun arose upon the world, he hailed the smoke of the early camp fire, and pressed on toward his hungry protectors.

Just at daylight the camp had been surprised and attacked by a squad of Federal soldiers. The rebels fled in confusion, leaving the camp in possession of the enemy, while they formed in the adjacent brush and prepared to re-take the camp. Just as Mr. Colburn rode into camp, all ignorant of what had occurred, Quantrell opened fire on the enemy, which was promptly returned. The preacher comprehended the situation in an instant, and, wheeling his horse, started to retreat. He was followed by a volley of whistling minnie balls from the new occupants of the camp, and fell from his horse instantly, by his sack of potatoes, and "went dead." The rebels re-took their camp, and in the precipitate retreat of the enemy they rode over the sack of potatoes and the body of the preacher, the horses every time clearing both at a bound. When the preacher was assured of safety, he got up, shouldered his potatoes and walked into camp with a broad smile on his face, to the great joy of his friends. By a timely *ruse* he saved both his bacon and potatoes.

Rev. J. M. Breeding.

The following account of the persecution of this excellent and faithful local preacher of the M. E. Church, South, is quite an abridgement of the statement furnished, but is amply sufficient to show that very few men in these perilous times suffered more, and escaped more frequently, as "with the skin of his teeth." How wonderful that special Providence which so often interposes to save the lives of his chosen servants!

In March, 1863, Mr. Breeding was residing on Barker's creek, in Henry county, Mo. His wife was very ill—not able to raise her head from her pillow. When they were alone, and at midnight, three armed men opened the yard gate, rode rapidly up to the house, and called for Mr. B. to come out. This he declined to do, telling them that he could hear what they had to say where he was. He saw from the door, which he held ajar, that they held their pistols well in hand, as if awaiting an object to shoot. They ordered him to come out a second time, and in no genteel language. He refused, saying to them that if they would come to see him in the day time he would see and talk with them like neighbors.

They asked him if he was armed. He told them that he was a civil man, and had some plows with which he expected to cultivate the ground in the summer; and did not let them know that he was wholly unarmed. They asked his politics, and were informed that he never meddled with the politics of the country; that his only platform was "Repentance toward God, and faith in the Lord Jesus Christ."

"You are a preacher, then?"

"Yes, I try to preach sometimes."

"A Southern Methodist preacher?"

"Yes, I belong to the Methodist Episcopal Church, South?"

"Well, that is just what we have understood, and we don't intend to let any such man live in this country. We have come with authority to order you to leave in six days, and if you are here at the expiration of that time it will not be well with you. We want to know whether you intend to leave or not."

Mr. B. asked for their authority, which they declined to give; whereupon he told them as he had not meddled in any way with their political strife he did not think any sane officer would send them at such a time on such business. They remarked that he could either obey or risk the consequences, and turned and rode off.

The excitement and alarm of this midnight interview proved well nigh fatal to his wife. As soon as they were gone, and he could renew his attentions to his wife, he thought that she was already passing down into the shadow of death. The anxiety and agony of the remaining part of that dreadful night no tongue can tell, no pen describe. About daylight she began to revive, and then to rest. On his knees, at her bedside, he determined that he would not leave her, though they should kill him.

A few days after this occurrence, Mr. B. learned from the nearest military post, through a friend, that no such order had been issued; but that the commander of the post, Captain Gallihar, would not be responsible for what his men did from under his eye.

During the following summer there were very few nights when one or more of these lawless men was not seen prowling about the premises and keeping the preacher in constant dread of arson or assassination. He had no peace and felt no security.

They, doubtless, meditated midnight mischief, but had not the courage to attempt it. They changed their plans, and began to report to the military officers various things on Mr. Breeding, to influence them to interfere for them and have him put out of the way.

In July his appointment in Calhoun was attended one Sabbath by a Lieut. Combs, with his company of men, whom he stationed at convenient places about the church and along the road near the church, as though they expected to encounter a desperate enemy.

As he approached the church and began to comprehend the situation, he discovered what he afterward learned were signals. When these signals were made the whole force moved out to the road and advanced rapidly toward the preacher; he was halted and his name demanded.

"You pray for 'Bushwhackers,' I learn," said the officer.

"No more than for other sinners," the preacher answered.

"But," said the officer, "some of the boys tell me they have heard you pray for the success of Bushwhackers. They say they have known you long, and that you are an original secessionist; that you have always believed in secession," &c.

The preacher appealed to those who had known him the longest, if they ever heard him utter disloyal sentiments or knew him to attend a political meeting of any kind. He was no political partisan, and never had been. They finally told him that he was a Southern Methodist preacher and that was enough, as they were all rebels.

While this conversation was going on and the most of the company were in disorder, a squad of men were drawn up in line in front of the preacher with their guns ready for use. Lieut. Combs stepped up in front of these men, when the conversation closed with the preacher, and talked to them for some time in a subdued tone of voice. At the close of the interview one of the men said, in a low voice: "Well, if you will not let us shoot him, we will egg him," and started off to a barn near by from which he soon returned with his hands full of eggs. The officer would not let him use the eggs, and after some further conversation he dismissed the preacher and took his company back to headquarters.

A few days after this Mr. Breeding had occasion to go to Windsor for medicine for his afflicted wife. There he again met these Calhoun soldiers. They were very annoying and insulting. A mounted squad of them started off before Mr. B. was ready and took the road leading to his house. When the preacher started home and had reached the forks of the road, he was minded to take the plainest and best road, but his horse pulled so obstinately for the other that he finally yielded and reached his home in safety. The next day a friend came to see if he was safe, and informed him that the squad of soldiers that left Windsor before him, waylaid the road to assassinate him. What a providential deliverance!

The next Sabbath Mr. Breeding had a regular appointment to preach at Windsor. With the Sabbath morning came a foraging party to his house demanding breakfast. They stayed and detained the preacher until it was too late to reach his appointment, and he had to remain at home. This detention saved him further trouble, and probably his life. He afterward learned that a band of twenty men were all that morning on the road that he was expected to pass. When it became so late that they supposed he had gone by some other way, they went to the church, surrounded it and entered, but to discover again their disappointment. The preacher was nowhere to be found; and in consultation some wanted to go immediately to his house and inflict summary punishment, but other counsels prevailed, and they determined to try him again the next Sabbath at his appointment at Moffat's School house.

The Sabbath came, and with its earliest rays came a messenger from a Mr. Owen, a Baptist friend, requesting Mr. Breeding to come to his house immediately as his son was at the point of death. Mr. B. went without delay several miles in a direction from the church. After detaining him as long as he could, Mr. Owen informed him of a trap set for him that day, and that he must remain at his house all day. The preacher was not aware of any evil designs, and only yielded to much earnest solicitation to keep out of harm's way.

After having so often and so narrowly escaped, Mr. Breeding thought it best to seek greater safety elsewhere. Accordingly he disposed of his effects, packed up and journeyed to Macon county, in North Missouri, and settled down near the old Hebron Church. This move was attended with much privation, suffering, danger and pecuniary loss. He found at his new home a faithful little band of men and women who met every Sabbath where prayer was wont to be made. To these he gladly joined himself.

By this time religious privileges were few and religious liberty greatly abridged by the operation of the "new Constitution." Ministers were afraid to preach, and the membership discouraged and depressed. The party in power were very vigilant in hunting out and dragging before the civil courts all non-juring ministers.

Mr. Breeding could not take the oath, and he contented himself for some time with an occasional exhortation to the faithful few who still kept the altar fires burning in a quiet way.

The meetings for prayer began to attract the attention of those in authority. They concluded that Mr. B. must be preaching, as the meetings were so regular and so well attended. The super-loyalists determined if such was the case they would take the law into their own hands and see what virtue there was in powder and ball.

The next Sabbath found eight armed men on the front seat to enforce the authority of the new Constitution. There appeared an equal number of orderly citizens prepared to protect the peaceful worship of the congregation. For a time matters wore quite a menacing aspect.

The usual prayer meeting exercises were had, and Mr. Breeding closed up with a warm and an earnest exhortation. The services were somewhat abbreviated, that the unfriendly parties might the sooner be separated.

The next Sabbath the same armed super-loyalists were present, but the friends of peace and order were absent. The preacher had great liberty in the service, and felt in no way intimidated by the presence of armed men on the front bench. During his earnest exhortation, founded upon a favorite text, the men became somewhat excited, but they had either not chosen a leader or the leader showed the white feather. They kept calling one upon the other to start—"You start, and I will follow." "No, you start, and I will follow," were expressions, though whispered, that could be distinctly heard by those near them. Such things did not deter the preacher. They could not browbeat him down, and finally, in their shame, they vented their *pique* on a luckless dog that lay stretched out on the floor near them.

After this frutless attempt to frighten these faithful and devout men and women, and to get some pretext for adding another name to the list of Missouri Martyrs, they surceased their persecutions, modified their prejudices, toned down their spirit, and from enemies some of them have become the fast friends and even the zealous converts of the sect that was "everywhere spoken against."

Such scenes of suffering, trial and danger, *simply* because the victim was a minister of the gospel, recalls the persecutions of other times, and re-enacts a history which we had vainly hoped would not darken the annals of the nineteenth century.

While the details of these dark scenes are stripped of all extra coloring that the naked facts may appear, the ever active imagination will, despite our soberest efforts, supply the want, and memory will be busy with the history of other times and other countries until Missouri is forgotten; the finest model of human government ever devised by man crumbles into dust; the much vaunted religious liberty expires upon its own desecrated altars; the light of a boasted civilization fades into darkness; the noblest and freest institutions go down in hopeless barbarism; a pure, non-political Christianity, with a non-juring ministry, are called upon to reproduce the agony of the Garden and the tragedy of Calvary without repeating the work and grace of atonement, and in memory we are living over the times of Charles the Fifth, Montmorenci and the Duke of Alva. The spirits of the French Huguenots, the Waldenses, Vaudois Martyrs and Bohemian Protestants have been reproduced in the ministry of Missouri. "Why do the heathen rage and the people imagine a vain thing? The kings of the earth set themselves, and the rulers take counsel together against the Lord and against his anointed, saying, 'Let us break their bands asunder and cast away their cords from us.'"

CHAPTER XIX.

REVS. R. N. T. HOLLIDAY AND GREEN WOODS.

Rev. R. N. T. Holliday—Statement of his Persecutions Furnished by Dr. Richmond, a Federal Officer—Could not War upon the Institutions of Heaven—Mr. Holliday aloof from Politics—Misconstrued—General W. P. Hall and his Militia Proclamation—General Hall and Mr. Holliday—General Bassett—Rev. Wm. Toole, Provost Marshal, and Mr. Holliday—A Renegade—Platte City Burned by Jennison and Mr. H. Ordered to be Shot on Sight—He Escapes—Is Arrested in Clinton County—Again Ordered to be Shot—Escapes to Illinois—Returns in 1865—Goes to Shelbyville and is Indicted for Preaching Without Taking the Oath—Crimes of the War—Common Law Maxim Reversed—Prominent Ministers of the M. E. Church, South, Assumed to be Guilty of Treason—Murder of *Rev. Green Woods*—Birth, Early Ministry and General Character—Gives up his District—Retires to his Farm in Dent County—Affecting Account of his Murder given by his Daughter—Extract from a Letter Written by his Wife—Details Published in the St. Louis *Advocate* of June 13, 1866—Reflections.

Rev. R. N. T. Holliday.

The following account of the persecutions of this good and useful minister of the gospel is furnished by Dr. Oregon Richmond, "who was an officer in the Federal army, and always anxious for the triumph of the Union forces." Upon that ground he properly claims the absence of undue bias from his statement. The whole case is so fully and minutely reported that it needs neither introduction nor comment to aid in a due appreciation of the facts:

"Canton, Mo., March 8, 1869.

"At the request of Rev. R. N. T. Holliday, I have consented to put together and transmit the somewhat remarkable events of that period of his life connected with the late war troubles. This request is the result of an antipathy on his part to acting the part of a self-eulogist. In my judgment no greater eulogy can be written of a minister of the gospel than that of a calm, unvarnished recital of the persecution to which that class of our citizens was subjected during the prevalence of, and immediately subsequent to, the late war.

"And perhaps, after all, it is but simple justice that these facts should be written by one who was an officer in the Federal army, and always anxious for the triumph of the Union forces. Though an officer in the Union army, he can thank God that his military life is unstained by a single act of cruelty or persecution; and, above all, is he thankful that he never made use of his military power to war against the institutions of Heaven or the chosen instruments ordained for their establishment amongst men. In other words, he was not attached to a Missouri regiment, is not a son of Missouri, and hence has never been instructed in the mysteries of that department of military tactics that teaches the wonderful doctrine that the truest patriotism consists in the abuse of defenseless women and children, and the subversion of the sublimest precepts of religion by the persecution and murder of its chosen apostles.

"In September, 1860, Rev. R. N. T. Holliday, the subject of this sketch, was appointed by the Missouri Conference of the M. E. Church, South, of which he has long been a member, to Rushville, in Buchanan county, Mo. In the ensuing spring the war commenced, but it was not until May, 1861, that he received the first intimation of the approaching trouble that would draw him into its clutches, and ultimately make him a wanderer and an exile from his chosen field of usefulness.

"About that time a Union meeting was held near Rushville, and addressed by Hon. Willard P. Hall and others from St. Joseph. Mr. Holliday was urged to be present and reply on behalf of the South; this he declined to do. He was not even present at the meeting, believing that ministers of the gospel should keep themselves unspotted from the political strifes of men. Yet his enemies said that he stayed away through personal fear, and he was henceforth the subject of various kinds of annoyances and petty persecutions.

"The Conference of September, 1861, returned Mr. Holliday to Rushville. He was not molested until March, 1862, when Brig.-General W. P. Hall issued a proclamation requiring all men subject to military duty to enroll themselves in the State militia. Mr. Holliday refused to enroll, upon the ground that ministers were exempt from military duty. Gen. Hall sent him word at once, that if he did not enroll he would have him arrested. Mr. Holliday replied that, being exempt from military duty by the laws of the State, he could but consider the demand extra-official, and if an arrest must be the result of non-compliance with an illegal demand, he preferred to be arrested. Upon this General Hall addressed a note to Mr. H. in the politest terms, requesting an interview to arrange the difficulty. Trusting the General's honor, Mr. Holliday complied; but, upon presenting himself at headquarters, the General refused to see him, and ordered him taken to the Provost-Marshal's office for enrollment. Gen. Bassett, the Provost-Marshal, had the entrance to his office securely guarded after Mr. H. was admitted, and informed him that he must enroll under Order 19, as a Union man, and submit to a physical examination, or under Order 24, as a rebel sympathizer, and pay a commutation fee of $30. Finding submission inevitable, or something worse, Mr. H. registered under Order 24, but refused to pay the commutation as an unlawful and an unauthorized exaction, and demanded his exemption papers as a minister of the gospel, at the same time producing his ordination parchments. General Bassett, after some delay, gave him exemption papers, and, after considerable annoyance, he gave him a pass also, which enabled him to travel back and forth and fill his appointments without further molestation than an occasional petty persecution, the instigation of malice, and an occasional threat of being shot.

"During the summer of 1862 Mr. Bassett was superseded in the office of Provost-Marshal by a Mr. W. Tool, who had been up to that period a minister in the M. E. Church, South. He had, however, apostatized, and joined the M. E. Church, North.

"Mr. Bassett's brief apprenticeship in villainy fitted him for, and he was appointed to, a higher office. Mr. Holliday was requested to fill the pulpit made vacant by the military prohibition upon Rev. W. M. Rush, of St. Joseph, and the ladies of the church in which Mr. Rush had been silenced waited on Provost-Marshal Tool and requested permission for Mr. Holliday to fill the silent pulpit. Mr. Tool, who was acting in the interest of the North Methodists, refused to permit Mr. H. to come to St. Joseph to preach the gospel.

"In September, 1862, Mr. Holliday was sent to Platte

City, and there remained unmolested until the following June, when soldiers from Kansas took his horse, which he never saw afterward. He borrowed another, which was also stolen and carried off. He thus lost two horses in as many weeks.

"About the middle of July, 1863, Col. Jennison, of Kansas, went to Platte City and burned the town. His men were ordered to shoot Mr. Holliday down at sight. Knowing the character of Jennison's men, and being apprised of the order by a Union man, Mr. H. made good his escape, leaving his family at Mr. Redman's. On the evening of his flght his house, containing all that he had in the world, except what the family had on, was given to the flames. His family were thus made destitute and reduced to beggary.

"The next day, at 3 P. M., Mr. Holliday was arrested, by order of a Clinton county militia captain, and taken to Plattsburg. He was there subject to some indignities, until Mr. Cockrell informed Captain Irvine, commander of the post, of the facts, who, being a gentleman and a Mason, ordered the instant release of Mr. Holliday.

"The next day Capt. Irvine was killed in an engagement with the rebels. This very much enraged the militia, and an order was issued again to shoot Mr. H. on sight. He again made his escape by flight and concealment. He remained ten days at the residence of Mr. Powell, of Clinton county, but upon hearing of the order to shoot him,he, with two other ministers, Messrs. Tarwater and Jones, took refuge in the woods, and made their way on foot to Osborn, where Mr. Holliday met his family, and all took the train to Quincy, Ill. They remained in Illinois until the war closed, in 1864, doing the best he could as a minister of the gospel. Returning to Missouri in 1865, he met the Conference at Hannibal, and was appointed to the Shelbyville circuit.

"By this time the New Constitution had been declared the fundamental law of the State, and under it all ministers of the gospel were required to take the iron-clad 'test oath' as a qualification for the work of the ministry, or subject themselves to arrest, indictment, fine or imprisonment.

"Actuated by the same motives of conscience that impelled all true ministers of the gospel, he promptly refused to take and subscribe said oath. He was, therefore, arrested and indicted by the grand jury of Shelby county for preaching and teaching as a minister of the gospel without having, under oath, attested his past and present loyalty to the Government of the United States. The said indictment bore the signatures of Wm. M. Boulware, Circuit Attorney, E. S. Holliday, Foreman of Grand Jury, and James Ralph, C. R. Colton and Wm. Colton as witnesses. A copy of the indictment is in Mr. Holliday's possession, to be handed down to his children as a memento of his sufferings and triumphs in the cause of his Master. It will doubtless make their faith doubly strong in the principles of that holy religion for which he endured so much privation, persecution and personal danger.

"Mr. Holliday was subsequently indicted for the same offense, and held in a bond of $500 for appearance at the November term of the Shelby Court. Mr. M. C. Hawkins, a lawyer of Canton, made an able argument on a motion to quash the indictment, which motion was not sustained, and the case was continued to the ensuing May term, when a *nolle pros equi* was entered and Mr. Holliday released.

"The facts above narrated I have received from Mr. Holliday's own lips. He was so reticent of matters concerning himself personally that I can not but regard this as a very meagre epitome of all that he was required to do and to suffer in the performance of the work his Master gave him to do. He evidently is already richly rewarded in the depths of his own consciousness, and justly decided that nothing man may say for him can serve in the smallest degree to increase that reward.

"[Signed] OREGON RICHMOND."

The persecutions in the early part of the war were not without a sharp discrimination in favor of the prominent ministers of the M. E. Church, South. Few were exempt. The exceptional cases were either in the large cities or under the protection of partisan loyalty. For some reason the leading ministers of the Church, South, were looked upon as the very ringleaders of the Southern revolt against the Government. So general was this belief amongst the officers of the Union army, that whoever escaped their surveillance had to prove a negative in the face of the most unwarranted and unfounded presumptions of guilt, supported and flanked by the deepest rooted prejudices and the most blinded passion. Nor is this putting the case too strongly. It is not in excess of the facts.

No matter how guarded, how prudent, how cautious in public or private life, the tongue of the accuser always reached the official ear before the accused was aware of his summons to the official bar.

That good old maxim of the English common law,

that assumed a man to be innocent until he was proven to be guilty, was reversed. Men were assumed to be guilty, and they had to prove their innocence if they could, or suffer the penalty of assumed guilt.

And, indeed, the right of trial was granted to but few. Many, very many, suffered imprisonment and death without ever being so much as informed of the crime for which they suffered.

The day of eternity alone will reveal the nameless crimes which men in authority, and men without authority, committed during the late civil war. May a merciful Providence forever spare the country a repetition of the horrible scenes through which it has so recently passed. These reflections are suggested by the murder of the

Rev. Green Woods.

The subject of this sketch was born in Bellevue, Washington county, Missouri, Feb. 27, 1814, where he grew up on a farm in sight of Caledonia.

He was received on trial in the Missouri Annual Conference M. E. Church in the fall of 1836, when the Conference was held in St. Louis, and was appointed by Bishop Roberts, junior preacher on the Farmington Circuit, with George Smith as his senior.

The next year he was returned by Bishop Soule to Farmigton, with Alvin Baird as his senior.

The next year his name does not appear in the minutes, nor does it appear again until the year 1853, when he rejoined the St. Louis Conference and was appointed by Bishop Andrew to Cape Girardeau and Jackson.

In 1854 he was appointed to Ste. Genevieve Circuit,

and at the Conference of 1855, at Springfield, he was received into full connection, and returned to Ste. Genevieve Circuit, with J. H. Cumming as junior preacher.

It is needless to follow his appointments in the Conference further than to say that everywhere he was well received and always well reported of for good works. He was a diligent and faithful laborer in his Master's vineyard, and few men stood higher in the estimation of the people or was more securely enthroned in their affections. He was a man of unblemished character, unswerving integrity, unwavering fidelity, deep and fervent piety, and of good preaching ability. He was unobtrusive, unostentatious, civil, courteous, gentle and kind to all; had many friends and few enemies—lived for his work, and attended strictly to his own business. The last man who would ever intermeddle with politics or make himself officious or offensive to any man or party of men. He had charity for all, and malice for none. This is written by one who knew him well, and loved him much, and was a member of the same class of undergraduates in the Conference.

When the war broke out Mr. Woods was Presiding Elder on the Greenville District, St. Louis Conference; was extensively known in Southern and Southeastern Missouri, and had been just as extensively useful. But the troubles thickened so fast and the country was so generally disturbed and distracted that with a heavy heart he gave up his regular work on the district and contented himself with such preaching as he could do near his home in Dent county, while he attended to the cultivation of his little farm.

The following account of the events of 1862, furnished

by his eldest daughter, will be read with deep interest, as they culminate in the awful tragedy of his murder:

"In the spring of 1862 the excitement in the country became so intense that my father could no longer travel his district, so he thought he would stay at home and try to make enough to support his family on his farm. As the people in the neighborhood desired him to preach to them, he made an appointment to preach, about three miles from home, the second Sunday in May. He filled this appointment, and announced another at the same place for the second Sunday in June. Before that time arrived he was advised by some of his friends not to go to his appointment, as they believed that he would be taken prisoner, and perhaps killed, that day by the soldiers if he attempted to preach. But he told them that he would go and preach, and if the soldiers wished to arrest him they could do so; that if necessary he could go to jail. He said that he did not believe that they would kill him, as he had not done anything to be killed for.

A man by the name of Silas Hamby, a member of the Methodist Church, North, had said some time before that no Southern Methodist preacher should preach at Mount Pleasant again. But my father thought it was an idle threat, as he had heard of no preacher being killed because he was a preacher.

"When Sunday morning came, father and my sister, younger than myself, went to Mount Pleasant, and he preached to a small congregation—the people being afraid to turn out on account of the soldiers—and returned home the same evening unmolested. The next morning he took my sister—just thirteen—and two little boys he had hired, and went out to a field one mile from home to finish planting corn. While they were at work the mother of the boys came by the field on her way to our house. She saw that they were nearly done, so she thought she would wait till they finished and come along with them. By this means there was one grown person present to witness his arrest. I think it was about the middle of the forenoon of that Monday, June 9, 1862, when sixteen men, armed and uniformed as Federal soldiers, came to our house and surrounded it. They inquired for father. Mother told them that he was not at home, but out in the field (father told her if they came and called for him, to tell them where he was). They made a general search, and then huddled up out in the yard and held a council a few minutes. Five of them were sent to the field, and while they were gone those at the house were stealing everything they could get their hands on that belonged to father, leaving very few things behind.

"When the five soldiers got to the field father was not quite done planting. They rode up and asked if his name was Green Woods; he told them it was. They told him that he was the man they were after, and ordered him to alight over the fence. He asked them if they would not wait until he could finish planting, as he had then but a few short rows; but they told him, with an oath, that they were in a hurry, and kept hurrying him while he was getting his horse ready to start. When they started from the field my sister asked them what they intended to do with father. They told her, with an oath, that it was uncertain where he would get to before he came back. They brought him to the house and allowed him to eat his dinner. But when he went to dress himself, he could not find a change of clothes, as the soldiers had taken all that he had, and would not even give him his pants and hat. They took him about three miles from home, to a man's house by the name of Jones, and pretended to get evidence against him. (This was north-west from where we live). They then took him about three miles from home, to where a man lived named Peter Skiles, who kept a blacksmith's shop. They stopped and staid there awhile, and searched the house, as Skiles was a Southern man. They then took father about half a mile and killed him, and left him lying out in the woods away from the road —no one knew where except those who placed him there. Two guns were heard after the soldiers left Skiles'.

"This was done on Monday, and his body was not found till the next Monday. We did not know that he was killed until his body was found. When found he was lying on his back with his overcoat spread on the ground under him; one arm was stretched out one way, and the other stretched out the other way, his hat drawn down over his face, his coat and vest and left glove lying on the ground near him, his right glove on, his left shirt sleeve torn off, and his left hand off and gone. He seemed to have been dragged some two or three hundred yards before he was shot, as there was but little blood along the trail, and was found as above described near a large tree and among some low bushes.

"We have heard several times that the Northern Methodist presiding elder, by the name of Ing, sent the men to kill my father. I have given you the substance of what we know of father's death.

(Signed) "JOSEPHINE M. A. M. WOODS,
"Eldest Daughter,
"E. A. WOODS, Wife, and
"MARY LOUISA, Daughter of
"Rev. Green Woods."

Mrs. Woods furnishes the following additional particulars:

"While eating his dinner the soldiers asked him if he did not think he ought to have taken the oath—meaning the oath of allegiance which all citizens were required to take. He replied that he would be candid with them, as he tried to be with all men; that it afforded no protection, as only the day before the soldiers had been taking the property and breaking the guns of those who had taken the oath, and he could not see that the oath had profited them any. They hurried him much to finish his dinner. He asked them for his hat, which they refused to give him. He said that he would then wear his old one, and be with his equals—meaning that he was about as near worn out as his hat.

"Thinking that it might have some good effect upon the soldiers, I reminded him, in their presence, that the meal was out, and asked what I must do, now that he was going away. He replied, 'the Lord will provide.' And, so far, it is literally true; the Lord has been merciful to give us our daily bread, as we have never had a single meal without bread.

"When he started he told me to do the best I could, and seemed to have a presentment that he would never return.

"On the way that evening he was stopped at the house of Dr. Boyd. While there he said to Mrs. Boyd, 'Tell Mrs Woods that you saw me here.' Mrs. Boyd also heard him tell the soldiers to hurry up and take him wherever they intended to take him; that they would keep him in the hot sun till he would be down sick. They replied that they had a good doctor. He had been very sick only a short time before. It was his custom to hold family worship night and morning, no matter what else was to do. The last day of his life he read for the morning lesson the thirty-seventh Psalm."

Strenuous efforts have been made to obtain the names of the guilty parties, with but little success. The following statement is the latest and most reliable:

"A man by the name of Dennis was the pilot, and it is said helped do the shooting. A man named Wells was in the company. We can not give the first names of either of these men now, but have the promise of them.

"A young man named Bill Fudge, the son of North Methodists who were once members of the Southern Methodist Church, and another named Harrison Ratliff, it is said, helped commit the murder."

To the question, "What evidence have you that Ing, the North Methodist presiding elder, sent the men to commit the murder?" the following reply was furnished:

"All the evidence we have that Ing sent the men is, that he was their commander at the time; and it has been told, by those who said they saw it, that father's hand was carried to Ing as proof that they had killed him, and that he still had it in his possession a year or two ago.

"Respectfully, JOSIE M. A. M. WOODS."

When Mr. Woods' dead body was found, "his left hand was off and gone." Common rumor in the community, and the statement of several reliable gentlemen —which may hereafter be given—go to confirm this horrible and savage report about the hand.

The following account of the affair was published in the *St. Louis Christian Advocate,* of June 13, 1866, and signed "R.," of Crawford county:

"REV. GREEN WOODS.—*Mr. Editor:* In the letter of your California correspondent, in last week's *Advocate,* the names of several ministers formerly connected with the St. Louis Conference are mentioned with that of the lamented Green Woods, who the writer too truly mentions as having been cruelly murdered in the summer of 1862. And, as the writer of this sketch had known the deceased for many years, and was living in an adjoining county at the time the cruel murder was committed, he may be able to furnish some facts relative thereto that would interest his many friends and acquaintances of by-gone days. He was at the time (1862) living at his home, in Dent county, Mo., on a little farm that he was quietly cultivating with his own hands, and had been guilty of no other offense that that of preaching through the county in which he lived every Sunday, and oftener as he found opportunity. And, at the time he was torn from his weeping wife and little ones, he was at home plowing in his field, when suddenly he was surrounded by men wearing the uniform of soldiers, and hailing from Kansas—regular 'Jaykawkers.' How many broken-hearted wives and mothers, and destitute orphan children, throughout Missouri will have cause to remember these cruel 'Kansas Jayhawkers!' The cruel assassination of loved husbands and fathers; the burnt and blasted homesteads, where lonely chimneys only are left to tell the tale of once happy and contented households now scattered and torn by the ruthless storm of war in the wake of these Kansas desperadoes. Truly the fate of Missouri has been hard; and of many it may be said they are strangers in their own land.

"When informed by them that he must go with them as a prisoner, and probably knowing from the fate of others what he might expect of them, he told them that he had violated no law, that he was a minister of the Methodist Church, South, and that if they intended to kill him, he was not afraid to die. Then taking, as he well believed, a sad and final farewell of his wife and little children, he started with his captors to the town of Salem, as he thought. But, alas! what must have been the agony of the fond wife when she learned, several days afterward, that he had not been taken to Salem at all! Diligent search but confirmed her worst fears. He had been taken about two miles from home by the road side and shot. There the mortal remains of Green Woods were found—a cold and lifeless corpse—with the fatal bullet shot through the head.

"In contemplating such a scene as this, how the heart saddens and sickens to know that humble and devoted ministers of the cross are put to death for no other cause than that of being ministers of the M. E. Church, South. Is it because that Church has been, and still is, in the way of those who profess to have all the piety, loyalty and religion in the land, that its members and ministers are specially denounced, proscribed and persecuted, and are the marks of special vengeance for every gang of raiding soldiers that chance to come into Missouri?

"I am credibly informed that the deceased had never taken any part in the excitement growing out of the war up to that time; that he had never mentioned politics in the pulpit, and had never left home on account of the troubles during all the dark days of '61 and '62.

"Rev. Green Woods was a native of Missouri, and through many portions of Southern and Southeastern Missouri will he be remembered, as his powerful and eloquent voice echoed and died away upon the gently murmuring breezes of his native hills and vales in calling sinners to repentance. But he now sleeps the long sleep of death. That clarion voice is now silent, and will no more be heard on earth proclaiming the good news and glad tidings of salvation which shall be unto all people. But we close, and drop a silent tear to his memory; knowing that He who holdeth the earth in the hollow of his hand, and who numbereth the very hairs of our heads, doeth all things well.

"We have good reason to believe that the religion he so long and faithfully preached to others sustained him in the last trying hour; and in the great day, when all mankind shall stand forth to be judged according to the deeds done in the body, many will rise up and call him blessed. R."

Thus passed away, by the hand of violence, one of the excellent of the earth, "of whom the world was not worthy." A faithful witness for the word of God and the testimony of Jesus, having committed no offense against the laws of God or man, he fell a martyr to the truth; gave his life for a principle and a cause, and offered himself upon the service and sacrifice of his chosen Church, and the faith she vindicates in his death, and ascended the thrones of martyrdom, to await, with the martyrs of all ages, the final and glorious triumph of the Kingdom of Messiah, in whose service he counted not his life dear unto himself. It is a grand thought that Infinite Goodness and Power has ordained that "Christ must reign till he hath put all enemies under his feet." "Then cometh the end." "Even so: come Lord Jesus."

CHAPTER XX.

REVS. A. MONROE, W. M. RUSH, NATHANIEL WOLLARD.

Rev. A. Monroe, the Patriarch of Missouri Methodism—Age, Honor and Sanctity not Exempt from Profanation—Mr. Monroe and his Wife Arrested in Fayette—Mrs. Monroe's Trials and Witty Retorts—How Mr. Monroe Escaped the Bond—Robbed of Everything by Kansas Soldiers in 1864—An Old Man Without his Mittens—A Tower of Strength—"Our Moses"—Calls the Palmyra Convention—***Rev. W. M. Rush***—The Character of Missouri Preachers—A Native Missourian—Settles in Chillicothe—In St. Joseph the First Year of the War—Caution in Public Worship—An Offensive Prayer by Rev. W. C. Toole—General Loan Closes the Church and Deposes Mr. Rush from the Ministry by Military Order—General W. P. Hall vs. Mr. Rush—Hall Publishes a Letter that Denies Mr. Rush Protection, and Exposes him to Assassination—Mr. Rush Returns to Chillicothe—His House a Stable and his Home a Desolation—Bold Attempt to Assassinate him—Correspondence with General Hall—Goes to St. Louis—Masonic Endorsement—In Charge of the Mound Church—Will Hear of Him Again—***Rev. Nathaniel Wollard*** Murdered in Dallas County—Horrible Details—Particulars—Reflections.

Rev. Andrew Monroe.

Even this venerable and honored servant of God—now the Patriarch of Missouri Methodism—was not exempt from trials and troubles during the late war. If a venerable form, erect and majestic; grey locks, long and flowing; lofty mien, benign and saintly; a pure life, long and useful; an honored name, associated with the history of the good and pure in the State; saintly beneficence, sanctified to the highest purposes of the gospel, and a meek and quiet spirit diffused through the toil, and suffering, and labor, and triumphs of half a century in the ministry could disarm malice, awe the passions into reverence, break the force of prejudice and shield the person and property, the home and happiness, the liberty and life from vicious violation and petty profanation, then Andrew Monroe had lived in peace unmolested, and his humble house, a freeman's sacred castle, been secure from the tread of vandalism and the hand of plunder. But no altar was too sacred, no home too pure, no name too greatly reverenced and no life too pure and holy to deter the invader or wither the sacrilegious hand of the spoiler. Meanness was not an incident of the war, and sacrilege was not confined to Mexican guerrillas. Men are naturally mean, and depravity is a fact of human nature. Nor did the war make thieves, and robbers, and murderers, and highwaymen; they were such before, the occasion only was wanting. The sunbeam does not create, it only reveals the motes in the atmosphere. The war furnished the occasion and unveiled the meanness of men; the pure gospel ministry rebuked it, and, naturally enough, provoked its malice and became its victim. Even Andrew Monroe, the noble old Roman, could not escape.

In the winter of 1862 the Rev. A. Monroe was traveling the Fayette Circuit, Missouri Conference M. E. Church, South, and living in the town of Fayette, Howard county. Fayette, like all other towns of importance in the State, was a military post, with one Major Hubbard in command.

One day of that winter Mr. Monroe and his family were surprised by the appearance of a Federal officer and a squad of men entering his humble home, placing him and his wife under arrest, and marching them off to headquarters, for what offense they never knew.

The soldiers had arrested many other ladies and gentlemen at the same time, and they had plenty of company when they reached headquarters, amongst whom was the Rev. Dr. W. H. Anderson, then President of Central College.

When Major Hubbard came in and saw the number of ladies present under arrest he affected surprise, and said that he had not ordered their arrest; that his subalterns had transcended his orders, and at once informed the ladies that they were released, remarking at the same time that when he wished to see them he would not send for them, but do himself the pleasure of calling at their homes. To which Mrs. Monroe promptly replied that she was obliged to him for releasing them so early, but as for seeing him, she had no desire whatever to see him at her house or anywhere else.

Many a true and modest woman had occasion during those troublous times to call upon her ready wit to reply to the various impertinent inquiries and demands of a ruffian soldiery; and while Mrs. Monroe was surprised at her own courage, her indignation was somewhat appeased when she observed the cutting effect of her retort. Not many days afterward she had occasion again for her ready wit and her Christian fortitude and forbearance. Very early in the morning five soldiers called and demanded breakfast. Mr. Monroe was at home, but he soon retreated from the front door and called upon his wife to meet the issue. She had no help, and the idea of cooking for so many, and these, too, whom she believed to be her enemies, and who would not hesitate to do her any injury, was very repulsive. But to get rid of them was a difficult question, as many ladies know. By the time she reached the front door and heard their request her answer was ready. She replied, "My Bible teaches me, 'If thine enemy hunger, feed him; if he thirst, give him drink;' upon these terms and no other you can get breakfast." To her surprise one of them said, "Madam, we will accept breakfast upon those terms, for I profess to be somewhat acquainted with the Bible." She thought they would turn and go away in a rage, but, on the contrary, she had to turn and get breakfast for "her enemies" with the best grace she could.

It turned out that the spokesman was a local preacher in the Northern Methodist Church, and at the table he remarked to Mrs. Monroe that his father was as great a rebel as she was. To which she replied, that it was a thousand pities that he had so far departed from the ways of his father as to be a degenerate son of an honored sire. Whereupon he said, "As a loyal man, I would hate awfully to have to live with such a rebel. Gen. Price could well afford to issue a commission to you, madam."

Not many days after this Mr. Monroe was just ready to mount his horse one morning for a tour of appointments in the country, when a soldier appeared with orders to arrest him and take him to the headquarters of Capt. Hale, then commanding the post. The venerable man of God was then marched up to headquarters at the point of the bayonet and required to take the military oath, (so-called), and give bond, with good security, for his future loyalty to the Government, and for the loyalty and good order of his family, the Captain remarking that "the secesh talk of the women of his family should be stopped." Mr. Monroe replied that he could take the oath if he would then let him go about his Master's work, but as for the bond, he must excuse him, as he did not wish to involve his friends and he had but little property. If it was his little property he was after, he might as well go and take charge of that at once and let him go about his business. The Captain saw the point and told him to take the oath then and "go preach the gospel to every creature."

"In 1864 Mr. Monroe was living on a farm about eight miles from Glasgow, in Howard county, when General Price made his famous raid into Central Missouri, and took Glasgow amongst other places. The day before the battle of Glasgow Mr. Monroe was out in a field on his little farm, and his family all away from home except a servant, when a company of Kansas soldiers passing along the road halted, entered the house and robbed it of everything of value they could find. The house was literally pillaged. Mr. Monroe's watch, a fine cloth coat, several pairs of bed-blankets, quilts, comforts, and, indeed, everything of any value to them. While thus engaged they saw a young man who lived near approaching the house, all unconscious of what was going on. He was arrested and relieved of all his money, $75. One rough-looking Dutch soldier rode out to the field and accosted the venerable man with an imperative demand for his money. When he found that he had but two dollars in the world, he would not take it, but rode back in disgust. A young man—Mr. Monroe's nephew—was met near the house on his uncle's only riding horse, with his only saddle and bridle. The young man was arrested, and the horse and equipments taken to Glasgow and never heard from afterward.

Thus, in one single hour, the venerable servant of God stood alone in his field, stripped of everything he had—horse, watch, clothes, blankets, bedding—everything of value. What must have been the feelings of Mrs. Monroe on returning home, after an absence of just one hour, to find her house plundered by a ruffian soldiery, and her husband beggared. To complete the work, a small squad of soldiers passed along soon afterward, and when they could find nothing else to steal or appropriate, a rough, drunken Dutchman demanded of the old man his woolen mittens, which a lady had but recently given him. He gave them up, and considered himself fortunate to get off so easy.

With such petty annoyances, involving privation and suffering, this faithful minister of the gospel—this pioneer and patriarch of Missouri Methodism—passed through the dark and trying scenes of the late civil war, always hopeful and joyful, and ready to rejoice that he was counted worthy to suffer for a cause of which himself was the finest type, and a principle to maintain which he was willing to go even to prison and to death. To the struggling cause of Christ and his suffering friends he was a tower of strength, to the discomfited and disheartened hosts of the Methodist Israel, he was "our Moses." When "these calamities were overpassed," and the shock of war had expended its fire and force—when the smoke of battle cleared away, and the storm-cloud hung low upon the horizon, he surveyed the field, marked the desolation, measured the extent of the wreck, discovered some remains of Zion's former beauty, while others, with indecent haste, sounded her funeral knell; and his voice, like that of a mighty chieftain, was heard over the prairies, along the railroads and in the cities of Missouri, calling the faithful to duty, and rallying the scattered forces for counsel. Upon his call a few ministers and friends convened in Palmyra, in June, 1865, and decreed the life of the Church, the resuscitation of her vital powers, the recovery of her lost ground, and the rehabilitation of her distinctive institutions and organs. (See the particulars of this Palmyra meeting in its appropriate place.)

REV. W. M. RUSH.

Few men suffered earlier, or more, than the subject of this notice. For many years the name of the Rev. W. M. Rush has been conspicuous on the rolls of Missouri Methodism. Prominent amongst her ablest and truest ministers and foremost in her aggressive evangelism, he has stood through many years of her history. Identified with her early struggles and a faithful laborer upon her broad foundations, he has grown with her growth and strengthened with her strength, until his life and her history are one. Few men have been more conspicuous in her councils or more distinguished in her fields of labor and conflict. The class-mate of Marvin, the senior and compeer of Caples, the companion of Monroe, and Jordan, and Smith, and Eads, and Johnson, and Redman, and the noble band of Methodist pioneers and patriots, his name will adorn the early annals of the Church, as it will illustrate her later persecutions.

Mr. Rush does not care to conceal the fact that he is a native of Missouri. He was converted to God July 8th, 1838, and united with the Methodist Church the following August. He was licensed to preach in Sept., 1841, and was admitted on trial in the Conference the following October, at Palmyra, Bishop Morris presiding and W. W. Redman acting as Secretary. He has ever been, since that date, an effective itinerant preacher—never sustained any other relation to the Conference.

While traveling the Brunswick district, in 1856, and by the advice of Bishop Pierce, he made arrangements to settle his family in a permanent home, and selected Chillicothe, Livingston county, as the most central and suitable location. He purchased eligible lots, with land adjoining the town, and erected an excellent and commodious residence for his large family. He also improved, furnished and stocked his adjoining lands to make them productive. Here he settled his family and remained until 1860, when he was appointed to St. Joseph station, and it became necessary for him to lease out his property in Chillicothe and move his family to St. Joseph, where he was living when the war broke out in 1861. He was deeply impressed with the necessity of caution and prudence in the conduct of his pulpit and public services, as the people to whom he ministered were divided on the questions at issue in the war. He was so careful not to give offense to any that he framed a somewhat formal prayer to be used in public services touching the troubles of the country.

It was about as follows: "O Thou, who art infinite in wisdom, in goodness and in power, we pray thee so to direct in the affairs of this country, that the events that are now transpiring may all result for thy glory and the well being of humanity. We pray that those in authority may have wisdom to direct them in adopting such measures as shall be promotive of the best interests of all the people."

To this form of prayer and the sentiments it contained he thought all good citizens of either party could say, Amen. He carefully abstained from every expression that would be offensive to the sectional feelings and views of any of his congregation. In this he was particular, and, he thought, successful. Matters passed on well enough until early in February, 1862, when, after preaching on Sabbath, he called on the Rev. W. C. Toole, a local preacher, to close the service with prayer. He was a strong partisan, and his language in the prayer was extremely bitter toward those in rebellion against the Government. Though the congregation was much divided in sentiment, they were at peace among themselves. This prayer was like a firebrand. It excited a good deal of feeling, and people of opposite views thought it much out of place. Upon reflection and consultation with his leading brethren, he determined thereafter to close his own services with prayer, which ministers should always do unless other ministers are present and in the pulpit. He pursued this course but one Sabbath afterward, and then a brother minister, the Rev. S. W. Cope, preached for him, when, during the week following, Brigadier-General B. F. Loan, then in command, sent for Mr. Rush to report himself at his headquarters. This he did, and Gen. Loan told him that he had concluded to close his church. Mr. Rush asked him on what account. He replied, "Because of disloyalty." He was then asked in what respects they were disloyal, and answered that he was informed that a prayer for the Government could not be offered in that church without giving offense.

The whole matter of the prayer of Mr. Toole and the general character of the service were then explained to Gen. Loan. Mr. Rush was careful to give the reasons for avoiding the introduction of anything savoring of sectional views into the public service; that they could not settle the troubles of the country in the church service; that such an effort would only destroy the peace of the church without in the least benefiting the country; that no prayer savoring of secession had ever been offered in the church or would be tolerated on any account; that the course pursued was the only proper one; and that if all the churches in the land would attend to their appropriate work and let politics alone it would be far better for the country. To all of this the General replied that the time had come when there must be a distinction in the churches between patriots and traitors. Mr. Rush told him that he could not discriminate in his church on account of political opinions; that he had been in the ministry more than twenty-five years, and in all that time he had not in a single instance, in prayer or sermon, given utterance to a word or sentence by which his opinions could be known upon any political questions at issue before the country, and that he did not expect in the future to depart from that course. He replied that his mind was made up to close the church. The interview ended, and the church was closed.

Soon afterward the General directed a special order to be issued forbidding Mr. Rush from preaching or conducting any kind of religious service within the bounds of his military district. Thus he was silenced—deposed from the ministry, and his ordination credentials revoked by a military satrap. An ambassador for God stricken down by one stroke of a pen to which bayonets imparted power! A messenger of salvation to dying men silenced by the caprice of shoulder-straps, and one to whom the risen Messiah by his spirit said, "Go into all the world and preach the gospel to every creature," suspended from his divine commission by the decree of human power! A "legate of the skies" at the feet of a miserable specimen of human weakness clothed with a little brief authority! Impious presumption! equaled only by sacrilegious contumely and prurient vanity.

After Gen. Loan was dismissed from the military service by Gov. Gamble, and Gen. W. P. Hall had succeeded him in command of the district, Mr. Rush addressed a note to Gen. Hall, calling his attention to the order of Gen. Loan, and asking its revocation. Mr. Rush hoped for much consideration at the hands of Gen. Hall from a somewhat intimate acquaintance of sixteen years, and the further fact that at the beginning of the troubles their views were in perfect harmony. He had no doubt whatever but that the silencing order of Gen. Loan would at once be revoked. But for once he had mistaken the man. Mr. R. did not then properly estimate the power of the German Radicals of the district nor the ambition of Gen. Hall—the necessity for him to manufacture a character for extreme loyalty, in doing which he would sacrifice any man or any principle that stood in the way of his personal promotion.

Gen. Hall not only refused to revoke the order of Gen. Loan, but published in the St. Joseph *Herald*, a paper that circulated extensively in the military camps, his letter to Mr. Rush, in which the latter was denounced as a traitor and unworthy the protection of the Government. While Gen. Loan, in his personal intercourse with Mr. Rush, was courteous and gentlemanly, Gen. Hall was abusive, ungentlemanly and tyrannical. His published letter unveiled his true character, while it subjected its helpless victim to suspicion, insult and attempts at brutal assassination.

Mr. Rush, in the midst of such trials and dangers, had to give up his charge and return to Chillicothe. Here he found his beautiful home laid waste; the fencing destroyed, the house broken up, horses stabled in three rooms on the first floor, and soldiers quartered on the second floor, and the fruit and shrubbery all destroyed.

He rented a house for his family, and while the officers of the post always treated him with courtesy and kindness, Gen. Hall's letter had stirred up the common soldiery until his life and the lives of his family were in constant peril. When he discovered this state of things, he wrote Gen. Hall a polite letter, protesting against his published letter, representing the injustice he had done him, and the danger to his person and life caused by it. Gen. Hall returned his letter, and in reply threatened him with a military commission.

About the 1st of May, 1863, a bold attempt was made to assassinate him in his own house. His house was first assailed with stones and brick-bats, by which the windows were crushed in and the door battered. Pistol shots were then fired through the doors and windows; but a kind Providence protected him and his family from serious injury.

Upon reporting the facts to the officers in command, protection was promptly furnished, and a guard stationed at the house. But, at the same time, the officers advised him to seek safety elsewhere; that with all their efforts to protect him the assassin's missile might any moment put an end to his life.

The week after this occurrence he went to St. Louis to attend the sessions of the Grand Masonic bodies of the State. These grand bodies gave to his ministerial and personal character their highest endorsement, by electing him Grand Chaplain of the Grand Lodge, also of the Grand Chapter, and also of the Convention of High Priests for the State of Missouri.

The following is the written order which Gen. Loan directed Col. King, his subordinate, to issue deposing Mr. Rush from the functions of the ministry in his military district:

"HEADQUARTERS REG'T M. S. M.,
CHILLICOTHE, Mo., April 24, 1862.

"*Rev. W. M. Rush, Chillicothe, Mo.:*

"Dear Sir—I am directed by the Brigadier-General commanding the district to notify you that it is deemed advisable and necessary to suspend you from the performance of your duties as a minister, or preacher, within this military district, so far as they relate to any of the public services in the church. This will, you observe, include all preaching, the conducting of prayer meetings, &c., &c. Of said suspension you are hereby notified.

"This, I will add, results from information, deemed entirely reliable, of your disloyal sentiments, and of your very great desire to actively promote the cause of the traitors.

"I am, sir, very respectfully,

"WALTER KING, Col. M. S. M.,
"Commanding Chillicothe Post."

Mr. Rush had been prohibited by verbal order from preaching in St. Joseph. After he left St. Joseph he preached once in Plattsburg and once in Chillicothe, whereupon General Loan ordered Colonel King to issue the above order. It was this order which Mr. Rush requested Gen. Hall to revoke.

The reply to the letter asking the revocation of Gen. Loan's order, besides being published, was sent as a private note also, and is as follows:

"HEADQUARTERS N. W. DIS.,
ST. JOSEPH, MO., February 17, 1863.

"*Rev. W. M. Rush, Chillicothe, Mo.:*

"My Dear Sir—I am in receipt of yours of the 16th inst. I regret that I am not able to comply with your request. According to my views, a religious congregation that can not endure prayers for its Government is disloyal; and a minister that encourages such a congregation in its course is also disloyal.

"I agree with you, that allegiance and protection are reciprocal. But allegiance requires the citizen to protect the Government against all enemies. This you not only refuse to do, but you are not willing to pray for the success of your Government over traitors. You claim to be neutral. A citizen has no right to be neutral when enemies are assailing his Government.

"I can not relieve you from Gen. Loan's order.

"Very respectfully,

"WILLARD P. HALL,
"Brig.-Gen. Com'dg."

The following letter was written to General Hall after Mr. Rush had suffered long and much from the effects of his published letter. It explains itself:

"CHILLICOTHE, MO., April 30, 1863.

"*Gen. W. P. Hall:*

"DEAR SIR: Some months ago I requested you to relieve me from Gen. Loan's order. This you declined to do, and at the same time (unintentionally, I hope,) inflicted upon me a severe injury. Your letter was published in the *Herald*, and was made the basis of various actions against me. Dr. Hughs, who classified those who were exempt from military duty as loyal and disloyal, enrolled me disloyal. I asked him on what ground he so enrolled me, and told him that I claimed to be as loyal as any man in the Government, and that I challenged any man to show the contrary. He told me that he acted upon your letter and did not feel himself authorized to go behind it. He assigned no other reason. Dr. Hughs, you may know, is an *extreme Radical* man.

"On the 1st of January Capt. Moore, Provost-Marshal of this post, gave what are called free passes to my negro woman and girl, and they are now in Kansas. I called on him to know on what ground he based his action. He said he concluded from your letter that I was rebellious, and, therefore, gave the passes without any charge or proof.

"On the first Monday of April, at our municipal election, my vote was challenged by a Lieutenant from St. Joseph, I believe. I asked on what ground. He said my name was on the disloyal list. I told him I did not put it there. Capt. Moore said it was put there by order of Gen. Loan.

"Such are some of the open effects of your published

letter, and, as a lawyer, you doubtless know the extent of your legal responsibility for such publication.

"In your published letter to me you regarded me as disloyal because, as you say, I encouraged a congregation that could not endure prayers for its Government. If by the *Government* you mean the country and the Constitution, I beg to inform you that prayers are regularly offered for the country, in the public congregation as well as in my private family; and in private I pray to Him who is infinite in wisdom, in goodness and in power, that he would so direct in the affairs of the nation, and so control the events that are now transpiring as that all things might yet result for his glory and the well being of humanity; that he would grant unto our rulers wisdom to adopt such measures as would speedily bring peace and prosperity to our distracted country.

"If by the Government you mean the measures of the *Administration*, I must say that I do not pray for the success of the President's Proclamation liberating the slaves of the South.

"Since these troubles began, I have claimed to be, and I believe I am, as loyal a man as there is in the country, and the Constitution does not permit you, nor any body of men, to prescribe a form of prayer as a test of my loyalty. Since the commencement of these troubles I have been a man of peace. I believed that war would be disastrous to the country, and that if persevered in it would tear down the fair fabric which my fathers helped to rear, and that my children would be left without a country.

"Sir, I boast not of family, but an ancestral name stands on the Declaration of Independence, and the family has represented the Government at Paris and at London. Sir, I can pray for peace, but I can not pray for war. I never in public or in private prayed for the success of the sword as wielded by any power on earth.

"What was my offense? I labored to preserve the peace of my congregation. I thought that the Church was not the proper arena for the strife of those contending opinions that were convulsing the nation.

"Why did not Colhoun and Lyon of the Presbyterian Church offer such prayers as that offered by W. C. Toole? I will answer. They had too high a sense of religious propriety. Sir, political preaching has sown the seeds that are bringing forth the death of the nation. In more than twenty years in the ministry I have never given utterance to a political sentiment in the pulpit. But now these political preachers are heroes, and I am without a pulpit.

"You have, also, published to the world that I have no claim upon the Government for protection. Thus I am published by you as an outlaw, to be slain by any one who may be so disposed. And this, notwithstanding I have constantly performed every duty enjoined upon me by the Constitution and laws of the country.

"On last Wednesday evening, just at dark, my son William, while feeding, was shot at by some one who had secreted himself but a few yards from him. The bullet entered his cap just over his forehead and passed out behind. An inch lower would have killed him. The shot was, no doubt, intended for me.

"When I wrote to you before, I did it that you might make your own record in my case. You had the opportunity of revoking Gen. Loan's order or of sustaining it. You saw proper to *exceed* very much the order of Gen. Loan.

"One word more. I had a financial interest of $1200 a year in my pulpit so long as my pastoral relation to the Church should continue. That relation still continues, but my financial interest in the pulpit has been confiscated, without the authority of law and contrary to a general order issued by the General commanding the department. I am advised by eminent legal counsel that yourself and General Loan are financially responsible to me.

"General, I have thus written to you *candidly*, as I think a man of conscious integrity has a right to write to one to whom he is willing to accord equal integrity. *If you think that order should still remain in force, so let it be.*

"Your obedient servant,

"W. M. Rush."

To this letter General Hall made the following reply:

"Headq'rs Seventh Military Dis't of Mo.,
St. Joseph, Mo., May 2, 1863.

"*Rev. Wm. Rush, Chillicothe, Mo.:*

"Sir—I return herewith your very extraordinary letter of the 30th ult. Notwithstanding the threats contained in it against myself, you surely did not consider what you were writing. My opinion was, and is, that it would do a serious injury to the public for me to rescind Gen. Loan's order with reference to yourself. To threaten an officer for the discharge of his duties, especially in times like these, is a serious offense, which a Military Commission would promptly punish. I bear you no malice. I have done what I have done in your case because I believed my duty required it. My advice to you is, to make no more threats.

"Very respectfully,

"WILLARD P. HALL,

"Brig.-Gen'l, E. M. M."

Neither explanation nor comment is necessary to the full meaning of this instance of heartless cruelty and wanton oppression. The fact that General Hall's mother-in-law, with whom he lived, was at the time one of the most devoted, pious and prominent members of Mr. Rush's Church, only shades the deeper and darker the character of this Missouri Nero.

General Hall's skepticism and political ambition made him a ready and a cruel instrument of religious persecution. Without the moral courage to avow his skepticism, and denied the force of character necessary to meet and master opposition, he was just the man to use the authority of shoulder-straps to make war upon the institutions of heaven and persecute God's chosen ministers of salvation; and he will feel very uncomfortable in the history he has made.

Mr. Rush found it necessary for his own safety to remove his family to St. Louis, and remain there until the close of the war. He found the Mound Church without a pastor, and by the appointment of the Presiding Elder took charge of that Church, and there remained until the quiet and safety that succeeded the war was restored to the State. Mr. Rush will appear again as a victim of the New Constitution, and a noble champion of the liberty of conscience and the supremacy of Christ in his Church, which the infidel provisions of that instrument endeavored to strike down.

It will be appropriate to close this chapter with an account of the murder of the

REV. NATHANIEL WOLLARD,

A minister of the Calvinistic, or, as generally termed, "Hard-Shell" Baptist Church.

Elder Wollard, or "Uncle Natty," as he was familiarly called, was an aged man, in his *seventy-second* year. He had lived a long time in Dallas county, Mo., where he was extensively known and very highly appreciated as a true man, a good neighbor, a kind father, an affectionate husband, a peaceable citizen and an acceptable minister—highly esteemed in love by his denomination for his character and work. He could not, nor did he desire to, take any part in the strifes, excitements and dangers of the war. He craved the boon of living at home unmolested, and spending the evening of his life in peace in the bosom of his family.

He had grown up in the olden times, and under the old *regime*, when men were outspoken, candid and fearless in the utterance of their sentiments; and, hence, he expressed himself in opposition to the "abolitionists," as he called the Union men, and in sympathy with the South. He did not make himself officious or offensive in the expression of his Southern sympathies. He was not a secessionist *per se*, but a Southern man, deeply impressed with the conviction that the Northern fanatics intended to break up the Government and destroy the foundations of republican liberty. He honestly believed that the success of the South in the struggle would vindicate the wisdom of the fathers of the Republic, and establish firmly and forever the vital principles of civil and religious liberty for which "Washington fought and freemen died."

The fact that he entertained such sentiments, however prudent and cautious in their utterance, "was sufficient to call forth the vengeful feelings and murderous purposes of the militia of this State."

A detailed account of his murder has been furnished by one acquainted with all the facts, in the following language:

"The murder was committed on the evening of Sept. 1, 1863—that dark and bloody year. A cheerful fire had been made in his sitting room, and he was peacefully enjoying an evening with his family, all unconscious of the approach of danger—not dreaming that his peace would so soon be disturbed, or that his long life was so near its end. While thus in domestic tranquillity, and unconscious of danger, a squad of militia scouts rode up to the door, dismounted and walked in without any ceremony. They addressed the old man in a very rough manner, ordering him out of his house, as they wished to speak with him. Father Wollard told them that they could talk to him where he was; that he was not going to leave his house.

"The intention of the militia was evidently to get him out of his house, feign that he made an effort to escape, and shoot him. If this was their intention they were defeated by the fact that Father Wollard supposed that if he left the house, one or two men would guard him and his family while the rest of them would pillage and then burn the house.

"When they found that they could not get him out of the house, one of the militia raised his pistol and shot him, the ball taking effect in the face and inflicting a mortal wound. He was removed from the house into the yard and laid on a bed prepared for him, his head resting on the bosom of his heart-broken companion, while his son, a youth of sixteen, was wiping the blood from his face, and keeping it from his mouth, as it flowed so freely from the wound that he feared it would strangle his father. In the meantime the militia had set the house on fire and committed everything they had to the flames.

"Having finished their work of destruction, one of them came to where the dying old man was lying, and, finding that he was not yet dead, shot him again, the ball taking effect in his forehead. He instantly expired.

"The only charge they made against him was that he fed 'bush-whackers,' which was not true. He had fed Southern and Federal soldiers alike when they came to his house, and some of these very men had been recently fed at his table who now turned upon him and brutally and barbarously murdered him.

"The men who committed this fatal and foul deed belonged to Capt. Morgan Kelly's company of militia. They were never punished, but are now living in Dallas county undisturbed, except by an accusing conscience. Capt. Kelly himself professes to be a minister of the gospel, of the Christian, or Campbellite, Church, yet he seems to live in peace, with this and many other crimes staring him in the face."

The heart sickens at such a recital of cold-blooded murder; and the evidence of savage, not to say inhuman, barbarity that characterized the horrible crime is sufficient to humiliate the whole race of men and send our much vaunted Christian civilization reeling back into the dark ages. The shadow on the dial of Ahaz went back ten degrees—it was a wonderful miracle—but here, in the noon of the nineteenth century, the shadow on the dial of human progress and Christian civilization has gone down forty degrees without a miracle, and reaches the grosser, the darker and the baser passions of our fallen nature, which instigate and then execute deeds of horror at which all Christendom revolts.

CHAPTER XXI.

REV. B. H. SPENCER.

His Character and Position as a Minister—Order of Banishment—Interview with General Merrill—Note to Colonel Kettle—Cause of Banishment—Letter to A. C. Stewart—Provost-Marshal at Danville—Frank, Manly Reply—Second Letter to Mr. Stewart, and Petition to General McKean—The Latter Treated with Silent Contempt—Strong Loyal Petition Endorsed by H. S. Lane, U. S. Senator, and O. P. Morton, Governor of Indiana—"Red Tape"—Petition Returned—Hon. S. C. Wilson Counsel for the Exiles—General Schofield Finally and Unconditionally Revokes the Order of Banishment—Indictment for Preaching Without Taking the "Test Oath."—Why he Declined to Take the Oath—Prayer for his Persecutors.

Rev. B. H. Spencer.

Neither goodness, kindness, humility nor usefulness in a minister of the gospel could disarm malice or shield the servant of God from the persecutions of wicked men. It is truly astonishing how many and how diverse the pretexts framed for the arrest, robbery, banishment, imprisonment or murder of those whose only crime was that they were ministers of the gospel in connection with the M. E. Church, South. Infidelity was never at a loss for expedients and Antichrist was never without efficient agents.

The Rev. B. H. Spencer is almost a native of Missouri, being only six months of age when his parents came to Missouri from North Carolina, and has received regular appointments from the Missouri Annual Conference,

M. E. Church, South, consecutively since 1843, when he was first admitted on trial. No man has a cleaner and purer record in the Church, both in his personal and ministerial character; and few men have occupied so many places of high trust and responsibility. He is one of the old Presiding Elders, and has often been called to represent his Conference on the floor of the General Conference, and has always proved himself to be prudent in council, wise in legislation, correct in administration and eminently useful in the pulpit; distinguished, perhaps, for his scriptural, practical and forcible expositions of the distinctive doctrines and duties of Bible Christianity. He is zealous, humble, earnest, energetic and Methodistic in all his ministerial work; extensively known and highly esteemed in love for his works' sake all over the State.

Long associated with the honored names that will live in the annals of Missouri Methodism, and taking a high rank with them, the sentiments that introduced the Rev. W. M. Rush to these pages, and the reader, may, with but little alteration, introduce Mr. Spencer.

Mr. Spencer is a representative man in his character and position in Missouri, and while his persecutions were severe and protracted, his was not an isolated case. He represents in his cruel and wanton exile a large class of Missourians, and especially of Missouri ministers, some of whom will, perhaps, never return to this State. B. T. Kavanaugh, L. M. Lewis, E. K. Miller, B. R. Baxter and many others are possibly lost to the State forever. They may have gone out for different causes, but the peculiar proscription and persecutions to which ministers in Missouri have been subjected kept them out.

Few if any cases of persecution in Missouri present more deliberate meditation, cooler cruelty and more heartless inhumanity than the one disclosed in the following narrative, made in Mr. Spencer's own quiet, clear and forcible style. His letters to the various military officials, written in exile, and while all the finer sentiments and feelings of his manly, Christian heart were writhing under the cruel injustice he had to bear without the means of vindication or the hope of redress, are worthy the pen of Cranmer, and would have given a higher tone and temper to the moral courage of Latimore.

The reader must, however, measure the man and his persecutors by the following paper:

"ORDER OF BANISHMENT.

"DEAR DOCTOR: The first item that I send you is in regard to my *banishment,* as an act of *ecclesiastical persecution.*

"In the town of High Hill, Mo., on the 16th January, 1863, I received from the hands of a Federal soldier the following order, viz.:

"'HEADQUARTERS N. E. DISTRICT MISSOURI,
"'WARRENTON, Mo., Jan. 13, 1863.

"'*Provost-Marshal, or Commanding Officer, Danville, Mo.:*

"'SIR: You will cause the following persons to leave the State of Missouri, within a reasonable time after the receipt of this order, and reside, during the war or until permitted to return, at some place north of Indianapolis, Indiana, and east of Illinois. They will be required to report to you, by letter, once a month, and are not permitted to leave the State by way of St. Louis, but directed to go by Macon City and Hannibal, Missouri. Rev. B. H. Spencer, * * * * * * *.

"'By command of Brigadier-General Merrill.

"'GEO. M. HOUSTON, A. A. G.'

"The above order was accompanied by the following:

"'HEADQUARTERS 67TH REGIMENT E. M. M.,
"'DANVILLE, Mo., Jan. 16, 1863.

"'*Rev. B. H. Spencer:*

"'SIR: The above is a true copy of Gen. Merrill's order to me. You will obey said order within six days from this date. You will report to these headquarters on the day of departure.

"'By order of J. G. Kettle, Col. Commanding.

"'J. F. ANDERSON, Adjutant.'

"On the day of receiving this order I went to Warrenton, being Gen. Merrill's headquarters, to see if I could not induce him to revoke it. I found him at tho supper table, and unwilling to give me a hearing anywhere else, when the following conversation took place between us:

"'Gen. Merrill, I have received from you an order of banishment from the State, and wish to see you in regard to it.'

"'Then what is your name and place of residence?'

"'My name is B. H. Spencer, High Hill, Mo.'

"General (in a passion)—'I can do nothing for you!'

"I replied—'It seems that the tongue of slander has reached you concerning me; will you hear evidence in my favor?'

"His reply was peremptorily, '*No, sir!*'

"I inquired, 'Will you then read documents?'

"Answer in same manner—'*No, sir!*'

"He then inquired—'Does the order allow you to go by St. Louis?'

"I answered, 'No, sir.'

"'Then,' said he, 'see that you *don't go that way!*'

"I replied, 'I don't expect to.'

"He said, "*see that you don't!*' And then added, 'You may think yourself very fortunate that you are not hung, and should feel that you are *very mercifully dealt by!*'

So the conversation ended, and I returned home and wrote the following note to Colonel Kettle:

"HIGH HILL, Mo., Jan. 19, 1863.

"'*Col. J. G. Kettle, Danville, Mo.:*

"'HONORED SIR: Some time ago I promised to marry a couple in this vicinity on to-morrow night, and as it will not be in violation of Gen. Merrill's order, and will furnish me some means with which to carry out that order, *will you permit me to do so?*

"'I am, very respectfully, B. H. SPENCER.'

"The following is his reply:

"'HEADQUARTERS 67TH REGIMENT E. M.M.,
"'DANVILLE, Mo., Jan. 19, 1863.

"'*Rev. B. H. Spencer:*

"'SIR: Your request to marry the couple and to preach is granted. I would say that you had better not speak of your banishment in your sermon.

"'Yours, &c., J. G. KETTLE, Colonel.'

"On the 25th of January, 1863, I preached the sermon alluded to; and then, in company with four others, made my report to military headquarters at Danville, Mo. But, in consequence of an accident on the railroad,

I was permitted to remain with my family until the 28th of that month, when, with a sad heart, I was compelled to leave my distressed wife and six little children and go into a land of strangers, and remain in exile for ten long months.

"Dr. H. W. Pitman, Rev. D. W. Nowlin, Rev. J. D. Gregory and Rev. Wm. A. Taylor were banished in company with me. We had no trial, either civil or military, nor would they condescend to tell us what were the charges against us, or whether, indeed, there were any. Nor to this day—September 7th, 1869—have we found out why it was done, except through private and unofficial sources. The information thus received as to the cause of my banishment was as I expected—*I was banished because I was a Southern Methodist preacher!* One of the officers was asked by one of my friends: 'What are the charges against Spencer?' He answered, *'I never heard that there are any; but he is a man of influence, and, if disposed, can do a great deal of harm!'* Another officer was asked by another friend, and he replied, 'The fact that he is a *Southern Methodist preacher is all I want to know!'* There never was a more clear case of ecclesiastical persecution than was my banishment. Certain men sought to produce secession, treason and rebellion in the M. E. Church, South, by way of showing how they professed to hate these things in the nation; I opposed them, and they became my enemies and had me banished. If any one doubts this let him attend to the following documents:

"'ASHBY'S MILLS, IND., April 22, 1863.

"'*Mr. A. C. Stewart, Provost-Marshal, Danville, Mo.:*

"'SIR—There are reasons which induce me to believe

that my case is wholly at the disposal of the officers and Union men of Danville and vicinity. If this be so, I wish to solicit your attention to a few considerations in regard to my case. And, first, I was banished from my home and family *without a trial or a knowledge of the charges against me*, or who preferred them. Now, sir, is this right? Is there any law, civil or military, that will punish an *innocent* man? How could the officer who banished me know that I was guilty of any crime without giving me a trial and hearing evidence in the case? Have I ever had such a trial? When? Where? Who were the judge, jury, witnesses *pro* and *con?* Where was the prisoner during the trial? And where was my legal counsel to see that justice was done me? With what was I charged, and who were my accusers? Three months have passed since my banishment, and I am still left in ignorance of why it was done. Was it done merely to gratify official ambition? or rather, was it not done to gratify the malice of *secret enemies?* Can the interests of the Government be secured or protected or its dignity increased by such treatment of one of its citizens? Do you say that I am a great rebel, and therefore such treatment is good enough for me? How do you know that I am a rebel at all, much less a great one? Did you learn it from mere *rumor*, or from a trustworthy witness, sworn to tell the truth before a proper tribunal and in the presence of the accused? In the absence of such evidence how can an intelligent gentleman make such a charge, if, indeed, any one does make it? If it be stated, or insinuated, that I have been, or am, disloyal or disobedient to the Constitution of the United States, or to any of the laws made in pursuance thereof, or to the constitution and laws of any State where I have ever lived, or to any military order or edict—*this most unjust and oppressive one banishing me from my home and family not excepted—I deny the allegation and defy proof by competent testimony!* Have I not silently borne injustice and oppression long enough? Can you blame me for entering my earnest protest against such treatment? Has it not been said by officers who ought to know, '*that there are no charges against me, but that I am a man of influence, and, if disposed, could do a great deal of harm?*' Now, if there are no charges against me, in the name of everything that an American citizen holds dear, why suffer me to be thus persecuted and oppressed without an effort to prevent it? Are you not a sworn officer—sworn to support and defend the Constitution of the United States? and does that Constitution allow such treatment of an American citizen against whom there are no charges? and can you allow it to be done without an effort to prevent it and be innocent? And suppose I have *influence,* is that a crime? and what reason has any one to fear that I would use it for evil? Is it proposed to banish men of character and influence from the State for fear they will exert their influence for evil? If not, why send off, and keep off, so humble a person as myself? Is this the way an officer should fulfill his oath of office? Was he clothed with authority for this purpose? Is this the only protection I am to expect from the officers of my native State? Is not my banishment, under the circumstances, an unmitigated outrage upon civil and military order, as well as upon my liberties as a citizen? I love and almost venerate the Government of the United States as established by our patriotic ancestors! Among earthly institutions I expect and want nothing better. With *it* I find no fault. My complaint is against certain of its *officers* for the injustice and oppression with which they treat me. If you were in my place and I in your's, what course would you wish me to pursue? If a peaceable and quiet citizen, such as I have always been, is not free from imprisonment or banishment, *who is safe?* Has justice forsaken the land? And is there no place where the oppressed may find redress? If there be any place where justice may be had, will you tell me where it is, and how to approach it? I must candidly believe that my banishment was caused by *ecclesiastical persecution*—that I am banished for an *ecclesiastical* and not for *a political* reason! Certain persons sought to produce secession, treason and rebellion in the M. E. Church, South, by way of showing how they professed to hate these things in the nation, and I opposed them, because I not only loved *union in the nation,* but also *in the Church*—hence they became my enemies, and for this cause *alone,* as I believe, they secured my banishment! I believe the officer who did it was deceived, and induced to believe me *a bad and dangerous man,* or surely he would not have acted so hastily and rashly! But you know, and so do all my enemies, that such is not my character. Who would be injured by my return to my family? Can anybody tell? Does anybody fear it? Shall my secret enemies be allowed to continue the gratification of their malignity at my expense under pretense of friendship to the Government? Will my continued *religious* persecution do the Government any good? Why, then, suffer its continuance? Why keep a man in exile without just cause, who is in feeble health, with limited means, and a wife and six dependent children needing his attention? *Will you not then allow me to come home at once?* Do not even the instincts of humanity, to say nothing of the higher obligations of justice and official duty, urge compliance with this request? I honestly believe that you and the Union men of your vicinity can get me home if you will—just as easily as to say the word. I may be mistaken, but I honestly believe that my whole case is in your hands, and that I remain in exile or return to my family, just as you will the one or the other. I have reasons for this opinion, and if I am mistaken would like to know it. I wish to say that in all that I have written I have not *intentionally* used a single word that was *disrespectful* toward those in authority. In all that I have said, I have *aimed* to speak plainly, candidly and *earnestly*, but also *respectfully*. I respect you on account of the *authority* with which you are invested and the *Government* which you *represent*. But I protest against the way I am treated, and who can blame me for it? And if this protest shall be disregarded now, perhaps it may live and speak in vindication of my character when I am dead, and when the voice of *injured justice* shall be *heard* and *respected*. If you can not release me, will you tell me who can? And will you answer this at your earliest possible convenience, and let me know what you intend to do in my case. I am, most respectfully,

"'B. H. SPENCER.'

"The answer of the Provost-Marshal was *prompt, frank* and *manly*, and does honor to the head and heart of its author. Unlike every other officer, civil or military, to whom I had applied for information or redress, he did not treat me with silent contempt. *He answered.* And the answer is important, because it shows clearly that he not only had no hand in the banishment of myself and my companions in exile, but that he also had been kept in ignorance of the intention to do it, as also for the reasons why it was done. Surely there could have been no public charges against us, or proper trial in our case, or the Provost-Marshal in our immediate vicinity could not have thus been kept in ignorance of such an intention till after it was done.

"It proves, furthermore, that by order of Gen. McKean, it was left to the so-called loyal men of Montgomery county, Mo., to say whether we should return or not. And we have the names of those who gave their sworn opinions as to whether it was *proper* for us to return or not, and could give them, but in mercy we withhold them. And, finally, it proves that our efforts to obtain a revocation of our order of banishment, to be successful, had to be kept to *ourselves.* Why? Simply because if our secret enemies found it out they would thwart our efforts at the headquarters of the Commanding General of the district. But the letter speaks for itself. It is as follows:

"'OFFICE PROVOST-MARSHAL, DANVILLE,
MONTGOMERY CO., MO., April 26, 1863.

"'*Rev. B. H. Spencer, Ashby's Mills, Ind.:*

"'DEAR SIR—I have just received yours of 22d inst., and must acknowledge I am utterly at a loss to comprehend it.

"'I want to say, once for all, to yourself, as also to Doct. Pitman and Judge Nowlin, that I had no hand in your banishment whatever, either as a private citizen or as an officer; that I never had, either directly or indirectly, an intimation that such a thing was contemplated. An order was issued by General McKean, who is Commanding General of this district, headquarters at Palmyra, to J. G. Lane, Provost-Marshal of Wellsville district, to take the testimony of the loyal men of Montgomery county in relation to the *propriety* of your return home. Lane was removed from office and his district thrown into mine, and the order was sent to me by General McKean, which I executed by taking the evidence of loyal men, both at High Hill and Montgomery City, as well as Danville. The evidence was sworn to and sent by order of the commanding General to his headquarters.

"'Now, sir, I have given you the facts in regard to everything I have had to do with this case. And, although you protest against any intention to insult or offend in your communication, I must frankly admit that the whole tenor of your letter seems to savor of both. 'How can you consent, without just cause, to keep one in exile who is in feeble health,' &c., is one extract from your letter. '*Will you not then allow me to come home at once?*' is another. Now, sir, you must know that I have no direct control of this matter! Why ask me such questions? Why not ask me, as a private citizen, to use my influence to obtain a revocation of the order? The authorities that issued the order of your banishment have never asked, neither have I *given*, my opinion as to the propriety of the order. Notwithstanding I consider your letter as invidious, and, as I understand it, full of insinuations against me, yet, under the circumstances, I will allow humanity to step in, discard all feeling that your letter may have excited, and give you the best advice I am capable of.

"'Judge Nowlin, Doct. Pitman and yourself get up a letter, directed to Brig.-Gen. McKean, Palmyra, Mo., through me as Provost-Marshal of Montgomery county. Take *humanity* for your text; appeal to him through the tears of your wife and helpless children; let Government officers alone; agree to report to me once a week in person, if it should be considered necessary; give every assurance that your lips will be sealed in future as to the utterance of treason, directly or indirectly; send the letter to me and I will forward it, with such recommendation as I may deem proper and right, and, if that fails, I am at the end of my row. The success of this thing will very much depend on keeping my advice to yourselves. I may be mistaken, but I believe your liberation may be effected in that way. Give my respects to Judge Nowlin and Doctor Pitman.

"'Yours, &c.,

"'A. C. STEWART, Prov.-Marshal.'

"To the above noble letter I made the following reply:

"'ASHBY'S MILLS, MONTGOMERY CO., INDIANA,
"'May 4, 1863.

"'*Mr. A. C. Stewart, Provost-Marshal, Danville, Mo.*:

"'DEAR SIR: Yours of the 26th April is to hand, has been read and contents noted. And in reply let me say, I regret that you considered my letter in its whole tenor 'invidious, offensive and insulting,' notwithstanding my protest against such a construction. I knew the task I had undertaken was difficult, for there seems to be something about *official position* which is always more or less *impatient of contradiction.* And hence it was reasonable to conclude that this is true of military officers, who feel that it is theirs to *command* and for others to *obey* or *submit,* and not to *reason* or *question.* The difficulty was to so employ language as to convey some idea of my *righteous indignation* at the injustice of my treatment, and which would at the same time be *respectful* and *courteous* toward those in authority. And I question very much whether you yourself, in my circumstances, would, if you could, have done better. I was, with only a few days' notice, forced away from the fellowship and pastoral oversight of hundreds of beloved brethren; from a most dependent and afflicted family; from my only means of their support; from the graves of my kindred, and every thing of earth that was dear; was denied the privilege of going by St. Louis, where I might have reached the ears of power and have gained a revocation of my order of banishment; with limited means, was compelled to travel a circuitous and expensive route to my place of exile; was denied the privilege of living in the loyal State of Illinois, where I had kindred, and it would have cost me nothing; was denied the sympathy of friends who would have helped me financially, but were afraid; was sent into a land of strangers, under Government censure, where, without *sympathy,* if without *money,* a man had better be dead; was not allowed to know the charges against me, who were my accusers, or even the semblance of a trial, though I had sought one of Gen. Merrill, of Gen. Curtis, of Gen. Halleck, of Gov. Gamble, of Attorney-General Bates, of Secretary Stanton and of President Lincoln, and had done this, directly and indirectly, through men of commanding in fluence, whose loyalty was above suspicion, and all this without success; felt, yea *knew,* that I was *innocent;* that there could be *no truthful* evidence of my being guilty of any crime; knew that I was suffering all this to gratify the malignity of secret enemies who had deceived the military commander and secured my banishment; enemies who, like the midnight assassin, did their work and then slunk away to gloat over the misery they had caused; felt satisfied that I was thus persecuted for an *ecclesiastical* and not for *a political* reason; was sure the Government could not be benefited by my persecution nor injured by my return to my family; and, finally, became thoroughly convinced that the *influence* that controlled the action of those who had the power to release me from the binding force of this order, or to keep me in exile, was in or near Danville; and, in a word, was satisfied that I had found out the *locality* of the authors of my trouble and why they persecuted me, but the identical names of my persecutors I did not know; and hence, in view of the foregoing considerations, I wrote you in the way I did. Now, interpret my leter in the light of my circumstances, and imagine *yourself in my condition,* and you will be able to 'comprehend it,' and to *excuse* anything that may *seem* 'discourteous or insulting,' especially when I *assur*e you nothing of the kind was *intended.* You have my thanks for your *prompt* and *manly* reply to my letter. There are times when I would rather a man would *abuse me a little than not answer me at all,* and this is one of those times. You are the only officer who had the condescension, kindness, humanity, or whatever else you may please to call it, to answer a single one of my numerous appeals for deliverance from oppression, or for instruction as to where or how I might obtain it. To your praise be this spoken. It affords me much pleasure, also, to learn from yourself that you had no hand in securing my banishment, or knowledge of it until after it occurred. I wish I could think the same of every other citizen of Danville.

"'And now that, in accordance with your wish, I am addressing you as *a private* citizen, may I ask, and confidently expect, that you will give me the names of my accusers, and the nature of their accusations against me, if there are any, together with the names of those loyal men whose sworn testimony was sent to Gen. McKean in regard to the '*propriety*' of allowing me to come home, and the substance of what each one said? As that is the nearest a trial of anything else I have had, should not the accused be allowed to know his accusers, the names of the witnesses and the nature of their testimony against him? You reprehend me very severely for insinuating that you have any 'direct control of my case.' Well, I did not suppose you had authority to *revoke* the order of banishment; but I did suppose, and do still suppose, that you and your friends of that vicinity can influence Gen. McKean to revoke the order or not, just as you wish; and that you have control of my case in *that way.* And hence it is that I am so thankful to you, and so much encouraged by your kind offer to use your influence with the commanding officer to set aside this order and permit me to return home. And I am sure if you do promptly and vigorously exert your influence in that direction you are *certain* of success.

"'Among your items of advice you say, 'Give every

assurance that your lips will be sealed in future as to the utterance of treason, directly or indirectly.' Now, as this is, to my mind, an intimation that some one, or all three of us, are charged with having been guilty of treasonable utterances, and hence are required to give assurance that we will do so no more, I wish to say for myself that, if such be the intimation, I deny the allegation *in toto;* for I have neither *uttered* nor *acted* treason, nor do I expect to do either in future. And if I am permitted to return, and you can protect me from the tongue of slander, and the *secret enemies* that with consummate mendacity hound my steps and torture and misrepresent my language and conduct, you will hear nothing of treason, either in *utterance* or *action.* But, if *that* can not be done—if the tongue of slander and falsehood against me can not be silenced in any other way—then give a *fair trial,* and make these *secret liars,* who *whisper* falsehoods into official ears against those they hate, '*face the music,*' and I will vindicate my *innocence.* Upon that subject I can make no further promises. A mere *charge of treason,* you know, is no *evidence of guilt.* The *immaculate* Son of Man was accused of *rebellion, sedition* and *treason,* with *blasphemy,* and with being the *agent* of the *prince of devils!* Of *Innocence itself* they said, '*He is not fit to live; away with him! crucify him! crucify him!*' And 'If they have done these things in the *green tree,* what will they not do in the dry?' And the same divine authority has said, 'If any man will live *godly in Christ Jesus,* he must suffer *persecution,*' and I have made my calculations accordingly. As to your other suggestions, I wish to say that I will herewith transmit to Gen. McKean, through you, a request, or petition, for the revocation of this order in my case, accompanied with a few of the reasons why I make it, which I will thank you to send to him, if you please, together with such remarks and recommendations as you may think proper to make. Please let me hear from you at an early day, and much oblige,

"'Most respectfully,

"'B. H. SPENCER.'

"The petition was sent to General McKean, through the Provost-Marshal of Montgomery county, Mo., together with the best appeal that he could make in our favor. But the only notice he seems to have given it was to treat it with silent contempt.

"The following is a copy of that petition:

"'ASHBY'S MILLS, IND., May 7, 1863.

"'*Brigadier-Gen. McKean, Com., Palmyra, Mo.:*

"'DEAR SIR—Will you please to revoke the order of Gen. Merrill, of the 13th January, 1863, banishing me from the State of Missouri? A few of the reasons why I ask you to do this are—

"'1st. *The order was unjust.* The General who issued this order did not *know* me, was dependent upon *others* for his information concerning me, and was evidently *deceived* by my *personal enemies,* or he never would have issued it.

"'2d. I have never engaged in this rebellion in any way, nor violated any law, civil or military; and, therefore, am *not deserving* of this punishment.

"'3d. I have a wife and six small, helpless children, whose ages range from *two* to *twelve* years, from whom I have been forcibly separated for more than *three months,* and who very much *need* my attention, and, therefore, *humanity,* to say nothing of the higher claims of *truth* and *justice,* demands compliance with this request.

"'4th. If permitted to return, *I expect to be, as I have ever been, a law-abiding and good citizen,* and, therefore, the Government can not be *benefited* by my remaining in exile nor *injured* by my return to my family.

"'5th. As it is the duty and glory of a Government to protect its citizens in the possession of all their *legitimate rights,* I ask, and hope it will be your *pleasure* to grant, that I may return to my family in the enjoyment of the *untrammeled liberty* that I had before my banishment.

"'This petition will be sent to your headquarters by Mr. A. C. Stewart, Provost-Marshal, Danville, Mo., accompanied by such remarks and recommendations as he may think proper to make.

"'In the confident expectation that you will grant this just and reasonable request at an early day,

"'I am, most respectfully,

"'B. H. SPENCER.'

"After being compelled to remain long enough in exile to form character and make friends amongst strangers, at the end of nine months some of the most prominent Union men of Indiana, on the 31st August, 1863, sent the following petition to the Provost-Marshal General of the department of the Missouri:

"'*To Lieut.-Col. J. O. Broadhead, P. M. G. of Missouri, St. Louis, Mo., or to whomsoever this petition should be addressed:*

"'The undersigned petitioners beg leave respectfully

to represent to the proper authorities in the State of Missouri, that we are citizens of the United States, residents of the counties of Montgomery and Putnam, in the State of Indiana; that we are now and ever have been loyal and devoted to the Government of the United States; that we are supporters of the present Administration thereof, and that we are in favor of using all lawful ways and means for suppressing the present rebellion and preserving the Union established by our fathers; we, therefore, cordially endorse all and every one of the measures of the Government having these much desired objects in view.

"'We beg leave further to represent that there have been residing in our midst, in our immediate vicinity, for the past six or seven months, three individuals, said to be citizens of Montgomery county, in the State of Missouri, and to have been banished from that State by the military authorities there, viz.: H. W. Pitman, B. H. Spencer and David W. Nowlin. While we can not know the causes that led to the banishment of these men, we would state that they came among us under the ban of the Government, and we looked upon them as objects of suspicion. They and their conduct have been closely observed and narrowly scrutinized, not to say strictly watched by our party, and we deem it but sheer justice to declare, candidly and emphatically, that after an observation of the length of time indicated above we have seen nothing in these men that in our judgment would require that they longer be kept in exile.'

"'They are represented to us as men having families dependent greatly on them for support, and every feeling of humanity is enlisted in their behalf, if the interests of the Government do not imperatively require their continuance in exile. With the lights before us, and in view of the facts that these men have resided for the past six or seven months in a population greatly excited on political issues, and among whom sundry disloyal practices have been rife, in which they have had ample opportunities to have partaken if they had been so inclined, and yet our observation has not been sufficient to detect them as aiders or abettors in these disloyal practices; we feel free, therefore, to declare emphatically our convictions that the interests of the Government will not be advanced by a longer continuance of their exile; but, on the contrary, we are satisfied that those interests would be promoted by a revocation of the order banishing them from Missouri. We, therefore, in behalf of these exiles, pray the authorities in Missouri who are empowered to do so to revoke the order banishing the said H. W. Pitman, B. H. Spencer and David W. Nowlin from the said State of Missouri, and to release them from further pains and penalties in the premises; and as loyal citizens in duty bound, we will ever pray, &c.

(Signed) "'JOHN W. HARRISON,
"'DR. H. LABARRE,
"'FRANKLIN M. MCMURRAY,
"'DR. GEORGE W. MILLER,
"'JAMES KNOX,
"'J. J. BILLINGSLEY,
"'A. D. BILLINGSLEY.'

"The undoubted loyalty of these petitioners, and their prominence in social and political circles during

Mr. Lincoln's Administration, received the following endorsement, which accompanied their petition and formed a part of it:

"'I have known the signers of this paper long and well; they are true and loyal citizens of Indiana, and are all supporters of the Administration. They are gentlemen of the highest character, and their statements are entitled to full credit.

"'H. S. LANE, U. S. Senator.'

"'The gentlemen who signed the foregoing statement are of undoubted loyalty, and their representations are worthy of credit.

"'O. P. MORTON, Gov. of Indiana.'

"And now, by way of showing how difficult it was for those in prison or exile to obtain a hearing at headquarters, in consequence of *official routine, etiquette,* or what is technically called '*Red Tape,*' I give the following *inscription,* which was written on the outside of the above petition before it was returned to the petitioners. It seems first to have come into the hands of some *sub*-official, who read it and then wrote on it a digest of its contents, as follows:

"'*Petition.* Citizens of Indiana. *P. 102 (P. M. G.) 63.* That H. W. Pitman, B. H. Spencer and D. W. Nowlin, exiles from Montgomery county, Mo., be permitted to return to their families and homes, as they have been closely watched while here and have always conducted themselves as Union men. These petitioners are indorsed by the Governor of Indiana.'

"This sub-official then seems to have sent it to the P. M. General of the Department, who, without granting or promising to grant the petition, sent it back to

Gov. Morton, with the following explanation written on it:

"'HEADQUARTERS DEPARTMENT OF THE MISSOURI,
"'OFFICE OF THE P. M. G.,
"'ST. LOUIS, MO., Sept. 3, 1863.

"'Respectfully returned to his Excellency, O. P. Morton, Governor of Indiana, with the information that there are no papers on the cases of the persons named in the within petition in this office. Neither does their names appear upon the records. They were probably banished by order of some district commander.

"'By order of Lieut.-Col. J. O. Broadhead.

"'H. H. HAINE,
"'Lieut. and A. P. M. G. Dept. of the Missouri.'

"Upon receiving it Governor Morton sent it to Senator Lane, who sent it to the petitioners with the following explanation:

"'This paper was to-day returned to me by Governor Morton, with the indorsements on it. Sept. 7, 1863.

"'H. S. LANE.'

"Just think of it! No trial, no charges, nothing for us or against us, not on the records, no papers in our cases, and yet we in exile and compelled to stay there! But we employed one of Indiana's noblest lawyers, the Hon. Samuel C. Wilson, of Crawfordsville, to take that petition and go with it in person to Gen. Schofield's headquarters. The result was an unconditional revocation of the order of banishment, on the 16th Sept., 1863, which is as follows:

"'HEADQ'RS DEPARTMENT OF THE MISSOURI,
ST. LOUIS, MO., Sept. 15th, 1863.

"'*Special Orders No. 252.*]

"'I. Dr. H. W. Pitman, David Nowlin and B. H.

Spencer, citizens of Montgomery county, Missouri, heretofore banished to Indiana, to remain there during the war, are permitted to remain in any part of the United States, outside of the limits of this Department. They will report their places of residence the first of each month during the war to the Provost-Marshal General of this Department.

"'By command of Major-General Schofield.

"'WM. W. ENO, Ass't Adj't-Gen'l.

"'B. H. Spencer, per Maj. Dunn.'

"The foregoing facts and documents are a mere tithing of what might be given to the same effect, and go to show most clearly that I was persecuted in various ways, and banished from my helpless family for ten long months, for no higher and *no other crime* than that I was a *Southern Methodist preacher!*

TEST OATH.

"The following is a mere sample of numerous other indictments against me for preaching without taking the Missouri *test oath:*

"'Know all men, by these presents, that we, B. H. Spencer, as principal, and Thomas Kemble and A. Bigelow, as securities, are held and firmly bound unto the State of Missouri in the sum of one thousand dollars, the payment whereof, well and truly to be made, we bind ourselves, our heirs, administrators and executors, firmly by these presents. The conditions of the above bond are, that whereas B. H. Spencer has been indicted by the Grand Jury of Montgomery county for preaching without taking the oath; Now, if the said B. H. Spencer shall personally appear before the Judge of our Circuit

Court on the first day of the next term of said Court, said term of said Court to be held at the court-house in the town of Danvi.le, in and for said county, on the fourth Monday of next May, and answer to said indictment, and not depart therefrom without the leave of said Court, then said bond to be void, otherwise to remain in full force and effect. Witness our signatures this the 18th day of May, A. D. 1866.

"'B. H. SPENCER,
"'THOMAS KEMBLE,
"'ABNER BIGELOW.'

"My refusing to take this oath was not the result of an unwillingness to obey the constitution and laws of the State of Missouri, for I had already taken the 'Convention oath,' the 'Halleck oath' and the 'Rosecrans oath,' and had sworn fealty to the State as often, and in as many ways as *reason, conscience* and *loyalty* would allow. And hence, when civil authority came between me and my Divine Master, and virtually said, *I will allow you to obey your Master if you will swear fealty to me first,* I believed it to be *wicked* thus to surrender the claims of Christ to the demands of Cæsar, and resolved, at the hazard of fines and imprisonments, yea, even of life itself, that I would refuse compliance with this unrighteous requirement. I believed they had as much right to say *what should be preached* as to say *who should preach it!* Hence I refused, and numerous indictments were the result.

"Having scarcely commenced the recital of my persecutions as a Southern Methodist preacher, I find this article already too long, and therefore close, with the kindest wishes for all my persecutors, and an earnest prayer for their salvation.

"I am, truly and fraternally,
"B. H. SPENCER."

CHAPTER XXII.

REVS. D. B. COOPER, H. N. WATTS AND THOS. GLANVILLE.

Rev. D. B. Cooper—Attempt Made to Ride him on a Rail—Defeated by the Timely Appearance of Soldiers—Particulars Furnished by Dr. N. W. Harris—*Rev. H. N. Watts*—A Native of Missouri—Efforts Made to Place the Old Ministers under Disability or Run them out of the State—Mr. Watts Arrested—Silenced—Correspondence with Provost-Marshals Reid and Sanderson—"Test Oath"—*Rev. Thos. Glanville*—An Englishman by Birth—Early Life—Peculiar Trials—Manner of Life as a Citizen and a Minister—Driven from Home in 1863—Returns and Obtains Written Permission to Preach—Warned not to fill his Appointment on Sabbath, September 20, 1863—Remains at Home—That Night he is Shot Through his Window—Shot a Second and Third Time, and Expires Praying for his Murderers—His Eldest Son Shot and Killed the Same Night—Details Furnished by J. H. Ross and Rev. John Monroe—Conclusion.

Rev. D. B. Cooper.

The following account of an attempt to mob and ride on a rail this humble and worthy minister of the gospel will be perused with interest, as it is furnished by an eye witness and an intelligent physician, whose statements will not be called in question. But for the fact that he is "not a professor of Christianity," and authorizes the use of his name with respectable references, the language would be somewhat toned down and tempered to a milder moral zone. But it is thought best to give the communication as received, as it details some important facts, and throws light upon the *animus* of others:

"Pilot Grove, Cooper Co., Mo., April 25, 1869.

"*Rev. P. M. Pinckard, St. Louis, Mo.* :

"In the summer of 1863 Rev. D. B. Cooper, now of Mt. Sterling, Ky., was on the circuit in Linn county,

Mo. He is one of the purest men I have ever known, and remarkably reticent. I knew him intimately and well, being his physician and a personal friend. He never preached or talked politics, even to his most intimate friends and acquaintances. If there was but one man in Missouri during those wicked years of horror walking humbly before God and acting uprightly toward his fellow-men, that man was D. B. Cooper.

"On Sunday he was preaching in Laclede, my then residence; some one whispered to me that some soldiers were outside intending to ride the preacher on a *rail.* I went out and sure enough there were some half-dozen soldiers who had come up from Brookfield, had gone into a 'loyal' doggery, imbibed freely, and meeting some 'loyal Methodists,' were told that a rebel was preaching. Under the *stimuli* of bad whisky and the worse hearts of the 'God and morality' Methodists, they had come to the church with a fence-rail intending to commit an outrage upon this gentleman. But 'man proposes and God disposes.'

"I tried to dissuade them from their purpose, but could not, and went back into church to a lieutenant of Col. McFerran's regiment, then stationed in Laclede, and told him to go to Col. McFerran and tell him to send a file of soldiers immediately. I knew McFerran could be relied on, as he was a Democrat and a gentleman. There was no time to lose; service was nearly over, and neither Mr. Cooper nor his congregation knew anything of the impending outrage. The upper floor of a 'loyal' Methodist's house near by was full of 'God's elect' to witness the fun. Just before the service closed the braves crowded into the house, and when the congregation was dismissed they, the soldiers, were so situated that they had to leave the house last. When they came out and were about to lift their rail at the side of the house and seize Mr. Cooper—who was yet in ignorance of their designs—they, and all but myself, were surprised to see two files of soldiers, with fixed bayonets, marching down on us so as to encompass the entire crowd. As no violence had been done, no arrests were made. The miserable tools of the bad-hearted fanatics slunk away like whipped curs, leaving their pious (?) instigators gnashing their teeth and calling down curses upon McFerran and myself. I don't think their prayers were ever answered.

"These maudlin soldiers were not to blame. They were mere tools in the hands of the base-hearted men and women who instigated the outrage. This act is only a type of the general conduct of this people during the war who are now whining for union with you.

"I am no professor of Christianity, but if such people are Christians, or your union with them would compose a Christian body, I pray the Giver of all good to incline my heart to heathenism rather than such a mongrel abomination.

"I was living in Boonville when they committed the theft of your church there, and know all about it; but you will get the particulars of that honest (?) act from others.

"I have given you the facts, but have taken no pains, as you see. You may have to re-write it. You are at liberty to insert it in your book over my signature if you wish.

"Your friend, N. W. HARRIS."

References were furnished amply sufficient to endorse the veracity of Dr. Harris, had it needed such endorsement.

A complete history of those perilous times would unveil many similar acts nipped in the bud, or plotted and projected, but defeated by the timely interference of good men.

Many Southern Methodist preachers were threatened with a ride on a rail and a coat of tar and feathers; but the presence of peaceable citizens and the fear of military interference deterred the rabble in most cases from committing the deeds to which they were instigated.

The Rev. B. R. Baxter, now in Montana, and the Rev. H. H. Hedgepeth, now in heaven, and others, were forced to leave their work in Andrew, Holt and adjoining counties in consequence of such threats. Even the persons and lives of all Southern Methodist ministers were in constant peril in that portion of the State until after the Supreme Court of the United States had declared the test oath of the New Constitution unconstitutional. Indeed, not until 1867 was it safe for one of the proscribed and threatened of the M. E. Church, South, to be seen or heard in that part of the State northwest of St. Joseph, as facts hereafter to be narrated will show.

But for the present, and for the sake of some little chronological order, events in Southeast Missouri claim attention; and, first,

REV. HENRY N. WATTS.

Why were native Missourians in the ministry marked as the special objects of displeasure? Were they sinners above all the men who lived and labored in this goodly State, that such exceptional notice should be taken of them in the administration of pious loyalty? Possibly the discrimination was made upon the ground of personal influence with the people. That they had more influence with the people and stood higher in public estimation than any imported men will not be questioned; but that their influence was used for evil purposes, either political, social or moral, is distinctly denied. That others were envious of their well-earned position, and jealous of their power over the people and consequent ability to control the moral forces of the State for ecclesiastical advancement and distinction, is too true to escape the notice of history; for upon this fact the only rational hypothesis can rest that accounts for the noteworthy pre-eminence given to the old native Missouri ministers in these persecutions. A man who had been so long and so well known in the Missouri pulpit as the Rev. H. N. Watts could not escape the heavy hand of the persecutor, and the distinction in suffering he had gained in the ministry.

Mr. Watts was admitted on trial in the Missouri Conference, M. E. Church, South, at St. Louis, in 1844, and appointed to Ripley Mission, Cape Girardeau District.

From that time on he has been a faithful laborer in his Master's vineyard—always ready to go where the Bishop appointed him without murmuring or gainsaying. At times he has been called to fill the chair of Presiding Elder, and also to represent his Conference in the General Conference. His fidelity to the sacred claims and obligations of the gospel ministry has only been equaled by his loyalty to the Church of his choice and his fidelity to her distinctive peculiarities. He was always a man of one work, and never concerned himself particularly about the civil and political affairs of the country.

The policy of the Church and the saving principles and power of the gospel of grace were more to him than all "the things which belong unto Cæsar." He thought that there were men enough to attend to Cæsar's business, but none too many ministers to keep God's business with men and man's interest in the "kingdom of heaven" from suffering. Hence he kept himself free from political strifes and attended, with singleness of heart and life, to his holy calling. Thus he was engaged when the war broke out, and up to the summer of 1863 he had suffered very little molestation. He had taken no part in the strife and committed no act of treason against the Government; was a peaceable, orderly citizen.

In 1863 Mr. Watts was living in Charleston, Mississippi county, Mo., and on the 23d of July was arrested at his house by a squad of soldiers, accompanied by Meeker Thurman, Aaron W. and John Grigsby, and taken to Columbus, Ky. He was charged with no crime, and no offense against the laws or peace of the Government was ever alleged against him. In vain did he plead the protection of the Constitution of the United States. He was threatened with banishment or imprisonment during the war, unless he would take and subscribe a military oath, which was as repugnant to his feelings as it was oppressive to the rights of conscience. After taking the oath to secure his liberty, and receiving some personal abuse as a minister of the gospel, he was released and permitted to return to his home after an absence of several days.

In the spring of 1864, and while Capt. Ewing's company of militia were stationed in Charleston, and Lieut. Jas. A. Reed was Ass't Provost-Marshal, Mr. Watts was prohibited from preaching the gospel for several weeks by military authority. He continued, however, to travel his circuit and hold religious services. He would read the word of God, sing, pray and exhort the people to "flee from the wrath to come" and "lead peaceable and quiet lives in all godliness and honesty."

The following is the correspondence between the Assistant Provost-Marshal and Mr. Watts. It will serve to develop the nature of the persecutions he suffered in the light of the official records:

"OFFICE ASSISTANT PROVOST-MARSHAL,
"CHARLESTON, Mo., March 17, 1864.

"*Parson Watts:*

"SIR: You will greatly oblige me, and at the same time not inconvenience yourself, perhaps, by calling at this office on or before the 19th inst., for the purpose of complying with 'Special Order No. 61,' issued by the Provost-Marshal General, St. Louis, Mo., March 7, 1864, requiring ministers of the gospel to take the oath of allegiance therein prescribed.

"Your non-compliance with this notice will be taken as a refusal and will be acted upon accordingly.

"JAMES A. REID,
"1st Lieut. and Ass't Provost-Marshal."

To which Mr. Watts returned the following reply:

"CHARLESTON, Mo., March 18, 1864.

"*Lieut. James A. Reid, Ass't Provost-Marshal:*

"SIR: Your note of the 17th inst. has been received, asking me to appear at your office on or before the 19th inst., to comply with 'Special Order No. 61,' concerning 'convocations, conferences, councils, assemblies,' &c.

"1. I have written to St. Louis for certain information on this and other subjects. I would greatly prefer getting said information before taking action in this matter.

"2. I assure you I have not violated said order by attending any synod, council, conference, or any such assembly under any other name, since said order was issued.

"3. And as you think preaching would be a violation of said order, I have ceased preaching since I have heard of this order. And a private citizen is not required to take that oath, yourself being judge.

"4. As a private individual I have taken the oath of allegiance, a copy of which I have; and,

"5. I have not at any time, and do not design violating that order, and with this assurance I hope I shall not be hurried in this matter.

"Respectfully, H. N. WATTS."

Mr. Watts addressed the following letter to the Provost-Marshal General, St. Louis:

"CHARLESTON, Mo., March 18, 1864.

"*J. P. Sanderson, Pro.-Marshal Gen'l, St. Louis, Mo.:*

"DEAR SIR—Special Order No. 61, from your office, dated the 7th inst., 'concerning religious convocations, synods, councils, conferences, or assemblies under any other name or title,' not being understood as to the extent of its application, will you be kind enough to answer the following inquiries:

"1. Under these terms, 'convocations, synods, &c., or assemblies *under any other name or title*,' does this include congregational worship, or a congregation met in open church, with free seats, for preaching and other public services? and will each one so assembled be required to take the oath prescribed in Special Order No. 61?

"2. When an assembly of divines have met to transact the business of the Church, and have taken the prescribed oath, are they expected then to oppose secession and treason publicly from the pulpit, or only in private circles?

"3. A minister who has within the past year taken the oath of allegiance in another State, but is now traveling in this State, must he again take the oath before he can meet his congregation for public worship?

"Answers to these inquiries will be gladly received, if you can find time to answer

"Your obedient servant,

"H. N. WATTS."

The Assistant Provost-Marshal at Charleston received the following letter from the Provost-Marshal General in answer to the inquiries of Mr. Watts:

"HEADQUARTERS DEPARTMENT OF THE MISSOURI,
OFFICE OF PROVOST-MARSHAL GENERAL.
ST. LOUIS, MO., March 24, 1864.

"SIR—I am in receipt of your letter of the 21st, enclosing your correspondence with the Rev. Mr. Watts, and asking for further instructions; and, also, I am in receipt of a letter from the same Rev. gentleman, propounding to me the following questions:

(*See questions above.*)

"It can not be necessary, either for your guidance or that of the Rev. gentleman who has propounded these questions to me, to answer them categorically.

"The order referred to is too plain and distinct to be misunderstood. It applies, as the language used unmistakably indicates, to conferences and all other representative assemblies convened to promote the cause of religion and morality, and *not* to the ordinary meetings of Christians assembled for the business purposes of a congregation, or benevolent society, or for the worship of God. All the objects of it are answered when its enforcement is confined to the assemblies indicated in it, and, as a matter of course, it forms no part of its purpose or requirements that persons should take the prescribed oath before proceeding to worship their Maker when assembled for that purpose.

"In case of the attendance at any assemblage of the character indicated in said order of any one who has already taken the oath of allegiance prescribed by the laws of this State for the clergy *to* legalize marriage, &c., any certificate or evidence of the fact will be sufficient to render him eligible without again taking the prescribed oath.

"But, while such is the liberal construction of the Order No. 61, requiring no oath of those divines who have already taken the required oath to enable them to perform all their functions, it is no less the determination of the undersigned to enforce a rigid compliance with the ordinance of the State Convention of June 10, 1862, requiring licensed and ordained preachers of the gospel to take the oath of allegiance therein prescribed before assuming to discharge the duties pertaining to their avocations under the laws of this State.

"Those who have failed to do so, and who, under the pretense of preaching or worshiping God, meet really for seditious purposes, and, in truth, to desecrate and violate the laws of God and their country, can not be allowed so to meet or carry on their seditious purposes, and will be held to a strict accountability.

"I have no inclination, nor do I conceive it to be any part of my duty, to answer the Rev. gentleman's second interrogatory, and thus instruct him in his ministerial duties. My respect for his profession obliges me to presume that he is familiar with the Bible, and needs no such instruction from me. For the information asked in that interrogatory he will, therefore, have to refer to the Bible, whose expounder he professes to be. He need but do so in the proper spirit, and with an earnest desire to be guided by its teachings, to insure unto him a flood of light as to his duty in the premises.

"You will furnish the Rev. Mr. Watts with a copy of this letter, and be guided in your own actions by its instructions.

"Respectfully, J. P. SANDERSON,
"Prov.-Mar. Gen'l.

"Lt. Jas. A. Reid, Ass't Pro-Mar'l, Charleston, Mo."

The letter of the Provost-Marshal General was forwarded to Mr. Watts, through the Assistant Provost-Marshal's office at Charleston, accompanied by an order from the latter office requiring him to take the Convention oath of '62, or cease to preach, and report himself at headquarters, St. Louis. He went to St. Louis, took what was called the "Gamble oath," returned home and resumed his ministerial labors.

The correspondence here given is specially valuable for the light it throws upon the spirit and bearing of the military authorities in the direct issue they made with the clergy of the State. Many ministers of the gospel were more oppressed and persecuted, but all of them did not so far yield to military authority on the one hand, nor so sharply contend for the rights of conscience on the other.

The "Special Order, No. 61," has a history of itself that will be unveiled in due time, and the true nature of the proscription and persecution under it will be better disclosed in another place.

This forcing the conscience of ministers by prescribing "test oaths" is not a new thing. It is as old as the second great persecution under Domitian, A. D. 81, and as cruel as the Spanish Inquisition.

When State Conventions and military commanders in Missouri prepared political "test oaths" for ministers of the gospel as a class, and ordered all non-juring ministers under disability, the object was not doubtful in the minds of those acquainted with the history of religious persecutions.

Another martyred minister of the gospel, the horrible murder of another of God's chosen messengers of salvation, and *scene first* of the great Missouri tragedy closes, the curtain falls, and both writer and reader may seek temporary relief from what Dr. Summers, in a private note, calls "a terrible narrative." When the curtain rises again it will unveil other scenes in this wonderful histrionic drama, of which those already presented are but the preparation and prelude.

The trials and persecutions of the faithful men of God already narrated are sufficient to present the moral and religious phases of the war in Missouri to an intelligent public. Would to God the pall of oblivion could settle down upon the whole history. But if the world still retains its interest in truth; if the Church is still the repository of the testimony of Jesus and the divinely accredited authority for works of righteousness; if the ministers of the gospel are yet responsible for the "faith once delivered unto the saints," for the purity of the gospel and the integrity of the kingdom of God on earth, and if history is valuable for the lessons it teaches and the principles it vindicates, then that truth, that righteousness, that faith, that history, all demand the record here made, the lessons taught and the principles vindicated in the trials and sufferings of God's annointed servants during the recent reign of terror.

The following shocking narrative of murder must, according to the decision of the publisher, close the first volume.

REV. THOMAS GLANVILLE AND SON.

The subject of this sketch was long and favorably known to the Church in Missouri, and was highly esteemed for his integrity, honesty and fidelity to principle as well as for his general usefulness as a minister.

Others who knew him better have furnished the following account of his life and labors, together with the circumstantial details of the dark and bloody tragedy which closed his career of usefulness on earth—one of the most heartless and cruel assassinations in all the dark history of martyrdom in Missouri.

The following sketch has been furnished by an intimate friend of the martyred minister, and will be read with mournful interest:

"*Rev. Thomas Glanville and Son.*—It was the privilege of the writer to be intimately acquainted with the subjects of this sketch for more than a score of years. Without reference to official documents or private papers, I write mostly from memory, hoping thereby to preserve the precious memory of two worthy men.

"Rev. Thomas Glanville was born in England about A. D. 1811, and came to America when about sixteen years of age. He was converted to God in early life, and after much mental agony yielded to the conviction that it was his duty to preach.

"Soon after he began to preach, he joined the St. Louis Conference M. E. Church, South, and traveled several years. But family afflictions came upon him—his wife died and left him three children. He married again and soon afterward located.

"Time rolled on and ever found him diligent in business, fervent in spirit, serving the Lord; and laboring efficiently as a local preacher.

"In the fall of 1852 a camp-meeting was held in his neigborhood by the lamented Leeper, Anthony and Bond. Bro. Glanville's three children were at the altar as penitents. All the tenderest sympathies of a father's heart went out after them. How pointed his instructions! and his prayers! O, how fervent!

"He told the writer that he had made a vow that if the Lord would accept his three children at that meeting, he would rejoin the Conference and travel and preach as long as his way seemed open. The Lord did mercifully accept his three children; and, true to his vow, he rejoined the Conference and remained an acceptable member till the day of his death.

"When the late civil war commenced and the flock in Southwest Missouri was left for the most part without a shepherd, he and the local preachers of his neighborhood met in council and went out 'two and two' and held meetings in the most destitute neighborhoods.

"After a time he was ordered by a militia Captain to discontinue his preaching. This grieved him much, but he yielded and remained silent for almost a year.

"In February, 1863, a meeting was appointed in one of those destitute neighborhoods, which he attended. The 'fire was shut up in his bones,' and in company with a friend he waited on the Captain then in command in that vicinity and requested permission to resume his duties as a minister. To his great joy he received a written permission, and the next night he preached a sermon full of joy and comfort.

"In July or August following three men called at his gate one dark night and ordered him to leave the country on pain of death. A few days after he remarked to the writer that he would love to live to see peace restored to the country, and he hoped he would, and then added, 'Those fellows may kill me, but I think not. Of one thing I am certain, they can't harm me; death has no terrors for me, and has not had *for fifteen years.*'

"He was a bold and fearless man. 'Conscious innocence knows no fear;' but through the entreaties of friends he left home for a month or more; and it is to be regretted that he made up his mind to return, and did so, saying that he would 'risk the consequences.'

"He published an appointment for preaching, and a few hours before the time came, two militia soldiers waited on him and informed him that he would not be permitted to hold the service. He remained at home that Sabbath, and remarked to a neighbor, 'Those fellows will kill me, I believe; but they shall never have it to say that they shot me in the back.' That holy Sabbath was his last on earth.

"When night came on and good men laid them down to peaceful slumbers, his murderers approached his quiet dwelling. A ball discharged from a revolver passed through his window, entered his face and he fell to the floor. To make sure of his victim the murderer raised the window and reaching in shot him through the chest. They then went round, forced the door and three men entered. After a few words with Bro. Glanville's son, one of them remarked that he had better finish the old man, and so saying shot him again. Thus died the Rev. Thomas Glanville, in the fifty-third year of his age.

"After threatening to burn the house and ordering the family to leave on short time, they rode two miles to the residence of Bro. Glanville's eldest son, Mr. A. C. Glanville, a man of fine mind and respectable literary attainments, with a meek and quiet spirit, and a member of the M. E. Church, South. They called him up, and, all unconscious of his father's fate and his own danger, he made a light. No sooner was the light made than a ball passed through his window, entered his head and he fell lifeless on the hearth. Thus perished father and son in one night.

"Since their death little has been said in reference to them; but they still live in the hearts of many friends, and it is well known that they bore the highest type of manhood.

"Bro. Glanville had for many years been an ordained elder in the M. E. Church, South, and while as a preacher he was neither profound nor brilliant, yet he possessed a sound mind, a good understanding in the things of God, was a good sermonizer and improved every year, so that his last days were his best. Peace to his memory.

"JOHN H. ROSS."

The Rev. John Monroe, of the St. Louis Conference, one of the oldest ministers in Missouri, furnishes the following sketch of the lamented Glanville:

"The Rev. Thomas Glanville was born in England, May 15, A. D. 1811. Came to this country about the year 1829 or 1830, and a short time afterward was married to Miss Donnell, of Green county, Mo. Not long after this event he embraced religion and united with the M. E. Church, and in 1841 was received on trial in the Missouri Conference.

"In 1843 he was appointed to Buffalo Circuit, where he endured much affliction, both of body and mind. His wife died and he married again, and the next year he located. For a time he traveled under the Presiding Elder and was readmitted into the St. Louis Conference in 1855, and then traveled regularly until the war came up. He did not cease to preach in his neighborhood. He had an appointment the day he met his awful fate, but dared not attend it, as his avowed enemies were watching his movements. This was Sabbath, Sept. 20, 1863. At night three outlaws, guided, no doubt, by another who was not responsible to any military organization, approached his peaceful home and shot him. And what for? No one knows. He, like all good men, was self-denying and made no compromise with sin, wicked men or devils; reproving sin in all its forms and in all places, he had enemies who threatened him years before, and this was a good time to put their designs into execution.

"At first he was ordered from home; he went, remained some three weeks and returned. Then they compelled him to take an oath and give bond, in which he was bound to stay at home—just what he wanted to do. But in a few days after giving bond there came a stripling of a boy, purporting to have orders from a Lieutenant of the same family whence all his troubles came, ordering him to again leave home forthwith, and be quick about it. He then, as a law-abiding man, went to Captain Allen, then at Hermitage, for protection to enable him to keep his obligation, and to know how to act under the circumstances. But the Captain refused to protect or instruct him, only to tell him that he had better leave quickly, knowing at the same time that such a course would forfeit his bond. He had made up his mind to leave the next morning, but, as stated, three armed men came after dark and shot him some three or four times, and he expired instantly. His last and dying words were, 'Lord, have mercy on my enemies.'

"He was buried without a song; not even a prayer was permitted to be offered in behalf of his disconsolate wife and weeping children. But the good man exchanged a world of woe for a land of rest.

"Thomas Glanville was always known to be a law-abiding man and a peaceable citizen. He often boasted of the privileges he enjoyed under this benign Government, and only claimed his rights under its Constitution and laws. He was never known to violate any law, abhorred a mean thing and would speak out against it.

He strenuously opposed all bushwhacking, stealing, murder, and any and all infringement upon the rights of others. He stood up squarely for the rights of the M. E. Church, South, and contended boldly for the principles of religious liberty. In view of these things it is not difficult to account for his shameful and brutal murder.

JOHN MONROE."

It is quite a relief to turn away, for a time at least, from the contemplation of such scenes of barbarity and more than savage cruelty as the history of the terrible past presents to our faith and philosophy.

Three long chapters, prepared for this volume, are laid over for the second, by the decree of the publisher, to prevent the enlargement of the present volume to an improper size. By it the next volume will be enriched beyond measure. What is lost to this will be gained for that, and neither the work, as a whole, nor the reader will be damaged.

The deferred chapters contain an account of the "Rosecrans oath," in "Special Order No. 61," of March 7th, 1864, and its designs upon the common laws and facts of religious liberty; the persecutions, trials, banishment, etc., of the Rev. Drs. McPheeters and Farris, of the Presbyterian Church, the Rev. Tyson Dynes, of the M. E. Church, South, the long imprisonment and peculiar sufferings of the Rev. Dr. McAnally; the effort to crush or confiscate the publishing house at St. Louis, and its preservation and security by the agent, the Rev. P. M. Pinckard; and a "Chapter of Martyrs," detailing with careful minuteness the cold-blooded murder of the Rev. John L. Wood, the Rev. George L. Sexton and the Rev. Edwin Robinson.

The history of the indictments, trials, imprisonment and persecutions of ministers under the "test oath" of the New Constitution will form a prominent and extensive feature of the second volume, with due attention to the particulars of the murder of the Rev. SAMUEL S. HEADLEE and others, which will invest the work with thrilling interest. The future historian will assign to these names a conspicuous place upon the long roll of martyrs, and the future Church will reap a rich harvest of souls, with multiplied agencies and resources, from the blood they shed "for the testimony of Jesus and the word of God."

"They lived unknown
Till persecution dragged them into fame,
And chased them up to heaven. Their ashes flew,
No marble tells us whither. With their names
No bard enbalms and sanctifies his song:
And history, so warm on meaner themes,
Is cold on this. She execrates, indeed,
The tyranny that doomed them to the fire,
But gives the glorious sufferers little praise.'

www.ingramcontent.com/pod-product-compliance
Lightning Source LLC
LaVergne TN
LVHW021141110826
845150LV00005B/1088

* 9 7 8 1 4 2 5 5 4 8 1 0 0 *